Th

Trinity & All Saints
ACCREDITED BY THE UNIVERSITY OF LEEDS

LIS LIBRARY
This book is due for return on or before the last date
stamped below

The

mar

like

the

und

Bibl

\

frar

anc

-
-
-
-
-
-
-
-

wishing to find   ntinuing cultural
significance.

You may also be interested in the following
Routledge Student Reference titles:

Religion: The Basics
Malory Nye

Fifty Key Christian Thinkers
Peter McEnhill and George Newlands

Fifty Key Medieval Thinkers
G. R. Evans

Who's Who in Christianity
Lavinia Cohn-Sherbok

Who's Who in the New Testament
Ronald Brownrigg

Who's Who in the Old Testament
Joan Comay

Key Writers on Art: From Antiquity to the Nineteenth Century
Edited by Chris Murray

Key Writers on Art: The Twentieth Century
Edited by Chris Murray

Literary Theory: The Basics
Hans Bertens

Poetry: The Basics
Jeffrey Wainwright

Shakespeare: The Basics
Sean McEvoy

The Bible in Western Culture

The Student's Guide

Dee Dyas and Esther Hughes

Consulting editor
Stephen H. Travis

Routledge
Taylor & Francis Group

LONDON AND NEW YORK

First published 2005
by Routledge
2 Park Square, Milton Park, Abingdon, Oxon OX14 4RN

Simultaneously published in the USA and Canada
by Routledge
270 Madison Ave, New York, NY 10016

Routledge is an imprint of the Taylor & Francis Group

Scripture quotations are from the New Revised Standard Version of the
Bible, copyright © 1989 by the Division of Christian Education of the
National Council of the Churches of Christ in the USA. Used by
permission. All rights reserved.

Typeset in Plantin by
HWA Text and Data Management Ltd, Tunbridge Wells
Printed and bound in Great Britain by
MPG Books Ltd, Bodmin

British Library Cataloguing in Publication Data
A catalogue record for this book is available from the British Library

Library of Congress Cataloging-in-Publication Data
Dyas, Dee
   The Bible in Western culture : the student's guide / Dee Dyas and
Esther Hughes.
       p.   cm.
   Includes bibliographical references.
1. Bible–Introductions. 2. Bible–Influence. 3. Christianity and culture.
I. Hughes, Esther (Esther Scott) II. Title.

BS475.3.D93 2005
220.6'1–dc22   2004020082

ISBN 0–415–32617–6 (hbk)
ISBN 0–415–32618–4 (pbk)

CONTENTS

ACKNOWLEDGEMENTS

We would like to thank all those who have generously provided advice, information and support, especially Stephen Travis, Jeremy Begbie, Paul Cavill, Richard Davey, Stuart Dyas, Angela Hughes, Ben Hughes, Helen Phillips, Roger Pooley, Peter Preston and Heather Wilson. We are grateful to the Bible Society for a generous research grant and to our editors, Rosie Waters, Susannah Trefgarne and Milon Nagi, for their guidance and endless enthusiasm for this project.

Dee Dyas and Esther Hughes
The Christianity and Culture Project,
University of York and St John's College, Nottingham

ABBREVIATIONS

The following abbreviations are used for the books of the Bible:

OLD TESTAMENT

Gen	Genesis
Ex	Exodus
Lev	Leviticus
Num	Numbers
Deut	Deuteronomy
Josh	Joshua
Judg	Judges
Ruth	Ruth
1 Sam	1 Samuel
2 Sam	2 Samuel
1 Kings	1 Kings
2 Kings	2 Kings
1 Chr	1 Chronicles
2 Chr	2 Chronicles
Ezra	Ezra
Neh	Nehemiah
Esth	Esther
Job	Job
Ps	Psalms
Prov	Proverbs
Eccl	Ecclesiastes

Song	Song of Solomon
Isa	Isaiah
Jer	Jeremiah
Lam	Lamentations
Ezek	Ezekiel
Dan	Daniel
Hos	Hosea
Joel	Joel
Am	Amos
Ob	Obadiah
Jon	Jonah
Mic	Micah
Nah	Nahum
Hab	Habakkuk
Zeph	Zephaniah
Hag	Haggai
Zech	Zechariah
Mal	Malachi

NEW TESTAMENT

Mt	Matthew
Mk	Mark
Lk	Luke
Jn	John
Acts	The Acts of the Apostles
Rom	Romans
1 Cor	1 Corinthians
2 Cor	2 Corinthians
Gal	Galatians
Eph	Ephesians
Phil	Philippians
Col	Colossians
1 Thess	1 Thessalonians

2 Thess	2 Thessalonians
1 Tim	1 Timothy
2 Tim	2 Timothy
Titus	Titus
Philem	Philemon
Heb	Hebrews
Jas	James
1 Pet	1 Peter
2 Pet	2 Peter
1 Jn	1 John
2 Jn	2 John
3 Jn	3 John
Jude	Jude
Rev	Revelation

INTRODUCTION

THE PURPOSE OF THIS BOOK

Anyone who explores art, literature, history or music in any depth swiftly recognises the Bible as a vital key to understanding and interpreting much of Western culture and history. For hundreds of years, human creativity was inspired and shaped by a Christian world view and a system of reference and allusion which has not only moulded our past but continues to affect our present. Phrases such as 'being a Good Samaritan', 'turning the other cheek', and 'going the extra mile' still pervade the English language; the physical landscape and material culture of many countries still bear the imprint of Christian belief and practice; the impact of biblical teaching can be seen in systems of law and ethics. Yet, for many today, the stories of the Bible are not so familiar and the network of allusions and references appear frustratingly elusive. This book therefore offers a way into the Bible for those who would like to explore its influence on Western culture. It is not intended as a guide to the Bible in all its aspects or to the huge area of Biblical Studies, but as an introduction to key stories which have inspired and influenced artists, writers and musicians in the past and which continue to do so today.

APPROACHING THE BIBLE

The Bible is not a single book but a collection of books, an anthology of different works by different authors in different genres. It was written in a small area of the eastern Mediterranean over a period lasting more than 1,200 years and completed nearly 2,000 years ago. The English word 'Bible' comes from the Greek plural *ta biblia* meaning 'the books', a term that came into use in the early Christian era. The Bible contains historical accounts, laws and ritual regulations; genealogies and family sagas; **prophecy**, proverbs and letters; short stories, songs and poetry. This diverse material was gathered together because religious communities, first Jewish and then Christian, believed that it was written under **divine inspiration** and as such did not just record God's actions but also revealed his nature.

The idea that God speaks through holy writings, or **scripture**, is common to Jews, Christians and Muslims, who for this reason are sometimes called 'People of the Book'. Jews continue to use the Hebrew Bible which was written between *c.*1300BCE and *c.*150BCE, though parts of it are probably based on earlier oral traditions. Christians refer to this portion of the Bible as the **Old Testament**, to which they add the **New Testament**, comprising twenty-seven further books by several different authors written in Greek between *c.*CE50 and *c.*CE100. The three main Christian Churches – the Orthodox, the Roman Catholic and the Protestant – each have their own preferred versions of the Bible which differ slightly in the books chosen for inclusion and in the order in which they are presented.

The holy scriptures of Islam, the Qur'an, do not form part of the Jewish or Christian Bible, although some Bible characters including **Abraham, Joseph, Moses, David, Mary** and **Jesus** appear in the Qur'an, often with different emphases or doctrines.

FORMATION

The process of selecting which books were to be included in the Bible took place over some eight centuries, and although it continues to be the subject of debate the differing lists of Bible books are now considered by Jewish and Christian authorities to be complete. The term **canonical**, from the Greek *kanon* (measuring rod or rule), is often used to describe the books accepted as authoritative.

The Jewish Bible comprises three sections which are presented in the order in which they became accepted as authoritative. The first section comprises five books, together known as the **Pentateuch** from the Greek meaning five scrolls, or as the **Torah** meaning teaching. These five books of early Israelite history and teaching, called **Genesis**, **Exodus**, **Leviticus**, **Numbers** and **Deuteronomy**, were frequently copied and circulated together after 400BCE. The second section, known as the **Prophets**, continues Israelite history and includes related prophecy and is thought to have gained recognition not later than 200BCE. The final section, the **Writings**, which includes poetry, short stories, proverbs and books of wisdom as well as some later Israelite history, completed the Jewish scriptures c.CE100.

Most of the early Jewish Christians did not read the Jewish Bible in the original Hebrew, but relied on a Greek translation called the **Septuagint**. This was probably produced during the third and second centuries BCE by Jewish scholars living in Alexandria, for use by Jews living outside Palestine. The Septuagint presents the Bible books in a different order, and includes some additional books of Jewish writing not considered authoritative by Hebrew-speaking Jews; books that later became known to Christians as the **Old Testament** *Apocrypha* (from the Greek meaning 'hidden'). There is also a large group of Jewish religious works not considered canonical, called the **Pseudepigrapha**, or 'false' writings because many claim to have been written by famous people who lived much earlier than the real authors.

The early Christians referred to the Septuagint to support their claims about Jesus. The earliest Christian writer is **St Paul**, whose letters date from CE50–60 and were collected together around CE100. To these were added the four **Gospels**, which tell the life story of **Jesus**, written between CE65 and CE100. The books of the New Testament were not finally agreed until 367CE when **Athanasius** listed 27 books which he termed the 'canon'. There is also a **New Testament** *Apocrypha*, comprising Christian documents of the second and third centuries CE, such as the *Gospel of Thomas* and the *Acts of Pilate*.

TRANSLATION

As Christianity spread across the Roman Empire in the early centuries of the Common Era (CE), the first Christian Bibles containing both the Jewish and Christian scriptures were produced. From the second century onwards, there were translations of at least parts of the Bible into languages such as Latin, Syriac and Coptic. In CE382 the scholar **Jerome** was commissioned by the Pope to begin a new Latin translation of this Bible from the original Hebrew and Greek, which became known as the **Vulgate**, from the Latin *vulgus*, or common language. Working initially from the Septuagint, Jerome included books not considered authoritative by Hebrew-speaking Jews on the grounds that they had been accepted by Christian scholars for three centuries. However, he distinguished them from the rest of the Jewish canon and gave them the name *Apocrypha*. Orthodox and Catholic Bibles still include these books. Protestant Bibles, following the German theologian **Martin Luther** (d.1546), tend to exclude the *Apocrypha* or to print them in a separate section within the book.

The **Vulgate** was the version of the Bible most widely used in the West and was the official Bible of the Catholic Church for over 1,000 years. Over the centuries, however, Latin ceased to be the common language and many ordinary people gained knowledge of the Bible through visual sources such as murals and stained glass in Churches, and oral sources such as the **mystery plays**. Portions of the Bible were translated or paraphrased into languages other than Latin. Some **Psalms** and the four **Gospels** were translated into Anglo-Saxon. However, after 1200 the Church became more cautious about such vernacular translations owing to their use by heretical groups. The first complete translation of the Bible into English was made by followers of **John Wyclif** (*c.*1330–84) towards the end of the fourteenth century but outlawed by the Archbishop of Canterbury soon afterwards.

The growing Protestant Reformation, informed by the writings of Luther, taught that **salvation** was a matter of personal response to the **grace** of God and did not rely on the mediation of the Church. The Reformers believed that the Bible should be removed from the control of the Church and made available to individual believers in their own languages. Luther himself began a translation into German, rejecting the Latin version used by the Church and returning to the original Hebrew and Greek texts. Protestantism took hold across Europe, particularly in countries with relatively high literacy rates, aided by the new technology of printing that enabled Bibles to be reproduced quickly and consistently.

The first printed English translation of the New Testament was produced by **William Tyndale** in 1525 or 1526 and was opposed by the Catholic Church which tried to destroy all copies. Tyndale was eventually put to death as a heretic. Using Tyndale's translations as a basis, Tyndale's assistant, Miles **Coverdale**, published the first complete Bible in English in 1535. The English Church, under Henry VIII, was more sympathetic to the Protestant cause and a reworked version of Coverdale's text was authorised for use in parish churches in 1539. The Catholic Queen, Mary Tudor, proved less tolerant and Protestants again fled to Europe. In 1560 English Protestants living in Geneva produced their own English translation of the Bible. Their *Geneva Bible*, sometimes called 'the Bible of Shakespeare', was popular for over a hundred years.

Under Queen Elizabeth I, Catholics fled to Europe and published a new version of the Bible in English, which was translated from the Vulgate. The New Testament of their *Douay Bible*, named after the place it was printed, was published in 1582; the Old Testament (published in Rheims) followed in 1610. The whole became known as the *Douay-Rheims Bible*. This became the standard text for English-language Catholics for three hundred years. Meanwhile, in 1568, Elizabeth I licensed a version called the *Bishop's Bible*, for use in the Church of England. The next monarch, James I, commissioned an entirely new English version, translated from the original texts.

First published in 1611, the *King James Version* (**KJV**) or *Authorised Version* (**AV**) was extensively used by English-speaking Protestants worldwide until well into the twentieth century. Arguably, it is the Authorised Version which has had the greatest influence on Western culture, with quotations and references in its rich, elegant language becoming common in ordinary speech as well as in literature in English for several centuries.

In recent decades, many new, contemporary language versions of the Bible have been produced, taking advantage of current scholarship in ancient languages and taking into account recently discovered manuscripts.

INTERPRETATION

The earliest Christian commentaries on the Jewish Bible are found in the New Testament itself, where the Hebrew texts are used to suggest that Jesus is the fulfilment of the Law and the Prophets. Based on this early intertextuality, the **Fathers of the Church** came to view the Hebrew and Christian scriptures as a divinely inspired unity. This view was supported by a complex symbolic system of interpretation known as **typology**, in which the Old Testament is seen as prophesying or prefiguring the New. This system saw, for example, **Abraham**'s willingness to sacrifice his son **Isaac** as a '**type**' of the sacrifice of Jesus by God.

From the Fathers of the Church onwards, it was believed that the Bible could be understood at more than one level. The predominant method of interpretation offered four levels: the literal or historical; the moral or tropological, which gives guidance on how to live in obedience to God; the allegorical, which interpreted events in the light of Christ and the Church, often using typology; and the spiritual or anagogical, which is concerned with **heaven** and **eternal life**. These approaches became the standard method of interpreting the Bible in the medieval West and were still popular in the seventeenth century, where they can be seen in the sermons of John Donne.

The Protestant Reformers not only criticised the restriction of the translation of the Bible by the Church, they also rejected the view that the Church had exclusive control of the interpretation of the text. **Luther** called for a return to *sola scriptura* (scripture alone) in which the individual reader, under the guidance of the **Holy Spirit**, was regarded as his or her own interpreter of the Bible. By the mid-nineteenth century, Protestant emphasis on straightforward rather than allegorical readings of scripture resulted in the development of the Historical Criticism approach to the study of the Bible. This academic approach sought to determine the dates of composition and the history of the Bible texts and to discern the identities of their original authors and the responses of their original readers by returning to the Hebrew, Aramaic and Greek manuscripts. It tended to believe that it was possible to approach the text neutrally and in so doing to discern a general meaning.

Postmodern study of the Bible rejected the possibility of these types of meanings, and scholars from different disciplines and perspectives are now seeking to reclaim the Bible text from predominantly western Christian interpretations. The Bible is subject to a range of readings and is recognised as having been just as influential on cultural, racial and sexual identities as it has been on religious belief. The Bible is being studied as history, anthropology and literature and its influence on the development of law, ethics, art and literature in Western culture recognised.

THE TRADITIONAL CHRISTIAN READING OF THE BIBLE

The Bible has been so influential on the development of Western culture because for centuries the majority believed it to be the key to interpreting their past, present and future. Writers such as Chaucer, Milton or Dickens, and artists such as Michelangelo, Rembrandt and Blake, whatever their personal beliefs, all lived and worked in periods when a Christian view of the world and the traditional Christian reading of the Bible were widely accepted.

Through the centuries, most Christians have understood the Bible as a commentary on God's relationship with humankind which gives coherence to the history of the world and purpose to the life of individuals.

In the beginning the Bible shows God creating the universe out of nothing and peopling it with human beings made in his image. **Adam**, the first man, and **Eve**, the first woman, live together in the **Garden of Eden**, a place of safety and plenty, and enjoy a close relationship with God. Adam and Eve are free to eat any fruit in the garden except that of the **tree of knowledge of good and evil**; to eat this fruit will bring death. **Satan**, taking the form of a serpent, tempts Eve to taste this fruit and in turn she tempts Adam to eat it too. For this disobedience, or **sin,** God condemns humankind to a life of exile and separation from him, characterised by hard labour, enmity and pain.

Ejected from the Garden of Eden, Adam and Eve have children, including **Cain**, the first murderer. Human beings continue to show evidence of sin. Those who, through pride, seek to build the **Tower of Babel** are thwarted by God who makes them speak in different languages so that they can no longer understand each other. The increasing evil of humankind continues to arouse God's anger and he causes the earth to **flood** so that it will be wiped out. **Noah** saves a few people by building an **ark**, or boat, at God's command.

God makes a new beginning by calling **Abram**, later renamed **Abraham**, to go out in search of a promised land and to be the father of a nation who will live in a special relationship to God. Abraham's descendants spend a long period in exile until, at God's command, **Moses** leads them out of slavery in Egypt and into the **wilderness**. Here, on **Mount Sinai**, God gives the **Ten Commandments** and sets out a complex set of rituals and sacrifices that are required to deal with impurity and sin. After forty years in the wilderness the **Israelites** re-enter the land promised to Abraham, and become a nation led by kings including **David** and **Solomon**, who builds a temple at **Jerusalem**. However, some do not worship God alone, and he sends a series of **prophets** to warn them of the consequences of their evil. Eventually, the nation is conquered and the people are deported to **exile** in **Babylon**, from where a small group is permitted to return and rebuild the temple. Although the nation is re-established in **Israel**, it continues to be subject to war and invasion, and prophets predict that a **Messiah**, a mighty king, will rise up and save them from their enemies.

The **New Testament** claims that the Messiah came in the person of **Jesus Christ**, the Son of God. His life, as recorded in the four **Gospels**, has two main components: the accounts of his birth and early child-hood, and the three-year public ministry which ends with his crucifixion. At about the age of 30, Jesus is **baptised** by his cousin, the prophet **John the Baptist**, and begins to perform miracles, teach with great wisdom and gather a group of **disciples** around him. After three years Jesus is arrested and condemned to death by the Jewish authorities and by **Pilate**, the province's Roman ruler. He is crucified just outside Jerusalem and buried. Three days later Jesus is resurrected from the dead and appears in physical form to groups of his followers. In the New Testament the **resurrection** is interpreted as showing that Jesus has conquered death and, with it, the power of evil and sin. By accepting Jesus' death as the ultimate sacrifice for sin which offers the possibility of forgiveness, human beings are able to once again live in close relationship with God. After forty days Jesus is shown ascending into heaven, giving his disciples a final command that they should take his message to all nations. In this task they are aided by the gift of the **Holy Spirit**, whose dramatic arrival on the Day of **Pentecost** begins a period in which the **Early Church** spreads across the Roman Empire. The **Epistles** (letters) to churches and individuals contained in the New Testament encourage Christians to live in obedience to God. The Book of **Revelation** concludes with a vision of the end of time when evil will finally be defeated, Jesus will return to judge human beings, and a **new heaven and new earth** will come into being.

HOW TO USE THIS BOOK

This book is an introduction to this traditional Christian reading of the Bible that has so influenced literature and art in Western culture. It offers a selection of the most influential passages of the Bible presented as fully as possible. Each passage from the Bible is introduced with brief notes on context, characters and concepts, and followed by indications of related Bible passages and some examples of the influence of the passage on specific works of art, literature and music. Due to limitations of space, these examples can only be illustrative rather than comprehensive. Important terms, characters and doctrines appear in bold type and are explained in more detail in the Reference Section at the end of the book. For clarity and accessibility, the text used is that of the **New Revised Standard Version**, though phrases from the **Authorised Version** have been included where they have particular resonance.

THE OLD TESTAMENT

The **Old Testament** (**OT**) is the name given to the Hebrew **Scriptures** by Christians, who add the later **New Testament** (**NT**) to form the Christian **Bible**. As much as a third of the Old Testament is poetry. The Old Testament begins with five books called the **Pentateuch**, traditionally attributed to **Moses**. **Genesis** tells the story of God's relationship with humankind from **Adam** and **Eve**, through his **Covenant** with **Abraham** to the emergence of the **Israelite** nation. **Exodus** tells the story of this nation's return to the **Promised Land**, under the leadership of Moses, to whom God gives the **Ten Command-ments**, and in **Leviticus**, **Numbers** and **Deuteronomy** the **Law** is developed further.

The story of Israelite history, from their return to **Canaan** to the destruction of **Jerusalem** and their **Exile** in **Babylon**, is continued through the books of **Joshua**, Judges and Kings. Chronicles, Ezra and Nehemiah chart the return to Jerusalem and the restoration of the **Temple** in the fifth century BCE. Throughout this period God sends **Prophets** to encourage and to warn **Israel**.

The remainder of the Old Testament, called the **Writings**, includes a variety of genres including short stories, love poetry, **Psalms** and **Proverbs**.

1 IN THE BEGINNING

THE CREATION OF THE WORLD

Creation is a key topic which has undergone a wide range of interpretations over the centuries. In the **Bible**, 'creation' can mean both
the process by which the universe was made and the created order
which emerged. The account with which the Book of **Genesis** opens
focuses less on the details of the process than on making clear God's
role as Creator of all things and his delight in what had been made.
Thus Chapter 1 shows God 'speaking' different elements of creation
into existence ('And God said, "Let there be ..." ') and evaluating what
has been made as 'good'.

Genesis contains two accounts of God's creation of the world. In
the first (1:1–2:3), creation takes place over six 'days': (1) Division of light
and darkness; (2) Division of the waters; (3) Creation of the dry land
and plant life; (4) Creation of the sun, moon and stars; (5) Creation of
sea creatures and birds; (6) Creation of animals and human beings. On
the seventh day God rested. The second account (2:4–10) focuses on
the place of humankind in creation. First, God creates man from the
dust and breathes life into him. God then plants the **Garden of Eden**,
containing both the Tree of Life and the **Tree of Knowledge of Good
and Evil,** and places man in the garden, warning him not to eat from

the Tree of the Knowledge of Good and Evil. In order to provide companionship for man, animals and birds are then created and named by man. Finally, God creates woman as a partner for the man.

Key concepts

God as Creator; God's pleasure in the created world; two narrative traditions; man placed in the Garden of Eden; woman created from man.

Genesis 1; 2:1–9, 15–25

In the beginning when God created the heavens and the earth, [2] the earth was a formless void and darkness covered the face of the deep, while a wind from God swept over the face of the waters. [3] Then God said, "Let there be light"; and there was light. [4] And God saw that the light was good; and God separated the light from the darkness. [5] God called the light Day, and the darkness he called Night. And there was evening and there was morning, the first day.

[6] And God said, "Let there be a dome in the midst of the waters, and let it separate the waters from the waters." [7] So God made the dome and separated the waters that were under the dome from the waters that were above the dome. And it was so. [8] God called the dome Sky. And there was evening and there was morning, the second day.

[9] And God said, "Let the waters under the sky be gathered together into one place, and let the dry land appear." And it was so. [10] God called the dry land Earth, and the waters that were gathered together he called Seas. And God saw that it was good. [11] Then God said, "Let the earth put forth vegetation: plants yielding seed, and fruit trees of every kind on earth that bear fruit with the seed in it." And it was so. [12] The earth brought forth vegetation: plants yielding seed of every kind, and trees of every kind bearing fruit with the seed in it. And God saw that it was good. [13] And there was evening and there was morning, the third day.

[14] And God said, "Let there be lights in the dome of the sky to separate the day from the night; and let them be for signs and for seasons and for days and years, [15] and let them be lights in the dome of the sky to give light upon the earth." And it was so. [16] God made the two great lights – the greater light to rule the day and the lesser light to rule the night – and the stars. [17] God set them in the dome of the sky to give light upon the earth, [18] to rule over the day and over the night, and to separate the light from the darkness. And God saw that it was good. [19] And there was evening and there was morning, the fourth day.

[20] And God said, "Let the waters bring forth swarms of living creatures, and let birds fly above the earth across the dome of the sky." [21] So God created the great sea monsters and every living creature that moves, of every kind, with which the waters swarm, and every winged bird of every kind. And God saw that it was good. [22] God blessed them, saying, "Be fruitful and multiply and fill the waters in the seas, and let birds multiply on the earth." [23] And there was evening and there was morning, the fifth day.

[24] And God said, "Let the earth bring forth living creatures of every kind: cattle and creeping things and wild animals of the earth of every kind." And it was so. [25] God made the wild animals of the earth of every kind, and the cattle of every kind, and everything that creeps upon the ground of every kind. And God saw that it was good.

[26] Then God said, "Let us make humankind in our image, according to our likeness; and let them have dominion over the fish of the sea, and over the birds of the air, and over the cattle, and over all the wild animals of the earth,and over every creeping thing that creeps upon the earth."

[27] So God created humankind in his image,
in the image of God he created them;
male and female he created them.

[28] God blessed them, and God said to them, "Be fruitful and multiply, and fill the earth and subdue it; and have dominion over the fish of the sea and over the birds of the air and over

every living thing that moves upon the earth." [29] God said, "See, I have given you every plant yielding seed that is upon the face of all the earth, and every tree with seed in its fruit; you shall have them for food. [30] And to every beast of the earth, and to every bird of the air, and to everything that creeps on the earth, everything that has the breath of life, I have given every green plant for food." And it was so. [31] God saw everything that he had made, and indeed, it was very good. And there was evening and there was morning, the sixth day.

Thus the heavens and the earth were finished, and all their multitude. [2] And on the seventh day God finished the work that he had done, and he rested on the seventh day from all the work that he had done. [3] So God blessed the seventh day and hallowed it, because on it God rested from all the work that he had done in creation.

[4] These are the generations of the heavens and the earth when they were created.

In the day that the LORD God made the earth and the heavens, [5] when no plant of the field was yet in the earth and no herb of the field had yet sprung up – for the LORD God had not caused it to rain upon the earth, and there was no one to till the ground; [6] but a stream would rise from the earth, and water the whole face of the ground – [7] then the LORD God formed man from the dust of the ground, and breathed into his nostrils the breath of life; and the man became a living being. [8] And the LORD God planted a garden in Eden, in the east; and there he put the man whom he had formed. [9] Out of the ground the LORD God made to grow every tree that is pleasant to the sight and good for food, the tree of life also in the midst of the garden, and the tree of the knowledge of good and evil. [...]

[15] The LORD God took the man and put him in the garden of Eden to till it and keep it. [16] And the LORD God commanded the man, "You may freely eat of every tree of the garden; [17] but of the tree of the knowledge of good and evil you shall not eat, for in the day that you eat of it you shall die."

¹⁸ Then the LORD God said, "It is not good that the man should be alone; I will make him a helper as his partner." ¹⁹ So out of the ground the LORD God formed every animal of the field and every bird of the air, and brought them to the man to see what he would call them; and whatever the man called every living creature, that was its name. ²⁰ The man gave names to all cattle, and to the birds of the air, and to every animal of the field; but for the man there was not found a helper as his partner. ²¹ So the LORD God caused a deep sleep to fall upon the man, and he slept; then he took one of his ribs and closed up its place with flesh. ²² And the rib that the LORD God had taken from the man he made into a woman and brought her to the man. ²³ Then the man said,

"This at last is bone of my bones
 and flesh of my flesh;
this one shall be called Woman,
 for out of Man this one was taken."

²⁴ Therefore a man leaves his father and his mother and clings to his wife, and they become one flesh. ²⁵ And the man and his wife were both naked, and were not ashamed.

Linked themes

Christian commentators saw in the creation accounts evidence of the **Trinity** at work, citing passages such as 'Let us make humankind in our image ... so God created humankind in his image' (Gen 1:26–7) as indicating the involvement of more than one person. In John 1, **Jesus Christ** is described as 'the **Word**' who shared in the work of creation, and the presence of the **Holy Spirit** has been inferred from Gen 1:2 where the Hebrew word *rûah*, which can be translated wind, breath or spirit, is used. Thus the **Authorised Version** reads 'the Spirit of God moved upon the face of the waters'. A number of **Psalms**, including Ps 19, declare that the created world reveals the character and power of God.

Related works

Art: Michelangelo, *God Dividing the Waters and the Earth*, 1508–12 (Sistine Chapel, Vatican, Rome); William Blake, *God as Architect (The Ancient of Days)*, 1794 (British Museum, London); Michelangelo, *The Creation of Adam*, 1508–12 (Sistine Chapel, Vatican, Rome); William Blake, *God Creating Adam*, 1795 (Tate Gallery, London); Jacopo Tintoretto, *The Creation of the* Animals, c.1550 (Gallerie dell'Accademia, Venice); Paulo Veronese, *The Creation of Eve*, 1570 (Art Institute, Chicago); Peter Paul Rubens and Jan Bruegel the Elder, *Adam and Eve in Paradise*, c.1615 (The Hague); Paul Nash, *Creation*, 1924 (Victoria and Albert Museum, London); Marc Chagall, *Creation*, 1960 (Galerie Art Chrudim); Barbara Hepworth, *Genesis*, 1969 (Tate Gallery, London).

Literature: *Caedmon's Hymn*, late seventh century; *The Creation* (York Cycle of Mystery Plays); Milton, *Paradise Lost*, 1667; Charlotte Brontë, *Jane Eyre*, Ch 38, 1847; Gerard Manley Hopkins, 'God's Grandeur', 1877; D.H. Lawrence, *The Rainbow*, 1915; Patrick White, *The Tree of Man*, 1955.

Music: Franz Joseph Haydn, *The Creation*, 1798; Aaron Copland, *In the Beginning*, 1947.

THE FALL OF HUMANKIND

The accounts of the creation of **Adam** and **Eve** are followed swiftly by the story of their **Fall**, a narrative which was subsequently read as an explanation of the problems of the world and human society. The serpent (identified by later Jewish and Christian writers as **Satan**) persuades Eve to use her **free will** to choose to disobey God's command, but yielding to the desire for the forbidden fruit brings the pair only loss of innocence and an experience of shame and guilt which damages their relationship with God and with one another. Adam and Eve are banished from **Eden**, becoming **exiles** who face hardship, pain, disharmony and death. Subsequent stories in the Book of **Genesis**, such as those of **Cain** and **Noah**, indicate that the descendants of Adam and Eve inherit not only the consequences of their **sin** but also their sinful nature (**Original Sin**).

Key concepts

Human free will; the nature of temptation; disobedience; loss of innocence; the consequences of sin (separation from God, mortality, exile of humankind on earth, disharmony, domination of women).

Genesis 3

Now the serpent was more crafty than any other wild animal that the LORD God had made. He said to the woman, "Did God say, 'You shall not eat from any tree in the garden'?" [2] The woman said to the serpent, "We may eat of the fruit of the trees in the garden; [3] but God said, 'You shall not eat of the fruit of the tree that is in the middle of the garden, nor shall you touch it, or you shall die.'" [4] But the serpent said to the woman, "You will not die; [5] for God knows that when you eat of it your eyes will be opened, and you will be like God, knowing good and evil." [6] So when the woman saw that the tree was good for food, and that it was a delight to the eyes, and that the tree was to be desired to make one wise, she took of its fruit and ate; and she also gave some to her husband, who was with her, and he ate. [7] Then the eyes of both were opened, and they knew that they were naked; and they sewed fig leaves together and made loincloths for themselves.

[8] They heard the sound of the LORD God walking in the garden at the time of the evening breeze, and the man and his wife hid themselves from the presence of the LORD God among the trees of the garden. [9] But the LORD God called to the man, and said to him, "Where are you?" [10] He said, "I heard the sound of you in the garden, and I was afraid, because I was naked; and I hid myself." [11] He said, "Who told you that you were naked? Have you eaten from the tree of which I commanded you not to eat?" [12] The man said, "The woman whom you gave to be with me, she gave me fruit from the tree, and I ate." [13] Then the LORD God said to the woman, "What is this that you have done?" The woman said, "The serpent tricked me, and I ate." [14] The LORD God said to the serpent,

"Because you have done this,
    cursed are you among all animals
    and among all wild creatures;
upon your belly you shall go,
    and dust you shall eat
    all the days of your life.
[15] I will put enmity between you and the woman,
    and between your offspring and hers;
he will strike your head,
    and you will strike his heel."
[16] To the woman he said,
"I will greatly increase your pangs in childbearing;
    in pain you shall bring forth children,
yet your desire shall be for your husband,
    and he shall rule over you."
[17] And to the man he said,
"Because you have listened to the voice of your wife,
    and have eaten of the tree
about which I commanded you,
    'You shall not eat of it,'
cursed is the ground because of you;
    in toil you shall eat of it all the days of your life;
[18] thorns and thistles it shall bring forth for you;
    and you shall eat the plants of the field.
[19] By the sweat of your face
    you shall eat bread
until you return to the ground,
    for out of it you were taken;
you are dust,
    and to dust you shall return."

[20] The man named his wife Eve, because she was the mother of all living. [21] And the LORD God made garments of skins for the man and for his wife, and clothed them.

[22] Then the LORD God said, "See, the man has become like one of us, knowing good and evil; and now, he might reach out

his hand and take also from the tree of life, and eat, and live forever" – [23] therefore the LORD God sent him forth from the garden of Eden, to till the ground from which he was taken. [24] He drove out the man; and at the east of the garden of Eden he placed the cherubim, and a sword flaming and turning to guard the way to the tree of life.

Linked themes

In Christian thought, the events of the Fall and its effects both prefigure and are reversed in the coming of **Christ** as described in the **New Testament**. 1 Corinthians states 'as in Adam all die, so in Christ shall all be made alive' (1 Cor 15:22, **AV**). Later commentators, particularly in the Middle Ages, drew a contrast between the rebellious **Eve** and the **Virgin Mary** who responded in willing obedience to the message brought by the **Angel Gabriel** at the **Annunciation** (Lk 1:26–38). The tree whose fruit brought death is mirrored by the **Cross** on which Christ dies to make **forgiveness** possible for all (1 Pet 2:24).

Related works

Art: Masaccio, *Expulsion of Adam and Eve from the Garden of Eden*, 1426–7 (Cappella Brancacci, Santa Maria del Carmine, Florence); Hugo van der Goes, *Fall of Adam*, before 1470 (Kunsthistorisches Museum, Vienna); Hieronymus Bosch, *Original Sin*, c.1504 (Metropolitan Museum of Art, New York); Albrecht Dürer, *Adam and Eve*, 1507 (Museo del Prado, Madrid); Michelangelo, *Temptation and Fall*, 1508–12 (Sistine Chapel Ceiling, Vatican, Rome); Rembrandt, *Fall*, 1638 (British Museum, London); William Blake, *Satan Exulting Over Eve*, c.1795 (Tate Gallery, London); Paul Gauguin, *Eve. Don't Listen to the Liar*, 1889 (Marion Koogler McNay Art Museum, San Antonio); Marc Chagall, *Adam and Eve (Temptation)*, 1912 (Saint Louis Museum); George Segal, *Expulsion*, 1986–7 (Sidney Janis Gallery, New York).

Literature: The Old English poem *Genesis*; *Fall of Man* (York Cycle of Mystery Plays); Edmund Spenser, *Faerie Queene*, Bk I; John Milton, *Paradise Lost*, 1667; Andrew Marvell, 'The Garden' published 1681; Nathaniel Hawthorne, 'Rappacini's Daughter', 1844; William Golding,

Lord of the Flies, 1954; William Golding, *Free Fall*, 1959; Ted Hughes, *Crow*, 1970.

Music: Carol: *Adam Lay y-bounden.*

CAIN, ABEL AND SETH

The expulsion of **Adam** and **Eve** from the **Garden of Eden** is followed by the birth of their sons, **Cain** and **Abel**. The story of Cain and Abel became an archetype of rivalry, hatred and violence, as the breakdown in human relationships hinted at in the aftermath of the **Fall** emerges in the next generation.

Cain is described as a farmer, Abel as a nomadic shepherd. Both offer sacrifices, a fundamental **Old Testament** concept signifying thankfulness, loyalty and submission to God. Cain's offering of 'the fruits of the earth' was rejected while Abel's sacrifice of lambs was accepted. The reason is not clear although Abel's offering of the 'fat portions' from the firstborn of his flock may have been seen as more costly and therefore, by implication, more heartfelt.

Rejection unleashes Cain's intense anger against God and his brother. Ignoring God's warnings to overcome his rage and avoid **sin**, Cain kills Abel in secret. God, however, sees and exposes his action and Cain's famous question, 'Am I my brother's keeper?', only serves to underline the horror of fratricide. God's judgement on Cain builds on that visited on Adam and Eve. The earth will not respond to his labour, he is to endure twofold exile, cast out of a community which has already lost its true home in Eden. Though the 'mark of Cain' will protect him from the vengeance of others, he becomes a wanderer, deprived of the presence of God. In time, Eve bears a further son, Seth.

Key concepts
Sacrifices offered to God; warning against anger; murder of a brother; judgement and exile; the mark of **Cain**; building of the first city.

Genesis 4:1–17, 25

Now the man knew his wife Eve, and she conceived and bore Cain, saying, "I have produced a man with the help of the LORD." ² Next she bore his brother Abel. Now Abel was a keeper of sheep, and Cain a tiller of the ground. ³ In the course of time Cain brought to the LORD an offering of the fruit of the ground, ⁴ and Abel for his part brought of the firstlings of his flock, their fat portions. And the LORD had regard for Abel and his offering, ⁵ but for Cain and his offering he had no regard. So Cain was very angry, and his countenance fell. ⁶ The LORD said to Cain, "Why are you angry, and why has your countenance fallen? ⁷ If you do well, will you not be accepted? And if you do not do well, sin is lurking at the door; its desire is for you, but you must master it."

⁸ Cain said to his brother Abel, "Let us go out to the field." And when they were in the field, Cain rose up against his brother Abel, and killed him. ⁹ Then the LORD said to Cain, "Where is your brother Abel?" He said, "I do not know; am I my brother's keeper?" ¹⁰ And the LORD said, "What have you done? Listen; your brother's blood is crying out to me from the ground! ¹¹ And now you are cursed from the ground, which has opened its mouth to receive your brother's blood from your hand. ¹² When you till the ground, it will no longer yield to you its strength; you will be a fugitive and a wanderer on the earth." ¹³ Cain said to the LORD, "My punishment is greater than I can bear! ¹⁴ Today you have driven me away from the soil, and I shall be hidden from your face; I shall be a fugitive and a wanderer on the earth, and anyone who meets me may kill me." ¹⁵ Then the LORD said to him, "Not so! Whoever kills Cain will suffer a sevenfold vengeance." And the LORD put a mark on Cain, so that no one who came upon him would kill him. ¹⁶ Then Cain went away from the presence of the LORD, and settled in the land of Nod, east of Eden.

¹⁷ Cain knew his wife, and she conceived and bore Enoch; and he built a city, and named it Enoch after his son Enoch. [...]

²⁵ Adam knew his wife again, and she bore a son and named

him Seth, for she said, "God has appointed for me another child instead of Abel, because Cain killed him."

Linked themes

Abel is cited as an example of faith in Hebrews 11:4. Later commentators saw Abel, a shepherd who was an innocent victim, as prefiguring **Christ**, described in the **New Testament** as the **Good Shepherd** and also as the **Lamb of God**, who offers himself as a sacrifice for the sins of the world. **Cain** became a symbol of anger and murder and a warning of the isolation and exile which breaking the bonds of society brings.

Related works

Art: Titian, *Cain kills Abel*, 1542–4 (S. Maria della Salute, Venice); Rembrandt, *Cain Kills Abel*, c.1650 (Staten Museum for Kunst, Copenhagen); William Blake, *The Body of Abel*, c.1826 (Tate Gallery, London); Georg Grosz, *Cain*, 1944 (Georg Grosz Estate).

Literature: In the Old English poem *Beowulf*, the murderous monster Grendel is described as being of the kin of Cain (102–14); *The Killing of Abel* (Towneley Cycle of Mystery Plays); William Shakespeare, *Hamlet*, c.1601–2; Byron, *Cain: A Mystery*, 1821; Samuel Taylor Coleridge, *The Rime of the Ancient Mariner*, 1817; Samuel Taylor Coleridge, *The Wanderings of Cain*, fragments published 1828 and 1834; Charles Dickens, *The Mystery of Edwin Drood*, published 1870.

NOAH AND THE FLOOD

The account of the **Flood** in Genesis 6–8 is one of several stories of a great deluge which appear in different cultures. The version closest to the Genesis narrative comes in the Babylonian *Epic of Gilgamesh*. The Flood story offers a further example of God acting in judgement, illustrating both his power and his hatred of human **sin**. God is shown as willing to destroy what he has created because it has become corrupt, yet also as ready to preserve those who live in obedience to him. Noah is warned of the coming flood and offered a way of escape:

an **ark**, or great ship, which will save him and his family, together with representatives of all living creatures.

The destruction visited on the earth and its inhabitants is graphically portrayed. Noah, safe within the ark, sends out first a raven, which fails to return, and then a dove which brings back an olive leaf, a sign of hope which shows that the waters are subsiding. Noah's first action on leaving the ark is to make a **sacrifice**. In this, the first **covenant** (solemn agreement) in the Bible, God promises that the Flood will never be repeated, a pledge sealed with the sign of the rainbow.

Key concepts

God's judgement on human **sin**; God's plan to save those who obey him; Noah's faith and obedience; Noah's **sacrifice** and God's **covenant**; the rainbow.

Genesis 6:9–14, 17–19, 22

[9] These are the descendants of Noah. Noah was a righteous man, blameless in his generation; Noah walked with God. [10] And Noah had three sons, Shem, Ham, and Japheth.

[11] Now the earth was corrupt in God's sight, and the earth was filled with violence. [12] And God saw that the earth was corrupt; for all flesh had corrupted its ways upon the earth. [13] And God said to Noah, "I have determined to make an end of all flesh, for the earth is filled with violence because of them; now I am going to destroy them along with the earth. [14] Make yourself an ark of cypress wood; make rooms in the ark, and cover it inside and out with pitch. [...]

[17] For my part, I am going to bring a flood of waters on the earth, to destroy from under heaven all flesh in which is the breath of life; everything that is on the earth shall die. [18] But I will establish my covenant with you; and you shall come into the ark, you, your sons, your wife, and your sons' wives with you. [19] And of every living thing, of all flesh, you shall bring two of every kind into the ark, to keep them alive with you; they shall be male and female. [...]

[22] Noah did this; he did all that God commanded him.

Genesis 7:11–22

[11] In the six hundredth year of Noah's life, in the second month, on the seventeenth day of the month, on that day all the fountains of the great deep burst forth, and the windows of the heavens were opened. [12] The rain fell on the earth forty days and forty nights. [13] On the very same day Noah with his sons, Shem and Ham and Japheth, and Noah's wife and the three wives of his sons entered the ark, [14] they and every wild animal of every kind, and all domestic animals of every kind, and every creeping thing that creeps on the earth, and every bird of every kind – every bird, every winged creature. [15] They went into the ark with Noah, two and two of all flesh in which there was the breath of life. [16] And those that entered, male and female of all flesh, went in as God had commanded him; and the LORD shut him in.

[17] The flood continued forty days on the earth; and the waters increased, and bore up the ark, and it rose high above the earth. [18] The waters swelled and increased greatly on the earth; and the ark floated on the face of the waters. [19] The waters swelled so mightily on the earth that all the high mountains under the whole heaven were covered; [20] the waters swelled above the mountains, covering them fifteen cubits deep. [21] And all flesh died that moved on the earth, birds, domestic animals, wild animals, all swarming creatures that swarm on the earth, and all human beings; [22] everything on dry land in whose nostrils was the breath of life died.

After forty days Noah sends out a raven and then a dove to see whether the waters have subsided. The dove initially returns with an olive leaf; sent out again seven days later, it fails to return and Noah knows that it has found refuge on land.

Genesis 8:15–22

[15] Then God said to Noah, [16] "Go out of the ark, you and your wife, and your sons and your sons' wives with you. [17] Bring out with you every living thing that is with you of all flesh – birds and animals and every creeping thing that creeps on the earth – so that they may abound on the earth, and be fruitful and multiply on the earth." [18] So Noah went out with his sons and his wife and his sons' wives. [19] And every animal, every creeping thing, and every bird, everything that moves on the earth, went out of the ark by families.

[20] Then Noah built an altar to the LORD, and took of every clean animal and of every clean bird, and offered burnt offerings on the altar. [21] And when the LORD smelled the pleasing odour, the LORD said in his heart, "I will never again curse the ground because of humankind, for the inclination of the human heart is evil from youth; nor will I ever again destroy every living creature as I have done.

[22] As long as the earth endures, seedtime and harvest, cold and heat, summer and winter, day and night, shall not cease."

Genesis 9:8, 11–13

[8] Then God said to Noah and to his sons with him, [...]
[11] I establish my covenant with you, that never again shall all flesh be cut off by the waters of a flood, and never again shall there be a flood to destroy the earth." [12] God said, "This is the sign of the covenant that I make between me and you and every living creature that is with you, for all future generations: [13] I have set my bow in the clouds, and it shall be a sign of the covenant between me and the earth.

Linked themes

The story of **Noah** was interpreted by Christian commentators as a **type** of both **judgement** and deliverance. The **Flood** was considered to foreshadow the water of **baptism** (1 Pet 3:20–1). **Tertullian** and **Jerome**, among others, argued that the ark prefigured the **Church**, within which sinners could take refuge and thus escape condemnation. Jesus is shown comparing the unexpectedness of the **Second Coming** with the suddenness of the flood which swept away Noah's contemporaries (Mt 24: 38–9). Noah is cited as an example of faith (Heb 11:7).

Related works

Art: Bedford Hours, *Noah Leaving the* Ark, c.1423 (British Library, London); Michelangelo, *The Flood,* 1508–12 (Sistine Chapel, Vatican, Rome); Raphael, *Noah and his Sons Building the Ark*, 1517 (Vatican, Rome); Nicolas Poussin, *Winter (The Deluge)*, 1660–4 (Louvre, Paris); William Turner, *The Deluge*, 1805 (Tate Gallery, London); William Turner, *Shade and Darkness: The Evening of the Deluge*, c.1805 (Tate Gallery, London); Wassily Kandinsky, *Improvisation Deluge*, 1913 (Städtische Galerie, Munich).

Literature: The Flood appears in a number of Old English poems, including *Genesis*, *Judgement Day* and *Christ II* and *Christ III*. The fourteenth-century poem, *Cleanness*, warns of God's anger against sin while painting a moving picture of those overwhelmed by the rising waters. The mystery plays also retell the story of Noah, drawing on eastern traditions to show Noah's wife stubbornly resisting her husband's pleas that she enter the ark (see the Chester, Towneley and York pageants). Chaucer's *Miller's Tale* includes a parody of the Flood. See also George Herbert (1593–1633), 'The Bunch of Grapes', Andrew Marvell (1621–78), 'First Anniversary'; D.H. Lawrence, *The Rainbow*, 1915; Julian Barnes, *A History of the World in 10½ Chapters*, 1989.

Music: Benjamin Britten, *Noye's Fludde*, 1958; Michael Flanders and Joseph Horowitz, *Captain Noah*, 1973.

THE TOWER OF BABEL

Genesis describes human beings moving from a nomadic lifestyle to building cities, and seeks to explain the existence of different languages and nations. It also makes the point that human **sin** was not completely washed away by the **Flood**. Proud of their developing technology and building skills, human beings decide to create a tower reaching up to **heaven**, possibly resembling the *ziggurats* (towers representing stairways from heaven to earth) in early Mesopotamian temple complexes. God thwarts human presumption by multiplying their languages and causing them to scatter, leaving the building incomplete. The Hebrew text suggests a play on the words *babel* (Babylon) and *balal* (to confuse). *Babel* is the Hebrew name for **Babylon**, which in the Bible often carries connotations of pride, idolatry and oppression.

Key concepts
Human pride and boasting; **Babylon**; God foils human pride; multiplication of languages.

Genesis 11:1–9
Now the whole earth had one language and the same words. [2] And as they migrated from the east, they came upon a plain in the land of Shinar and settled there. [3] And they said to one another, "Come, let us make bricks, and burn them thoroughly." And they had brick for stone, and bitumen for mortar. [4] Then they said, "Come, let us build ourselves a city, and a tower with its top in the heavens, and let us make a name for ourselves; otherwise we shall be scattered abroad upon the face of the whole earth." [5] The LORD came down to see the city and the tower, which mortals had built. [6] And the LORD said, "Look, they are one people, and they have all one language; and this is only the beginning of what they will do; nothing that they propose to do will now be impossible for them. [7] Come, let us go down, and confuse their language there, so that they will not understand one another's speech." [8] So the LORD scattered them abroad from there over the face of all the earth, and they left off building the city. [9] Therefore it was called Babel, because there the LORD confused the language of all the earth; and from there the LORD scattered them abroad over the face of all the earth.

Linked themes

Some later commentators, including **Augustine** of Hippo, saw the events of **Pentecost**, when the **Holy Spirit** enabled the **disciples** of **Jesus** to praise God in a number of languages, as a reversal of the confusion of languages following the attempt to build the **Tower of Babel** (see Chapter 8: The Birth of the Church (Pentecost)).

Related works

Art: Bedford Hours, *Building of the Tower of Babel*, c.1423 (British Library, London); Pieter Brueghel the Elder, *Tower of Babel*, 1563 (Kunsthistorisches Museum, Vienna); Abel Grimmer, *Building of the Tower of Babel*, 1604; Josef Szubert, *Tower of Babel*, 1976 (Zimmerer Collection, Warsaw).

Literature: William Cowper, *The Task*, Bk V, 1785; James Joyce, *Finnegan's Wake*, 1939; J.R.R. Tolkien, *The Two Towers*, 1954–5; William Golding, *The Spire*, 1964; A.S. Byatt, *Babel Tower*, 1996.

Music: Anton Rubenstein, *Der Turm zu Babel*, 1870; Igor Stravinsky, *Babel*, 1944.

2 THE HISTORY OF ISRAEL

ABRAHAM, ISAAC AND ISHMAEL

Abram, later renamed **Abraham**, is a key figure in Jewish, Christian and Muslim traditions.

God calls Abram

Genesis shows God calling Abram to leave his home and family and journey to a land which God will show him. God promises that Abram will be the father of a great nation and that through him all the nations of the earth will be blessed.

Key concepts

God's promises to Abram; Abram's obedience to God's call.

Genesis 12:1–5

Now the LORD said to Abram, "Go from your country and your kindred and your father's house to the land that I will show you. [2] I will make of you a great nation, and I will bless you, and make your name great, so that you will be a blessing. [3] I will bless those who bless you, and the one who curses you I will curse; and in you all the families of the earth shall be blessed."

[4] So Abram went, as the LORD had told him; and Lot went with him. Abram was seventy-five years old when he departed from Haran. [5] Abram took his wife Sarai and his brother's son Lot, and all the possessions that they had gathered, and the persons whom they had acquired in Haran; and they set forth to go to the land of Canaan.

Linked themes

Abraham is cited as an example of obedient trust in God in Heb 11:8–19. Here Abraham, **Abel**, **Noah**, **Isaac** and **Jacob** are described as 'strangers and foreigners (**AV** 'strangers and pilgrims') on the earth' whose true home is in **heaven**.

Related works

Art: Jacopo Bassano, *Departure of Abraham*, c.1570–1 (National Gallery of Canada).

Literature: Edwin Muir, *Abraham*.

God's covenant with Abraham

God's original promise to Abram was later incorporated into a series of formal agreements or covenants. Thus in Genesis 17 the promise of the land is confirmed, the patriarch's name is changed from Abram ('exalted father') to Abraham ('father of a multitude'), and **circumcision** becomes the outward sign of belonging to the people of God. Because his wife Sarai (later **Sarah**) was barren, Abram has had a son called **Ishmael** by his wife's maidservant Hagar, but God still plans that Sarah will bear a child.

Key concepts
God's promises to Abram; Abram's name is changed to indicate the number of his descendants; circumcision as a mark of belonging; Sarah promised a son.

Genesis 17:1, 3–5, 8, 10, 15–16
When Abram was ninety-nine years old, the LORD appeared to Abram [...] ³ ... and God said to him, ⁴ "As for me, this is my covenant with you: You shall be the ancestor of a multitude of nations. ⁵ No longer shall your name be Abram, but your name shall be Abraham; for I have made you the ancestor of a multitude of nations. [...] ⁸ And I will give to you, and to your offspring after you, the land where you are now an alien, all the land of Canaan, for a perpetual holding; and I will be their God. [...]¹⁰ This is my covenant, which you shall keep, between me and you and your offspring after you: Every male among you shall be circumcised." [...]

¹⁵ God said to Abraham, "As for Sarai your wife, you shall not call her Sarai, but Sarah shall be her name. ¹⁶ I will bless her, and moreover I will give you a son by her. I will bless her, and she shall give rise to nations; kings of peoples shall come from her."

Linked themes
God's promise of a son for Sarah is fulfilled in the birth of **Isaac**. Abraham's descendants eventually settle in the land of **Canaan**.

Related works
Art: Barnett Newman, *Covenant*, 1949.

The hospitality of Abraham
God appears to Abraham at Mamre in the form of three men and once again promises that his wife Sarah, though past the age of child-bearing, will indeed have a son. God later warns Abraham of the impending destruction of the evil cities of **Sodom and Gomorrah** and his nephew, Lot, is saved.

Key concepts

Three heavenly visitors meet Abraham; Abraham offers hospitality; **Old Testament** 'Trinity'; Abraham, the friend of God; birth of Isaac foretold.

Genesis 18:1–5, 8–10

The LORD appeared to Abraham by the oaks of Mamre, as he sat at the entrance of his tent in the heat of the day. [2] He looked up and saw three men standing near him. When he saw them, he ran from the tent entrance to meet them, and bowed down to the ground. [3] He said, "My lord, if I find favour with you, do not pass by your servant. [4] Let a little water be brought, and wash your feet, and rest yourselves under the tree. [5] Let me bring a little bread, that you may refresh yourselves, and after that you may pass on – since you have come to your servant." So they said, "Do as you have said." [...]
[8] Then [Abraham] took curds and milk and the calf that he had prepared, and set it before them; and he stood by them under the tree while they ate.

[9] They said to him, "Where is your wife Sarah?" And he said, "There, in the tent." [10] Then one said, "I will surely return to you in due season, and your wife Sarah shall have a son."

Linked themes

The writer of Hebrews urges his readers not to neglect to welcome strangers for, by so doing, 'some have entertained angels unawares' (**AV** Heb 13:2). Both the Old Testament and the **New Testament** contain a number of stories of children conceived despite barrenness, old age or other factors (e.g. **Samuel**, **Samson**, **John the Baptist** and **Jesus** himself). The three men in this account were later understood by Christian commentators to be a manifestation of the Trinity.

Related works

Art: Andrei Rublëv, *Hospitality of Abraham*, c.1407 (Monastery of the Holy Trinity in Sergiev Posad); Giovanni Domenico Tiepolo, *Angels*

Appearing to Abraham, 1773 (Gallerie dell'Accademia, Venice); Raphael, *Abraham and Three Angels*, 1517 (Loggia, Vatican, Rome); Jan Provost, *Abraham, Sarah, and the Angel*, c.1500 (Louvre, Paris); Marc Chagall, *Abraham and the Three Angels*, 1960–6 (Musée National Message Biblique Marc Chagall, Nice).

Literature: William Blake, *Holy Thursday* (*Songs of Innocence*), 1794.

Isaac and Ishmael

Sarah at last bears a son. However, her jealousy of Hagar and **Ishmael**, **Abraham's** son by Hagar, means that Abraham is forced to send them away. Nevertheless, God promises that Ishmael's descendants will become a great nation, a pledge which according to tradition was fulfilled through the Arab peoples.

Key concepts

God keeps his promise to Abraham and Sarah; Ishmael is sent away but God promises to care for him.

Genesis 21:1–3, 9–13

The LORD dealt with Sarah as he had said, and the LORD did for Sarah as he had promised. [2] Sarah conceived and bore Abraham a son in his old age, at the time of which God had spoken to him. [3] Abraham gave the name Isaac to his son whom Sarah bore him. [...]

[9] But Sarah saw the son of Hagar the Egyptian, whom she had borne to Abraham, playing with her son Isaac. [10] So she said to Abraham, "Cast out this slave woman with her son; for the son of this slave woman shall not inherit along with my son Isaac." [11] The matter was very distressing to Abraham on account of his son. [12] But God said to Abraham, "Do not be distressed because of the boy and because of your slave woman; whatever Sarah says to you, do as she tells you, for it is through Isaac that offspring shall be named for you. [13] As for the son of the slave woman, I will make a nation of him also, because he is your offspring."

Linked themes

In the letter to the Galatians (4:21–31), Hagar is used as an image of slavery to the **Old Testament law.**

Related works

Art: Rembrandt, *Sarai Complains to Abram about Hagar*, c.1640–5; Rembrandt, *Abraham sends Hagar and Ishmael away*, c.1640–3 (Musée Bonnat, Bayonne); Giovanni Francesco Guercino, *Expulsion of Hagar and Ishmael*, 1658 (Brera, Milan); Giovanni Lanfranco, *Hagar in the Wilderness*, c.1640 (Louvre, Paris); Jean-Francois Millet, *Hagar and Ishmael*, c.1849 (Rijksmuseum, The Hague).

Literature: The Old English poem *Genesis A*; Herman Melville, *Moby Dick*, 1851.

The sacrifice of Isaac

God tests **Abraham's** trust in him by commanding that he sacrifice his beloved young son **Isaac.** Obediently, Abraham travels to the appointed place and prepares for the sacrifice. At the last moment he is stopped by an **angel** and instead sacrifices a ram found nearby.

Key concepts

Abraham asked to sacrifice his much-loved son; Abraham's obedience to God; God intervenes; an alternative sacrifice is provided.

Genesis 22:1–18

After these things God tested Abraham. He said to him, "Abraham!" And he said, "Here I am." [2] He said, "Take your son, your only son Isaac, whom you love, and go to the land of Moriah, and offer him there as a burnt offering on one of the mountains that I shall show you." [3] So Abraham rose early in the morning, saddled his donkey, and took two of his young men with him, and his son Isaac; he cut the wood for the burnt offering, and set out and went to the place in the distance that God had shown him. [4] On the third day Abraham looked up and saw the place far away. [5] Then Abraham said to his young men, "Stay here with the donkey; the boy and I will go over there; we will worship, and then we will come back to you." [6] Abraham took the wood of the burnt offering and laid it on his son Isaac, and he himself carried the fire and the knife. So the two of them walked on together. [7] Isaac said to his father Abraham, "Father!" And he said, "Here I am, my son." He said, "The fire and the wood are here, but where is the lamb for a burnt offering?" [8] Abraham said, "God himself will provide the lamb for a burnt offering, my son." So the two of them walked on together.

[9] When they came to the place that God had shown him, Abraham built an altar there and laid the wood in order. He bound his son Isaac, and laid him on the altar, on top of the wood. [10] Then Abraham reached out his hand and took the knife to kill his son. [11] But the angel of the LORD called to him from heaven, and said, "Abraham, Abraham!" And he said, "Here I am." [12] He said, "Do not lay your hand on the boy or do anything to him; for now I know that you fear God, since you have not withheld your son, your only son, from me." [13] And Abraham looked up and saw a ram, caught in a thicket by its horns. Abraham went and took the ram and offered it up as a burnt offering instead of his son. [14] So Abraham called that place "The LORD will provide"; as it is said to this day, "On the mount of the LORD it shall be provided."

[15] The angel of the LORD called to Abraham a second time from heaven, [16] and said, "By myself I have sworn, says the LORD: Because you have done this, and have not withheld your son, your only son, [17] I will indeed bless you, and I will make your offspring as numerous as the stars of heaven and as the sand that is on the seashore. And your offspring shall possess the gate of their enemies, [18] and by your offspring shall all the nations of the earth gain blessing for themselves, because you have obeyed my voice."

Linked themes

This episode was later interpreted by Christian commentators as prefiguring God's sacrifice of his own son, Jesus **Christ**, at the

Crucifixion. Romans 8:32 speaks of God 'who did not withhold his own Son, but gave him up for all of us'.

Related works

Art: Andrea del Sarto, *Sacrifice of Abraham*, c.1520 (Dresden); Mantegna, *Abraham and Isaac*, c.1500; Caravaggio, *Sacrifice of Isaac*, 1603 (Uffizi Gallery, Florence); Rembrandt, *Sacrifice of Abraham*, 1635 (The Hermitage, St Petersburg); Marc Chagall, *Sacrifice of Isaac*, 1960–6 (Musée National Message Biblique Marc Chagall, Nice); Jack Levine, *Sacrifice of Isaac*, 1974 (Kennedy Galleries, New York).

Literature: *Abraham and Isaac* (Chester Mystery Cycle); *Sacrifice of Isaac* (Brome Mystery Cycle); Søren Kierkegaard, *Fear and Trembling*, 1843; Wilfred Owen, 'The Parable of the Old Man and the Young'.

Music: Benjamin Britten, *Canticle II: Abraham and Isaac*, 1952; Igor Stravinsky, *Abraham and Isaac*, 1962–3.

JACOB

The story of **Jacob**, son of **Isaac** and Rebekah and a key figure in the **Old Testament**, offers stark illustrations of human greed, dissension and trickery interwoven with accounts of life-changing encounters with God.

Jacob and Esau

Jacob and his twin brother **Esau** are depicted as rivals even in the womb. Eventually Jacob obtains his brother's inheritance through opportunism, when Esau trades his birthright for a meal of lentil stew (**AV** 'mess of pottage'), and deception, when Jacob pretends to be Esau in order to gain his father's blessing.

Key concepts

Rivalry between Jacob and Esau; Jacob tricks Esau; Jacob gains **Isaac's** blessing through deception.

Genesis 25:21–3, 27–33

[21] Isaac prayed to the LORD for his wife, because she was barren; and the LORD granted his prayer, and his wife Rebekah conceived. [22] The children struggled together within her; and she said, "If it is to be this way, why do I live?" So she went to inquire of the LORD. [23] And the LORD said to her,

"Two nations are in your womb,
and two peoples born of you shall be divided;
the one shall be stronger than the other,
the elder shall serve the younger." [...]

[27] When the boys grew up, Esau was a skilful hunter, a man of the field, while Jacob was a quiet man, living in tents. [28] Isaac loved Esau, because he was fond of game; but Rebekah loved Jacob.

[29] Once when Jacob was cooking a stew, Esau came in from the field, and he was famished. [30] Esau said to Jacob, "Let me eat some of that red stuff, for I am famished!" (Therefore he was called Edom.) [31] Jacob said, "First sell me your birthright." [32] Esau said, "I am about to die; of what use is a birthright to me?" [33] Jacob said, "Swear to me first." So he swore to him, and sold his birthright to Jacob.

In old age, Isaac plans to bestow his blessing on Esau, his first-born. He asks Esau to find and prepare game for him to eat. However, Rebekah overhears and, while Esau is out hunting, she instructs Jacob to take food to his father in Esau's place. Isaac, whose sight is failing, is deceived and gives Jacob his blessing.

Genesis 27:30–6

[30] As soon as Isaac had finished blessing Jacob ... his brother Esau came in from his hunting. [31] He also prepared savoury food, and brought it to his father ...[32] His father Isaac said to him, "Who are you?" He answered, "I am your firstborn son, Esau." [33] Then Isaac trembled violently, and said, "Who was it then that hunted game and brought it to me, and I ate it all before you

came, and I have blessed him? – yes, and blessed he shall be!" [34] When Esau heard his father's words, he cried out with an exceedingly great and bitter cry, and said to his father, "Bless me, me also, father!" [35] But he said, "Your brother came deceitfully, and he has taken away your blessing." [36] Esau said, "Is he not rightly named Jacob? For he has supplanted me these two times. He took away my birthright; and look, now he has taken away my blessing."

Linked themes

In the **New Testament**, Esau is condemned because he did not value his birthright (Heb 12:16).

Related works

Art: Matthias Stomer, *Esau Selling Jacob his Birthright for a Bowl of Lentils*, c.1640 (Hermitage Museum, St Petersburg); Rembrandt, *Esau Sells his Birthright to Jacob*, c.1640–5 (Historisch Museum, Amsterdam); Govert Flinck, *Isaac Blessing Jacob*, 1635 (Rijksmuseum, Amsterdam); Rembrandt, *Jacob Asks his Father Isaac for a Blessing*, c.1655 (British Museum, London); Bartolomé Esteban Murillo, *Isaac Blessing Jacob*, 1665–70 (Hermitage Museum, St Petersburg).

Jacob's ladder

Jacob is forced to flee Esau's anger and journeys to the home of his uncle Laban. On the way, he experiences a dream-vision of God in which he sees a ladder or stairway reaching from earth to **heaven** with **angels** ascending and descending. God speaks to Jacob, renewing the promises he made to Abraham. On waking, Jacob names the place Bethel, 'the house of God'.

Key concepts

God renews his promises.

Genesis 28:10–19

[10] Jacob left Beer-sheba and went toward Haran … Taking one of the stones of the place, he put it under his head and lay down in that place. [12] And he dreamed that there was a ladder set up on the earth, the top of it reaching to heaven; and the angels of God were ascending and descending on it. [13] And the LORD stood beside him and said, "I am the LORD, the God of Abraham your father and the God of Isaac; the land on which you lie I will give to you and to your offspring; [14] and your offspring shall be like the dust of the earth, and you shall spread abroad to the west and to the east and to the north and to the south; and all the families of the earth shall be blessed in you and in your offspring. [15] Know that I am with you and will keep you wherever you go, and will bring you back to this land; for I will not leave you until I have done what I have promised you." [16] Then Jacob woke from his sleep and said, "Surely the LORD is in this place – and I did not know it!" [17] And he was afraid, and said, "How awesome is this place! This is none other than the house of God, and this is the gate of heaven."

[18] So Jacob rose early in the morning, and he took the stone that he had put under his head and set it up for a pillar and poured oil on the top of it. [19] He called that place Bethel.

Linked themes

Receiving guidance or instruction from God through dream-visions is a common theme in the **Bible**. Other examples occur in the lives of **Joseph** the son of **Jacob**, **Daniel**, **Joseph** the husband of the **Virgin Mary**, and the **Magi** who visit the infant Jesus.

Related works

Art: Raphael, *Jacob's Dream*, 1519 (Loggia, Vatican, Rome); Rembrandt, *Jacob's Dream*, c.1640–5 (Louvre, Paris); William Blake, *The Dream of Jacob's Ladder*, c.1790 (British Museum, London); Marc Chagall, *Jacob's Ladder*, 1930–2.

Literature: Walter Hilton (d.1396), *The Scale [Ladder] of Perfection*; John Milton, *Paradise Lost*, Bk 3, 1667; John Dryden, *The Hind and the Panther*, Bk 2, 1687.

Jacob, Rachel and Leah

Jacob falls in love with Rachel, his uncle's younger daughter, but now it is his turn to be tricked as Laban manoeuvres him into marrying her older sister first. Jacob becomes the father of twelve sons: six by Leah (Reuben, Simeon, **Levi**, **Judah**, Issachar and Zebulun), two by her maid Zilpah (Gad and Asher); two by Rachel's maid, Bilhah (Dan and Naphtali) and finally his two favourite sons **Joseph** and Benjamin, by Rachel. The sons are named as the ancestors of the **Twelve Tribes of Israel**.

Key concepts

Jacob's love for Rachel; Jacob tricked by Laban.

Genesis 29:16–30

[16] Now Laban had two daughters; the name of the elder was Leah, and the name of the younger was Rachel. [17] Leah's eyes were lovely, and Rachel was graceful and beautiful. [18] Jacob loved Rachel; so he said, "I will serve you seven years for your younger daughter Rachel." [19] Laban said, "It is better that I give her to you than that I should give her to any other man; stay with me." [20] So Jacob served seven years for Rachel, and they seemed to him but a few days because of the love he had for her.

[21] Then Jacob said to Laban, "Give me my wife that I may go in to her, for my time is completed." [22] So Laban gathered together all the people of the place, and made a feast. [23] But in the evening he took his daughter Leah and brought her to Jacob; and he went in to her. [24] (Laban gave his maid Zilpah to his daughter Leah to be her maid.) [25] When morning came, it was Leah! And Jacob said to Laban, "What is this you have done to me? Did I not serve with you for Rachel? Why then have you deceived me?" [26] Laban said, "This is not done in our country – giving the younger before the firstborn. [27] Complete the week of this one,

and we will give you the other also in return for serving me another seven years." [28] Jacob did so, and completed her week; then Laban gave him his daughter Rachel as a wife. [29] (Laban gave his maid Bilhah to his daughter Rachel to be her maid.) [30] So Jacob went in to Rachel also, and he loved Rachel more than Leah. He served Laban for another seven years.

Linked themes

Christian commentators later saw in Rachel and Leah personifications of the '**active life**' of involvement in the everyday world and the '**contemplative life**' of withdrawal and prayer. In this they functioned as **Old Testament** counterparts of **Mary** and **Martha**, the sisters of **Lazarus** (Lk 10:38–42).

Related works

Art: Michelangelo, *Rachel and Leah* (Tomb of Pope Julius II), 1542–55; Raphael, *Jacob's Encounter with Rachel*, 1518–19 (Loggia, Vatican, Rome); Valerio Castello, *Rebecca at the Well*, c. 1650 (The Hermitage, St Petersburg).

Jacob wrestles with the angel

After many years in exile, **Jacob** is told by God to return home. Though afraid of **Esau's** anger, Jacob gathers his family and flocks and sets off for **Canaan**. Alone at night, he wrestles with a stranger who, unable to overpower Jacob, touches his hip, injuring him. Jacob is told that he has wrestled with God and is renamed **Israel**, meaning 'one who fights with God'. Jacob calls the place *Peniel*, meaning 'the face of God'. Jacob returns to Canaan where he meets Esau and they are reconciled, though their descendants remain hostile.

Key concepts

Jacob encounters God face to face.

Genesis 32:24–30

[24] Jacob was left alone; and a man wrestled with him until daybreak. [25] When the man saw that he did not prevail against

Jacob, he struck him on the hip socket; and Jacob's hip was put out of joint as he wrestled with him. [26] Then he said, "Let me go, for the day is breaking." But Jacob said, "I will not let you go, unless you bless me." [27] So he said to him, "What is your name?" And he said, "Jacob." [28] Then the man said, "You shall no longer be called Jacob, but Israel, for you have striven with God and with humans, and have prevailed." [29] Then Jacob asked him, "Please tell me your name." But he said, "Why is it that you ask my name?" And there he blessed him. [30] So Jacob called the place Peniel, saying, "For I have seen God face to face, and yet my life is preserved."

Linked themes

Jacob was named by Jesus as a man of faith with whom he would eat in the **Kingdom of God** (Mt 8:11).

Related works

Art: Rembrandt, *Jacob's Struggle with the Angel*, *c*.1659–60 (Berlin); Eugène Delacroix, *Jacob Wrestling the Angel*, 1850–61 (S. Sulpice, Paris); Paul Gauguin, *Vision after the Sermon* (*Jacob Wrestling with the Angel*), 1888 (National Gallery of Scotland); Odilon Redon, *Jacob Wrestling with the Angel*, Pre-1909 (Brooklyn Museum, New York).

Literature: Isaak Walton, *Life of Dr John Donne*, 1640; Charles Wesley, 'Wrestling Jacob', 1742; Ernest Hemingway, *The Sun also Rises*, 1926.

JOSEPH

Joseph's life, as portrayed in **Genesis**, is a story of alternating privilege and suffering, during which God brings him through a series of setbacks to play a crucial role in preserving not only the people of Egypt but also his own family.

Joseph and his brothers

Joseph was the son of **Jacob's** favourite wife, Rachel, and the preferential treatment he received fuelled his brothers' jealousy. Dreams and their interpretation will continue to play an important role in Joseph's life.

Key concepts

Joseph is Jacob's favourite; Joseph's dreams; his brothers' resentment.

Genesis 37:3–8, 12, 17–20, 23–4, 26–8

3 Now Israel loved Joseph more than any other of his children, because he was the son of his old age; and he had made him a long robe with sleeves (**AV** 'coat of many colours'). 4 But when his brothers saw that their father loved him more than all his brothers, they hated him, and could not speak peaceably to him.

5 Once Joseph had a dream, and when he told it to his brothers, they hated him even more. 6 He said to them, "Listen to this dream that I dreamed. 7 There we were, binding sheaves in the field. Suddenly my sheaf rose and stood upright; then your sheaves gathered around it, and bowed down to my sheaf." 8 His brothers said to him, "Are you indeed to reign over us? Are you indeed to have dominion over us?" So they hated him even more because of his dreams and his words. [...]

12 Now his brothers went to pasture their father's flock near Shechem [...] 17 ... Joseph went after his brothers, and found them at Dothan. 18 They saw him from a distance, and before he came near to them, they conspired to kill him. 19 They said to one another, "Here comes this dreamer. 20 Come now, let us kill him and throw him into one of the pits; then we shall say that a wild animal has devoured him, and we shall see what will become of his dreams." [...]

23 So when Joseph came to his brothers, they stripped him of his robe, the long robe with sleeves that he wore; 24 and they took him and threw him into a pit. The pit was empty; there was no water in it. [...]

[26] Then Judah said to his brothers, "What profit is it if we kill our brother and conceal his blood? [27] Come, let us sell him to the Ishmaelites, and not lay our hands on him, for he is our brother, our own flesh." And his brothers agreed. [28] When some Midianite traders passed by, they drew Joseph up, lifting him out of the pit, and sold him to the Ishmaelites for twenty pieces of silver. And they took Joseph to Egypt.

Linked themes
Dreams, as a means of receiving God's guidance and foretelling the future, appear in the stories of **Daniel**, **Joseph**, the husband of the **Virgin Mary**, and the **Magi** who visit the infant **Jesus**.

Related works
Art: Rembrandt, *Joseph Recounts his Dreams*, c.1637 (Rijksmuseum, Amsterdam); Jan Victors, *Joseph Telling his Dreams to his Family*, 1651; Gioacchino Assereto, *Joseph Being Sold by his Brothers*, c.1625 (Private Collection); Rembrandt, *Joseph is Sold by his Brothers*, c.1650 (Berlin); Velasquez, *Joseph's Bloody Coat brought to Jacob*, 1630 (Monastery of San Lorenzo de El Escorial).

Literature: Thomas Mann, *Joseph and His Brothers*, 1934–44.

Music: Handel, *Joseph and His Brethren*, 1744; Tim Rice and Andrew Lloyd-Webber, *Joseph and the Amazing Technicolour Dreamcoat*, 1968.

Joseph and Potiphar's wife
Having been taken to Egypt by slave traders, Joseph is bought by Potiphar, an officer of Pharaoh. Eventually Joseph is placed in charge of the household. However, his good looks attract his master's wife who tries and fails to seduce him. Angered, she makes false accusations against him and Joseph is thrown into prison.

Key concepts
God helps Joseph prosper; Potiphar's wife tempts Joseph; Joseph resists temptation; Joseph unjustly accused.

Genesis 39:1–4, 7–17, 19–21

Now Joseph was taken down to Egypt, and Potiphar, an officer of Pharaoh, the captain of the guard, an Egyptian, bought him from the Ishmaelites who had brought him down there. [2] The LORD was with Joseph, and he became a successful man ...[3] His master saw that the LORD was with him, and that the LORD caused all that he did to prosper in his hands. [4] So Joseph found favour in his sight and attended him; he made him overseer of his house and put him in charge of all that he had. [...]

[7] And after a time his master's wife cast her eyes on Joseph and said, "Lie with me." [8] But he refused and said to his master's wife, "Look, with me here, my master has no concern about anything in the house, and he has put everything that he has in my hand. [9] He is not greater in this house than I am, nor has he kept back anything from me except yourself, because you are his wife. How then could I do this great wickedness, and sin against God?" [10] And although she spoke to Joseph day after day, he would not consent to lie beside her or to be with her. [11] One day, however, when he went into the house to do his work, and while no one else was in the house, [12] she caught hold of his garment, saying, "Lie with me!" But he left his garment in her hand, and fled and ran outside. [13] When she saw that he had left his garment in her hand and had fled outside, [14] she called out to the members of her household and said to them, "See, my husband has brought among us a Hebrew to insult us! He came in to me to lie with me, and I cried out with a loud voice; [15] and when he heard me raise my voice and cry out, he left his garment beside me, and fled outside." [16] Then she kept his garment by her until his master came home, [17] and she told him the same story [...] [19] When his master heard the words that his wife spoke to him, saying, "This is the way your servant treated me," he became enraged. [20] And Joseph's master took him and put him into the prison ...[21] But the LORD was with Joseph and showed him steadfast love; he gave him favour in the sight of the chief jailer.

Linked themes
Temptation is a key theme in the **Bible** from the story of **Adam** and **Eve** onwards. Joseph was seen by later commentators as prefiguring **Jesus** as someone who overcomes temptation and is falsely accused.

Related works
Art: Tintoretto, *Joseph and Potiphar's Wife* c.1555 (Museo del Prado, Madrid); Guido Reni, *Joseph and Potiphar's Wife*, c.1620 (Holkham); Rembrandt (or his workshop), *Joseph Accused by Potiphar's Wife*, 1655 (National Gallery of Art, Washington); Guercino, *Joseph and Potiphar's Wife*, 1649 (National Gallery of Art, Washington).

Literature: Henry Fielding, *Joseph Andrews*, 1742.

Pharaoh's dreams
Pharaoh's dreams not only provide a warning of approaching famine but offer an opportunity for **Joseph's** gifts to be demonstrated and for him to achieve great influence in Egypt. Eventually his own family come to buy grain: they too are saved from famine and are reconciled to Joseph.

Key concepts
God speaks through dreams; Joseph's gift of interpretation; seven years of plenty and seven of famine foretold; Joseph's God-given wisdom brings him great rank.

Genesis 41:1–8
After two whole years, Pharaoh dreamed that he was standing by the Nile, [2] and there came up out of the Nile seven sleek and fat cows, and they grazed in the reed grass. [3] Then seven other cows, ugly and thin, came up out of the Nile after them, and stood by the other cows on the bank of the Nile. [4] The ugly and thin cows ate up the seven sleek and fat cows. And Pharaoh awoke. [5] Then he fell asleep and dreamed a second time; seven ears of grain, plump and good, were growing on one stalk. [6] Then seven ears, thin and blighted by the east wind, sprouted after them.

[7] The thin ears swallowed up the seven plump and full ears. Pharaoh awoke, and it was a dream. [8] In the morning his spirit was troubled; so he sent and called for all the magicians of Egypt and all its wise men. Pharaoh told them his dreams, but there was no one who could interpret them to Pharaoh.

Joseph, whose ability to interpret dreams has been demonstrated during his time in prison, is summoned and asked to explain Pharaoh's experience.

Genesis 41:25–30, 33–7, 39–41

[25] Then Joseph said to Pharaoh, "Pharaoh's dreams are one and the same; God has revealed to Pharaoh what he is about to do. [26] The seven good cows are seven years, and the seven good ears are seven years; the dreams are one. [27] The seven lean and ugly cows that came up after them are seven years, as are the seven empty ears blighted by the east wind. They are seven years of famine. [28] It is as I told Pharaoh; God has shown to Pharaoh what he is about to do. [29] There will come seven years of great plenty throughout all the land of Egypt. [30] After them there will arise seven years of famine [...]
[33] Now therefore let Pharaoh select a man who is discerning and wise, and set him over the land of Egypt. [34] Let Pharaoh proceed to appoint overseers over the land, and take one-fifth of the produce of the land of Egypt during the seven plenteous years. [35] Let them gather all the food of these good years that are coming, and lay up grain under the authority of Pharaoh for food in the cities, and let them keep it. [36] That food shall be a reserve for the land against the seven years of famine that are to befall the land of Egypt, so that the land may not perish through the famine."

[37] The proposal pleased Pharaoh and all his servants. [...] [39] So Pharaoh said to Joseph, "Since God has shown you all this, there is no one so discerning and wise as you. [40] You shall be over my house, and all my people shall order themselves as you command; only with regard to the throne will I be greater than you." [41] And Pharaoh said to Joseph, "See, I have set you over all the land of Egypt."

Linked themes
Joseph's saving of the population of Egypt and preservation of his own family from famine was seen as foreshadowing the coming of **Jesus** the **Saviour** of humankind.

Related works
Art: Andrea del Sarto, *Life of Joseph the Hebrew*, c.1520 (Galleria Palatina, Florence).

MOSES AND THE EXODUS

Moses is a very significant figure within Judaism, Christianity and Islam. He is viewed as a prophet who transmits God's **law** and a worker of **miracles**, as well as the one who leads the **Exodus** from Egypt.

The birth of Moses
The birth of Moses takes place against the background of the oppression of the **Israelites** by the Egyptians. **Joseph** is no longer remembered and the rapidly expanding population of Israelite slaves is seen as a threat. **Pharaoh** orders that all male Jewish infants should be killed at birth but Moses is saved through the ingenuity of his family and adopted into Pharaoh's own household.

Key concepts
Moses saved from the threat of death.

Exodus 2:1–10
Now a man from the house of Levi went and married a Levite woman. [2] The woman conceived and bore a son; and when she saw that he was a fine baby, she hid him three months. [3] When she could hide him no longer she got a papyrus basket for him, and plastered it with bitumen and pitch; she put the child in it and placed it among the reeds on the bank of the river. [4] His sister stood at a distance, to see what would happen to him.

[5] The daughter of Pharaoh came down to bathe at the river, while her attendants walked beside the river. She saw the basket among the reeds and sent her maid to bring it. [6] When she opened it, she saw the child. He was crying, and she took pity on him. "This must be one of the Hebrews' children," she said. [7] Then his sister said to Pharaoh's daughter, "Shall I go and get you a nurse from the Hebrew women to nurse the child for you?" [8] Pharaoh's daughter said to her, "Yes." So the girl went and called the child's mother. [9] Pharaoh's daughter said to her, "Take this child and nurse it for me, and I will give you your wages." So the woman took the child and nursed it. [10] When the child grew up, she brought him to Pharaoh's daughter, and she took him as her son. She named him Moses, "because," she said, "I drew him out of the water."

Linked themes

This story of threat and deliverance was later seen as prefiguring the birth of **Jesus**, who had to flee the threats of a king, and the linked story of the **Massacre of the Innocents**.

Related works

Art: Raphael, *Moses Saved from the Water*, 1518–19 (Loggia, Vatican, Rome); Paulo Veronese, *Finding of Moses*, c.1570–5 (National Gallery of Art, Washington); Johann Liss, *The Finding of Moses*, 1626–7; Rembrandt, *The Discovery of Moses*, c.1635 (Philadelphia Museum of Art); Sébastien Bourdon, *Finding of Moses* c.1650 (National Gallery of Art, Washington); Nicolas Poussin, *Moses Being Placed in the Waters*, 1654 (Ashmolean Museum, Oxford); James Ensor, *Finding of Moses*, 1924 (Berkeley Art Museum, University of California).

The burning bush

In exile following his killing of an Egyptian who was beating an **Israelite** slave, **Moses** encounters God and is commanded to lead his people out of slavery.

Key concepts
Moses encounters God; God's plans to deliver his people.

Exodus 3:1–8, 10, 19–20

Moses was keeping the flock of his father-in-law Jethro, the priest of Midian; he led his flock beyond the wilderness, and came to Horeb, the mountain of God. ² There the angel of the LORD appeared to him in a flame of fire out of a bush; he looked, and the bush was blazing, yet it was not consumed. ³ Then Moses said, "I must turn aside and look at this great sight, and see why the bush is not burned up." ⁴ When the LORD saw that he had turned aside to see, God called to him out of the bush, "Moses, Moses!" And he said, "Here I am." ⁵ Then he said, "Come no closer! Remove the sandals from your feet, for the place on which you are standing is holy ground." ⁶ He said further, "I am the God of your father, the God of Abraham, the God of Isaac, and the God of Jacob." And Moses hid his face, for he was afraid to look at God.

⁷ Then the LORD said, "I have observed the misery of my people who are in Egypt; I have heard their cry on account of their taskmasters. Indeed, I know their sufferings, ⁸ and I have come down to deliver them from the Egyptians, and to bring them up out of that land to a good and broad land, a land flowing with milk and honey [...]¹⁰ So come, I will send you to Pharaoh to bring my people, the Israelites, out of Egypt." [...]

¹⁹ I know, however, that the king of Egypt will not let you go unless compelled by a mighty hand. ²⁰ So I will stretch out my hand and strike Egypt with all my wonders that I will perform in it; after that he will let you go.

Linked themes
Moses encounters God directly again on **Mount Sinai** when he is given the **Ten Commandments**.

Related works

Art: Botticelli, *Moses and the Burning Bush*, 1481–2 (Sistine Chapel, Vatican, Rome); Matteo Rosselli, *Burning Bush*, before 1623 (Pisa Cathedral); Rembrandt, *Moses and the Burning Bush*, c.1655; D. Feti, *Moses before the Burning Bush*, 1613–14 (Kunsthistorisches Museum, Vienna).

Literature: R.S. Thomas, 'The Bright Field', *Laboratories of the Spirit*, 1975.

Music: Handel, *Israel in Egypt*, 1739; Rossini, *Mosè in Egitto*, 1818.

The Passover

Moses and his brother **Aaron** confront **Pharaoh** but their request that the **Israelites** be allowed to leave Egypt is refused. The Egyptians then face ten 'plagues': a series of disasters (the Nile turning to 'blood', frogs, gnats, flies, livestock disease, boils, hail and locusts), culminating with the most devastating blow of all – the death of all the first-born in the land. The Israelites are protected by the blood of sacrificed lambs placed on their doorposts and lintels, so that the destroyer 'passes over' their homes.

Key concepts

God protects his people; the Israelites are delivered from slavery.

Exodus 12:21–3, 25–7

[21] Then Moses called all the elders of Israel and said to them, "Go, select lambs for your families, and slaughter the passover lamb. [22] Take a bunch of hyssop, dip it in the blood that is in the basin, and touch the lintel and the two doorposts with the blood in the basin. None of you shall go outside the door of your house until morning. [23] For the LORD will pass through to strike down the Egyptians; when he sees the blood on the lintel and on the two doorposts, the LORD will pass over that door and will not allow the destroyer to enter your houses to strike you down. [...] [25] When you come to the land that the LORD will give you, as he has promised, you shall keep this observance. [26] And when your children ask you, 'What do you mean by this observance?' [27] you

shall say, 'It is the passover sacrifice to the LORD, for he passed over the houses of the Israelites in Egypt, when he struck down the Egyptians but spared our houses.'" And the people bowed down and worshipped.

At midnight all the first-born in the land of Egypt, both humans and animals, are struck down. Pharaoh summons Moses and Aaron and urges that the Israelites should leave Egypt.

Exodus 12:34–6

[34] So the people took their dough before it was leavened, with their kneading bowls wrapped up in their cloaks on their shoulders. [35] The Israelites had done as Moses told them; they had asked the Egyptians for jewellery of silver and gold, and for clothing, [36] and the LORD had given the people favour in the sight of the Egyptians, so that they let them have what they asked. And so they plundered the Egyptians.

Linked themes

The details of this event – the eating of the **lamb** and the baking of unleavened bread – were adopted as the hallmarks of the great **Passover** festival in Judaism. According to the **Gospels**, it was during the Passover meal before his death (the **Last Supper**) that Jesus instituted the **Eucharist**, comparing himself to a sacrificial lamb whose blood would save sinners (see Mt 26:26–9).

Related works

Art: Tintoretto, *Passover of the Hebrews*, 1577 (Scuola di San Rocco, Venice); Bouts, *Feast of the Passover*, 1464–7 (Sint Pieterskerk, Leuven).

Music: Handel, *Israel in Egypt*, 1739; Arnold Schoenberg, *Moses and Aaron*, 1931–2; Spiritual, 'Go Down Moses'.

Crossing the Red Sea

Though pursued by Pharaoh's army, the Israelites are saved by the miraculous parting of the 'Red Sea' which subsequently flows back together, drowning the Egyptian army.

Key concepts

The threat from Pharaoh's army; God saves his people.

Exodus 14:5, 8–9, 21–8

⁵ When the king of Egypt was told that the people had fled, the minds of Pharaoh and his officials were changed toward the people, and they said, "What have we done, letting Israel leave our service?" [...]

⁸ The LORD hardened the heart of Pharaoh king of Egypt and he pursued the Israelites, who were going out boldly. ⁹ The Egyptians pursued them, all Pharaoh's horses and chariots, his chariot drivers and his army; they overtook them camped by the sea [...]

²¹ Then Moses stretched out his hand over the sea. The LORD drove the sea back by a strong east wind all night, and turned the sea into dry land; and the waters were divided. ²² The Israelites went into the sea on dry ground, the waters forming a wall for them on their right and on their left. ²³ The Egyptians pursued, and went into the sea after them, all of Pharaoh's horses, chariots, and chariot drivers. ²⁴ At the morning watch the LORD in the pillar of fire and cloud looked down upon the Egyptian army, and threw the Egyptian army into panic. ²⁵ He clogged their chariot wheels so that they turned with difficulty. The Egyptians said, "Let us flee from the Israelites, for the LORD is fighting for them against Egypt."

²⁶ Then the LORD said to Moses, "Stretch out your hand over the sea, so that the water may come back upon the Egyptians, upon their chariots and chariot drivers." ²⁷ So Moses stretched out his hand over the sea, and at dawn the sea returned to its normal depth. As the Egyptians fled before it, the LORD tossed

the Egyptians into the sea. [28] The waters returned and covered the chariots and the chariot drivers, the entire army of Pharaoh that had followed them into the sea; not one of them remained.

Linked themes
Christian commentators later saw in the Crossing of the Red Sea a parallel to **baptism**.

Related works
Art: Rosselli, *Crossing of the Red Sea*, 1481–3 (Sistine Chapel, Vatican, Rome); Bernardino Luini, *The Overwhelming of Pharaoh´s Host*, 1510–20 (Brera Gallery, Milan); Lucas Cranach the Elder, *The Passage of the Red Sea*, 1540 (Alta Pinakothek, Munich).

Literature: The Old English poem *Exodus*; Steinbeck, *The Grapes of Wrath*, 1939.

Manna from heaven
The Israelites spend forty years in the wilderness before they are allowed to enter **Canaan**. This story offers examples both of their constant tendency to complain and of God's provision for their needs.

Key concepts
God provides for his people.

Exodus 16:2–4, 13–15, 31
[2] The whole congregation of the Israelites complained against Moses and Aaron in the wilderness. [3] The Israelites said to them, "If only we had died by the hand of the LORD in the land of Egypt, when we sat by the fleshpots and ate our fill of bread; for you have brought us out into this wilderness to kill this whole assembly with hunger."

[4] Then the LORD said to Moses, "I am going to rain bread from heaven for you, and each day the people shall go out and gather enough for that day [...] [13]... in the morning there was a

layer of dew around the camp. [14] When the layer of dew lifted, there on the surface of the wilderness was a fine flaky substance, as fine as frost on the ground. [15] When the Israelites saw it, they said to one another, "What is it?" For they did not know what it was. Moses said to them, "It is the bread that the LORD has given you to eat. [...]

[31] The house of Israel called it manna; it was like coriander seed, white, and the taste of it was like wafers made with honey.

Linked themes
In John 6:1–14, Jesus feeds five thousand people. Later in the same chapter he compares himself to the **manna** provided in the desert and announces, 'I am the living bread that came down from heaven' (6:51).

Related works
Art: Tintoretto, *Fall of Manna, c.*1577 (Scuola di San Rocco, Venice); Luini, *Gathering of the Manna*, 1520–3 (Brera Gallery, Milan); Guido Reni, *Gathering of the Manna*, 1614–15 (Cathedral, Ravenna).

Literature: George Herbert, 'The Sacrifice', 1633; Milton, *Paradise Regained*, 1671.

The Ten Commandments
In the central event of the **Exodus, Moses** is shown ascending **Mount Sinai** to receive the **Ten Commandments**, together with other laws and the terms of a covenant from God. The first four commandments are about humankind relating to God; the remaining six deal with relationships between human beings.

Key concepts
Worshipping God alone; loving others.

Exodus 20:1–17
Then God spoke all these words:

[2] I am the LORD your God, who brought you out of the land of

Egypt, out of the house of slavery; [3] you shall have no other gods before me.

[4] You shall not make for yourself an idol, whether in the form of anything that is in heaven above, or that is on the earth beneath, or that is in the water under the earth. [5] You shall not bow down to them or worship them; for I the LORD your God am a jealous God, punishing children for the iniquity of parents, to the third and the fourth generation of those who reject me, [6] but showing steadfast love to the thousandth generation of those who love me and keep my commandments.

[7] You shall not make wrongful use of the name of the LORD your God, for the LORD will not acquit anyone who misuses his name.

[8] Remember the sabbath day, and keep it holy. [9] Six days you shall labour and do all your work. [10] But the seventh day is a sabbath to the LORD your God; you shall not do any work – you, your son or your daughter, your male or female slave, your livestock, or the alien resident in your towns. [11] For in six days the LORD made heaven and earth, the sea, and all that is in them, but rested the seventh day; therefore the LORD blessed the sabbath day and consecrated it.

[12] Honour your father and your mother, so that your days may be long in the land that the LORD your God is giving you.

[13] You shall not murder.

[14] You shall not commit adultery.

[15] You shall not steal.

[16] You shall not bear false witness against your neighbour.

[17] You shall not covet your neighbour's house; you shall not covet your neighbour's wife, or male or female slave, or ox, or donkey, or anything that belongs to your neighbour.

Linked themes

The Ten Commandments, which are also listed in Deut 5:6–21, have been extremely influential in both Jewish and Christian thought. Jesus offered a summary of the law in Mk 12:30–1: 'You shall love the Lord your God with all your heart, and with all your soul, and with all your mind, and with all your strength' … 'You shall love your neighbour as yourself.'

Related works

Art: Rembrandt, *Moses with the Tablets of the Law*, 1659 (Berlin).

Literature: John Bunyan, *The Pilgrim's Progress*, 1678; A. H. Clough, 'The Latest Decalogue', 1862; Thomas Hardy, *Tess of the D'Urbervilles*, 1891.

The bronze serpent

A further episode of grumbling by the people brings the punishment of an invasion of poisonous snakes which kills many. God tells **Moses** to place a bronze serpent on a pole and all who look at it are healed.

Key concepts

God's judgement on sin; Moses prays for the people; God provides a means of healing.

Numbers 21:5–9

[5] The people spoke against God and against Moses, "Why have you brought us up out of Egypt to die in the wilderness? For there is no food and no water, and we detest this miserable food." [6] Then the LORD sent poisonous serpents among the people, and they bit the people, so that many Israelites died. [7] The people came to Moses and said, "We have sinned by speaking against the LORD and against you; pray to the LORD to take away the serpents from us." So Moses prayed for the people. [8] And the LORD said to Moses, "Make a poisonous serpent, and set it on a pole; and everyone who is bitten shall look at it and live." [9] So Moses made a serpent of bronze, and put it upon a pole; and whenever a serpent bit someone, that person would look at the serpent of bronze and live.

Linked themes

This episode is referred to in **John's Gospel** where a parallel is drawn with the lifting up of Jesus on the **cross** to bring **forgiveness** and **eternal life** to all who will receive it (Jn 3:14–15).

Related works

Art: Michelangelo, *Brazen Serpent*, 1511; Anthony van Dyck, *Moses Raising the Brazen Serpent*, 1620 (Museo del Prado, Madrid); Tintoretto, *Brazen Serpent*, 1575–6 (Scuola di San Rocco, Venice); Bourdon, *Moses and the Brazen Serpent* 1653–4 (Museo del Prado, Madrid).

THE PROMISED LAND

After forty years spent wandering in the wilderness, the **Israelites** finally enter **Canaan**, the land which represented the fulfilment of God's promises to **Abraham**. However, entry into Canaan is fiercely contested by the groups which already occupy this area. The books of Joshua and Judges relate the struggles of the Israelites to live in peace and to remain faithful to the God of Abraham while surrounded by those who worship other gods, problems which continue to characterise the history of Israel.

Key concepts

God fulfils his promise; the need to live in obedience to God.

Joshua 1:1–3, 5–6, 8

After the death of Moses the servant of the LORD, the LORD spoke to Joshua son of Nun, Moses' assistant, saying, [2] "My servant Moses is dead. Now proceed to cross the Jordan, you and all this people, into the land that I am giving to them, to the Israelites. [3] Every place that the sole of your foot will tread upon I have given to you, as I promised to Moses. [...] [5] ... As I was with Moses, so I will be with you; I will not fail you or forsake you. [6] Be strong and courageous; for you shall put this people in possession of the land that I swore to their ancestors to give them. [...]

[8] This book of the law shall not depart out of your mouth; you shall meditate on it day and night, so that you may be careful to act in accordance with all that is written in it.

Linked themes
The need to obey God as a condition of remaining in the land is a continuing theme in the story of the Israelites.

Related works
Art: Rembrandt, *The Lord Appearing to Joshua*, c.1625; Marc Chagall, *Josué (Joshua)*, 1931 (Musée Marc Chagall, Nice).

Crossing the Jordan
Under Joshua's leadership, the people finally enter the **Promised Land**. The **Ark of the Covenant**, a portable shrine containing the tablets of the **Law** which **Moses** had been given by God, symbolised God's presence with the **Israelites**.

Key concepts
God miraculously opens the way for the people to enter Canaan.

Joshua 3:14–17
[14] When the people set out from their tents to cross over the Jordan, the priests bearing the ark of the covenant were in front of the people. [15] Now the Jordan overflows all its banks throughout the time of harvest. So when those who bore the ark had come to the Jordan, and the feet of the priests bearing the ark were dipped in the edge of the water, [16] the waters flowing from above stood still ... while those flowing toward the sea of the Arabah, the Dead Sea, were wholly cut off. Then the people crossed over opposite Jericho. [17] While all Israel were crossing over on dry ground, the priests who bore the ark of the covenant of the LORD stood on dry ground in the middle of the Jordan, until the entire nation finished crossing over the Jordan.

Linked themes

This incident recalls the **Crossing of the Red Sea** when the waters parted to allow the Israelites to escape the pursuing Egyptians. The Jordan remains an important symbol. It is in the same river that Jesus is baptised at the beginning of his ministry.

Related works

Art: Raphael, *Crossing the River Jordan*, 1518–19 (Loggia, Vatican, Rome).

Music: Spiritual, *Deep River*.

DAVID

David, a key **Old Testament** figure, is presented in a wide range of roles: the young shepherd guarding his sheep; the future king anointed by the prophet **Samuel**; the skilled musician; the young hero who overcomes **Goliath**; the king who captured **Jerusalem** and made it his capital; the adulterous lover of **Bathsheba**; the father of the rebellious **Absalom** and the wise **Solomon**. David is also identified as the author of a number of **Psalms**.

David anointed by Samuel

Israel's first king, **Saul**, was rejected by God for his disobedience. The prophet Samuel is therefore instructed to seek out God's chosen replacement, anointing him with oil as a sign of God's choice and empowering.

Key concepts

David chosen by God as successor to Saul.

1 Samuel 16:1, 10–13

The LORD said to Samuel, "How long will you grieve over Saul? I have rejected him from being king over Israel. Fill your horn with oil and set out; I will send you to Jesse the Bethlehemite, for I have provided for myself a king among his sons." […]

^{10} Jesse made seven of his sons pass before Samuel, and Samuel said to Jesse, "The LORD has not chosen any of these." ^{11} Samuel said to Jesse, "Are all your sons here?" And he said, "There remains yet the youngest, but he is keeping the sheep." [...] ^{12} ... Now [David] was ruddy, and had beautiful eyes, and was handsome. The LORD said, "Rise and anoint him; for this is the one." ^{13} Then Samuel took the horn of oil, and anointed him in the presence of his brothers; and the spirit of the LORD came mightily upon David from that day forward ...

Linked themes

David and Jesse are listed in the **Gospels** of **Matthew** (1:1–17) and **Luke** (3:23–38) as forebears of **Jesus**. In the Middle Ages this ancestry was traced visually in the **'Jesse Tree'**, based on the reference in Isaiah 11:1–3 that the **Messiah** would come from 'the stump of Jesse'.

David defeats Goliath

When the gigantic **Philistine** warrior **Goliath** challenges the **Israelite** army to face him in single combat, only the young shepherd **David** is brave enough to accept the challenge. Trusting in God's power, he confronts Goliath armed only with the slingshot he uses to defend his sheep.

Key concepts

David's trust in God; David overcomes a powerful opponent through relying on God's help.

1 Samuel 17:4–5, 7–9, 11, 32–5, 37–40, 45–6, 49, 51

^{4} And there came out from the camp of the Philistines a champion named Goliath, of Gath, whose height was six cubits and a span. ^{5} He had a helmet of bronze on his head, and he was armed with a coat of mail [...] ^{7} The shaft of his spear was like a weaver's beam [...] ^{8} He stood and shouted to the ranks of Israel, "Why have you come out to draw up for battle? [...] Choose a man for yourselves, and let him come down to me. ^{9} If he is able to fight with me and kill me, then we will be your servants; but if I prevail against him and kill him, then you shall be our servants and serve us." [...]

[11] When Saul and all Israel heard these words of the Philistine, they were dismayed and greatly afraid. [...]

[32] David said to Saul, "Let no one's heart fail because of him; your servant will go and fight with this Philistine." [33] Saul said to David, "You are not able to go against this Philistine to fight with him; for you are just a boy, and he has been a warrior from his youth." [34] But David said to Saul, "Your servant used to keep sheep for his father; and whenever a lion or a bear came, and took a lamb from the flock, [35] I went after it and struck it down, rescuing the lamb from its mouth ..." [...]

[37] David said, "The LORD, who saved me from the paw of the lion and from the paw of the bear, will save me from the hand of this Philistine." So Saul said to David, "Go, and may the LORD be with you!"

[38] Saul clothed David with his armour; he put a bronze helmet on his head and clothed him with a coat of mail. [39] David strapped Saul's sword over the armour, and he tried in vain to walk, for he was not used to them. Then David said to Saul, "I cannot walk with these; for I am not used to them." So David removed them. [40] Then he took his staff in his hand, and chose five smooth stones from the wadi, and put them in his shepherd's bag, in the pouch; his sling was in his hand, and he drew near to the Philistine. [...]

[45] ... David said to the Philistine, "You come to me with sword and spear and javelin; but I come to you in the name of the LORD of hosts, the God of the armies of Israel, whom you have defied. [46] This very day the LORD will deliver you into my hand, and I will strike you down and cut off your head ..." [...]

[49] David put his hand in his bag, took out a stone, slung it, and struck the Philistine on his forehead; the stone sank into his forehead, and he fell face down on the ground. [...] [51] Then David ran and stood over the Philistine; he grasped his sword, drew it out of its sheath, and killed him; then he cut off his head with it.

Linked themes
Christian commentators later drew parallels between David the shepherd rescuing his flock and **Jesus** who described himself as the **Good Shepherd** (Jn 10:14–18).

Related works
Art: Donatello, *David*, c.1430 (Uffizi, Florence); Andrea del Castagno, *The Youthful David*, c.1450 (National Gallery of Art, Washington); Michelangelo, *David*, 1501–4 (Florence); Caravaggio, *David*, 1606–7 (Kunsthistorisches Museum, Vienna); Caravaggio, *David with the Head of* Goliath, c.1610 (Galleria Borghese, Rome).

Literature: D.H. Lawrence, *David*, 1925.

David and Bathsheba
In this story **David** is shown committing adultery and then abusing his power and committing murder in order to cover up his sin. Only with the intervention of Nathan the prophet is he forced to confront his actions.

Key concepts
Covering up sexual **sin** leads to murder; abuse of power; facing God's judgement.

2 Samuel 11:1–4
In the spring of the year, the time when kings go out to battle, David sent Joab with his officers and all Israel with him ... But David remained at Jerusalem.

² It happened, late one afternoon, when David rose from his couch and was walking about on the roof of the king's house, that he saw from the roof a woman bathing; the woman was very beautiful. ³ David sent someone to inquire about the woman. It was reported, "This is Bathsheba daughter of Eliam, the wife of Uriah the Hittite." ⁴ So David sent messengers to get her, and she came to him, and he lay with her ... Then she returned to her house.

When **Bathsheba** tells David that she is pregnant, he recalls her husband Uriah and attempts to persuade him to return home to sleep with Bathsheba and thus conceal her adultery. However, Uriah, a conscientious soldier, refuses to visit his wife while his comrades are still at war. David therefore instructs his commander, Joab, to ensure that Uriah dies in battle. After Uriah's death, Bathsheba becomes David's wife and bears his son.

2 Samuel 11:27–12:7, 9, 13–14

[27] ... But the thing that David had done displeased the LORD. [1] And the LORD sent Nathan to David. He came to him, and said to him, "There were two men in a certain city, the one rich and the other poor. [2] The rich man had very many flocks and herds; [3] but the poor man had nothing but one little ewe lamb, which he had bought. He brought it up, and it grew up with him and with his children; it used to eat of his meagre fare, and drink from his cup, and lie in his bosom, and it was like a daughter to him. [4] Now there came a traveller to the rich man, and he was loath to take one of his own flock or herd to prepare for the wayfarer who had come to him, but he took the poor man's lamb, and prepared that for the guest who had come to him." [5] Then David's anger was greatly kindled against the man. He said to Nathan, "As the LORD lives, the man who has done this deserves to die; [6] he shall restore the lamb fourfold, because he did this thing, and because he had no pity."

[7] Nathan said to David, "You are the man! [...] [9] Why have you despised the word of the LORD, to do what is evil in his sight? You have struck down Uriah the Hittite with the sword, and have taken his wife to be your wife [...] [13] David said to Nathan, "I have sinned against the LORD." Nathan said to David, "Now the LORD has put away your sin; you shall not die. [14] Nevertheless, because by this deed you have utterly scorned the LORD, the child that is born to you shall die."

Linked themes
David's penitence is traditionally understood to have been expressed in Psalm 51 (see Chapter 3).

Related works
Art: Hans Memling, *Bathsheba Bathing*, 1485 (Staatsgalerie, Stuttgart); Raphael, *David and Bathsheba*, c.1515 (Loggia, Vatican, Rome); Massys, *David and Bathsheba*, 1562 (Louvre, Paris); Rembrandt, *Bathsheba with the Letter from King David*, 1654 (Louvre, Paris); Rembrandt, *Nathan before King David*, c.1650–5 (Berlin).

Literature: George Peele, *Love of King David and Fair Bathshebe*, 1599; John Dryden, *Absolom and Achitophel*, 1681–2; Christopher Smart (1722–70), *A Song to David*; Thomas Hardy, *Far from the Madding Crowd*, 1874; William Faulkner, *Absolom, Absolom!*, 1936.

Music: Mozart, *Davidde Penitenti*, 1785; Arthur Honnegar, *King David*, 1921.

SOLOMON

Solomon, second son of **David** and **Bathsheba** and the third king of **Israel**, was famous for his wisdom and wealth, and for building a magnificent palace and temple. Traditionally, the books of Proverbs, Ecclesiastes and the Song of Solomon (see Chapter 3) have been ascribed to him. However, he is said to have 'loved many foreign women' (1 Kings 11:1) whose influence led him to worship other gods. He was therefore told by God that after his death the greater part of his kingdom would pass not to his son but to one of his followers. Solomon is an ambivalent figure: highly gifted, yet also someone whose disobedience ultimately lost him God's favour.

God gives Solomon wisdom
When, in a dream, God offers Solomon a choice of gift, Solomon asks for wisdom so that he may govern his people well. Pleased, God is said

to have also promised him riches, honour and, if he remained obedient, long life. Solomon's wisdom was tested and proved by the case of two prostitutes who claimed the same child.

Key Points
Solomon asks God for wisdom to rule well.

1 Kings 3:5–7, 9–14
[5] … the LORD appeared to Solomon in a dream by night; and God said, "Ask what I should give you." [6] And Solomon said, "You have shown great and steadfast love to your servant my father David […] [7] And now, O LORD my God, you have made your servant king in place of my father David […] [9] Give your servant therefore an understanding mind to govern your people, able to discern between good and evil; for who can govern this your great people?"

[10] It pleased the Lord that Solomon had asked this. [11] God said to him, "Because you have asked this, and have not asked for yourself long life or riches, or for the life of your enemies, but have asked for yourself understanding to discern what is right, [12] I now do according to your word. Indeed I give you a wise and discerning mind; no one like you has been before you and no one like you shall arise after you. [13] I give you also what you have not asked, both riches and honour all your life; no other king shall compare with you. [14] If you will walk in my ways, keeping my statutes and my commandments, as your father David walked, then I will lengthen your life."

Solomon's wisdom is tested by the case of two prostitutes who share a house. Both have borne children, one of whom has died; both claim the living child as their own.

1 Kings 3:24–8
[24] So the king said, "Bring me a sword," and they brought a sword before the king. [25] The king said, "Divide the living boy in two;

then give half to the one, and half to the other." ²⁶ But the woman whose son was alive said to the king – because compassion for her son burned within her – "Please, my lord, give her the living boy; certainly do not kill him!" The other said, "It shall be neither mine nor yours; divide it." ²⁷ Then the king responded: "Give the first woman the living boy; do not kill him. She is his mother." ²⁸ All Israel heard of the judgment that the king had rendered; and they stood in awe of the king, because they perceived that the wisdom of God was in him, to execute justice.

Linked themes
1 Kings 10:1–7 states that the Queen of Sheba tested Solomon and concluded that his wisdom and prosperity exceeded his reputation. Tradition has credited Solomon as the author of two examples of biblical Wisdom literature: Proverbs and Ecclesiastes.

Related works
Art: Giorgione, *Judgement of Solomon*, 1505 (Uffizi, Florence); Raphael, *Judgment of Solomon*, 1519 (Loggia, Vatican, Rome); Nicolas Poussin, *Judgement of Solomon*, 1649 (Louvre, Paris); Luca Giorano, *Dream of Solomon*, 1693; Giovanni Battista Tiepolo, *Judgement of Solomon*, 1729 (Palazzo Patriarcale, Udine).

Literature: The Old English poem *Solomon and Saturn II*; Francis Bacon, *The New Atlantis*, 1626; Thomas Browne, *Religio Medici*, c.1634; Joseph Conrad, *Typhoon*, 1919.

Music: Handel, *Zadok the Priest*, 1737, *Solomon*, 1749.

Solomon dedicates the temple
One of **Solomon's** greatest achievements was building a splendid **Temple** in **Jerusalem** on a site provided by his father, **David**. Construction is said to have taken seven years. The Temple, made of stone and lined with cedar wood and gold, was built to honour God and to house the **Ark of the Covenant** which symbolised God's presence with his people.

Key concepts

The Ark of the Covenant, containing the **Tablets of the Law**, is placed in the Temple: the glory of God fills the Temple like a cloud; God cannot be contained within a single place; Solomon asks God to listen to the prayers of the people focused on the Temple.

1 Kings 8:1, 6, 9–11, 22–3, 30

Then Solomon assembled the elders of Israel and all the heads of the tribes, the leaders of the ancestral houses of the Israelites, before King Solomon in Jerusalem, to bring up the ark of the covenant of the LORD out of the city of David, which is Zion. [...]

⁶ Then the priests brought the ark of the covenant of the LORD to its place, in the inner sanctuary of the house, in the most holy place, underneath the wings of the cherubim. [...]

⁹ There was nothing in the ark except the two tablets of stone that Moses had placed there at Horeb, where the LORD made a covenant with the Israelites, when they came out of the land of Egypt. ¹⁰ And when the priests came out of the holy place, a cloud filled the house of the LORD, ¹¹ so that the priests could not stand to minister because of the cloud; for the glory of the LORD filled the house of the LORD. [...]

²² Then Solomon stood before the altar of the LORD in the presence of all the assembly of Israel, and spread out his hands to heaven. ²³ He said, "O LORD, God of Israel, there is no God like you in heaven above or on earth beneath, keeping covenant and steadfast love for your servants who walk before you with all their heart [...]

³⁰ Hear the plea of your servant and of your people Israel when they pray toward this place; O hear in heaven your dwelling place; heed and forgive.

Linked themes

The Temple remained a focal point of God's presence with his people and a place of pilgrimage. Solomon's Temple was destroyed in 587BCE and replaced after the exile. **Herod the Great** began to build a new temple in the time of **Jesus** but this was destroyed by the Romans in CE70.

Related works
Art: Raphael, *Construction of the* Temple, 1518–19 (Loggia, Vatican, Rome); James Tissot, *Solomon Dedicates the Temple at Jerusalem*, 1896–1900.

Music: Handel, *Solomon*, 1749.

The Queen of Sheba visits Solomon
The **Queen of Sheba** visits **Solomon** to test his wisdom and concludes that his wisdom and prosperity exceed everything she has heard.

Key concepts
Solomon's fame; Solomon's wisdom praised.

1 Kings 10:1–3, 6–7
When the queen of Sheba heard of the fame of Solomon (fame due to the name of the LORD), she came to test him with hard questions. [2] She came to Jerusalem with a very great retinue, with camels bearing spices, and very much gold, and precious stones; and when she came to Solomon, she told him all that was on her mind. [3] Solomon answered all her questions; there was nothing hidden from the king that he could not explain to her. [...]

[6] So she said to the king, "The report was true that I heard in my own land of your accomplishments and of your wisdom, [7] but I did not believe the reports until I came and my own eyes had seen it. Not even half had been told me; your wisdom and prosperity far surpass the report that I had heard.

Linked themes

Some Christian commentators later saw the visit of the **Queen of Sheba** with her lavish gifts as prefiguring the visit of the **Magi** to the **Christ** child (see Chapter 5: The Visit of the Wise Men (Magi)). Jesus compares himself with Solomon in Luke 11:31.

Related works

Art: Lorenzo Ghiberti, *Solomon and the Queen of Sheba*, 1425–52 (Duomo, Florence); Konrad Witz, *King Solomon and the Queen of Sheba*, 1435 (Staatliches Museum, Berlin); Francesco del Cossa, *Meeting of Solomon and the Queen of Sheba*, 1436–78; Edward Poynter, *Visit of the Queen of Sheba to King Solomon*, 1890 (Art Gallery of New South Wales, Sydney).

Music: Handel, *Solomon*, 1749.

EXILE AND RESTORATION

Following the death of Solomon in 922BCE, the kingdom was divided in two. Both parts were to suffer the experience of **exile**. In the **Old Testament** exile is frequently portrayed as a punishment for the failure of the **Israelites** to live in obedience to God. This important theme is woven through a number of books: the prophets warn that exile will be a consequence of disobedience, while the books of **Daniel** and **Esther** give insights into life in exile, with a vulnerable minority living in an alien culture and longing to return home. Yet there are also promises of restoration and the books of Nehemiah and Ezra illustrate the process of return and rebuilding.

Exile in Assyria

The northern kingdom (Israel) was conquered by the powerful Assyrian Empire in 722BCE and its people taken into captivity by stages.

Key concepts

The link between sin and exile.

2 Kings 17:5–8, 19–20

[5] Then the king of Assyria invaded all the land and came to Samaria; for three years he besieged it. [6] In the ninth year of Hoshea the king of Assyria captured Samaria; he carried the Israelites away to Assyria. He placed them in Halah, on the Habor, the river of Gozan, and in the cities of the Medes.

[7] This occurred because the people of Israel had sinned against the LORD their God, who had brought them up out of the land of Egypt from under the hand of Pharaoh king of Egypt. They had worshipped other gods [8] and walked in the customs of the nations whom the LORD drove out before the people of Israel, and in the customs that the kings of Israel had introduced. [...]

[19] Judah also did not keep the commandments of the LORD their God but walked in the customs that Israel had introduced. [20] The LORD rejected all the descendants of Israel; he punished them and gave them into the hand of plunderers, until he had banished them from his presence.

Exile in Babylon

The southern kingdom (**Judah**) was conquered by **Babylon** under Nebuchadnezzar in the sixth century BCE and the temple in Jerusalem destroyed in 587BCE. The population was taken into exile in stages.

Key concepts

God's warnings are fulfilled; the **temple** built by **Solomon** is destroyed.

2 Kings 25:8–11

[8] In the fifth month, on the seventh day of the month – which was the nineteenth year of King Nebuchadnezzar, king of Babylon – Nebuzaradan, the captain of the bodyguard, a servant of the king of Babylon, came to Jerusalem. [9] He burned the house of the LORD, the king's house, and all the houses of Jerusalem; every great house he burned down. [10] All the army of the Chaldeans who were with the captain of the guard broke down the walls around Jerusalem. [11] Nebuzaradan the captain of the guard

carried into exile the rest of the people who were left in the city and the deserters who had defected to the king of Babylon – all the rest of the population …

Linked themes
The Book of Lamentations, attributed to the prophet Jeremiah, contains reflections on the exile. The theme of exile is also expressed in Psalm 137:1–4.

[1] By the rivers of Babylon –
    there we sat down and there we wept
      when we remembered Zion.
[2] On the willows there
    we hung up our harps.
[3] For there our captors
    asked us for songs,
      and our tormentors asked for mirth, saying,
      "Sing us one of the songs of Zion!"
[4] How could we sing the LORD's song
    in a foreign land?

Related works
Art: Rembrandt, *Jeremiah Lamenting the Destruction of Jerusalem*, 1630 (Rijksmuseum, Amsterdam); Nicolas Poussin, *Destruction of the Temple at Jerusalem*, 1638 (Kunsthistoriches Museum, Vienna).

Music: Giuseppe Verdi, *Nabucco*, 1841.

Restoration
Promises of restoration are frequent in the writings of the **prophets** and eventually the **Israelites** return from **Babylon** to rebuild **Jerusalem** and its **Temple**.

The promise of return

Though this passage contains a warning that their time in exile will not be short, it also promises God has not abandoned his people and will bring them back to their homeland.

Key concepts
The length of the exile; the need for **repentance** and prayer; God's promise of restoration.

Jeremiah 29:1, 10–14

These are the words of the letter that the prophet Jeremiah sent from Jerusalem to the remaining elders among the exiles, and to the priests, the prophets, and all the people, whom Nebuchadnezzar had taken into exile from Jerusalem to Babylon. [...]

^{10} ... thus says the LORD: Only when Babylon's seventy years are completed will I visit you, and I will fulfil to you my promise and bring you back to this place. ^{11} For surely I know the plans I have for you, says the LORD, plans for your welfare and not for harm, to give you a future with hope. ^{12} Then when you call upon me and come and pray to me, I will hear you. ^{13} When you search for me, you will find me; if you seek me with all your heart, ^{14} I will let you find me, says the LORD, and I will restore your fortunes and gather you from all the nations and all the places where I have driven you, says the LORD, and I will bring you back to the place from which I sent you into exile.

Return to Jerusalem
In 538BCE Babylon itself was captured by the Persians and King Cyrus issued an edict allowing the Jews to begin their return home.

Key concepts
Fulfilment of God's promise; the people encouraged to rebuild the Temple.

Ezra 1:1–3

In the first year of King Cyrus of Persia, in order that the word of the LORD by the mouth of Jeremiah might be accomplished, the LORD stirred up the spirit of King Cyrus of Persia so that he sent a herald throughout all his kingdom, and also in a written edict declared:

² "Thus says King Cyrus of Persia: The LORD, the God of heaven, has given me all the kingdoms of the earth, and he has charged me to build him a house at Jerusalem in Judah. ³ Any of those among you who are of his people – may their God be with them! – are now permitted to go up to Jerusalem in Judah, and rebuild the house of the LORD, the God of Israel ..."

WOMEN IN THE OLD TESTAMENT

The **Old Testament** may at first sight appear to have an almost exclusively male cast in terms of **prophets**, rulers and heroic figures. In fact there are female examples in all these categories, though their portrayal is usually less prominent with only **Ruth** and **Esther** (and Judith and Susannah in the **Old Testament** *Apocrypha*) having books named after them. **Miriam**, described as a prophet, is depicted alongside Moses in the Exodus; **Deborah** is a significant leader and prophetess in the period of the Judges; and Huldah is also shown as a prophet consulted by the King in 2 Kings 22:14–20. Esther and Judith both show considerable courage and resourcefulness in saving their people from enemies and Ruth is a model of faithfulness and self-sacrifice.

As in the case of male Old Testament figures, there are also very negative portraits. Thus **Eve** not only succumbs to sin but becomes the agent of temptation for **Adam** (see Chapter 1: The Fall of Humankind); Lot's wife dies for her disobedience during the destruction of **Sodom and Gomorrah** (Gen 19:1–29); **Delilah** is the means of **Samson**'s betrayal; **Bathsheba**, as the object of King **David**'s desire, is the catalyst for acts of adultery and murder; and Queen Jezebel leads her husband Ahab into the worship of idols and seeks to destroy God's prophets. The book of Proverbs both praises good women and warns against those who may lead men astray. The portrayal of women in the Old and **New Testaments** has been subject to a wide range of interpretations from the earliest days of the **Church** to the present day. Many patristic and medieval commentators adopted a strongly anti-feminist stance, using figures such as Eve, Delilah and Bathsheba to argue their case.

Delilah and Samson

Samson was one of the great leaders of Israel in the period between entry into **Canaan** and the rise of the monarchy. He was dedicated to God from before his birth as a **Nazirite** whose vows included avoiding strong drink and not cutting his hair. His extraordinary strength enabled him to defend the **Israelites** against their enemies the **Philistines** until eventually he was betrayed by his Philistine wife. Blinded and imprisoned, he pulled down the temple of the god Dagon on his enemies, killing himself in the process.

Key concepts

Samson gives in to Delilah and she betrays him to the Philistines; Samson's disobedience causes him to lose his strength.

Judges 16:15–21

[15] Then [Delilah] said to him, "How can you say, 'I love you,' when your heart is not with me? You have mocked me three times now and have not told me what makes your strength so great." [16] Finally, after she had nagged him with her words day after day, and pestered him, he was tired to death. [17] So he told her his whole secret, and said to her, "A razor has never come upon my head; for I have been a nazirite to God from my mother's womb. If my head were shaved, then my strength would leave me; I would become weak, and be like anyone else."

[18] When Delilah realized that he had told her his whole secret, she sent and called the lords of the Philistines, saying, "This

time come up, for he has told his whole secret to me." Then the lords of the Philistines came up to her, and brought the money in their hands. [19] She let him fall asleep on her lap; and she called a man, and had him shave off the seven locks of his head. He began to weaken, and his strength left him. [20] Then she said, "The Philistines are upon you, Samson!" When he awoke from his sleep, he thought, "I will go out as at other times, and shake myself free." But he did not know that the LORD had left him. [21] So the Philistines seized him and gouged out his eyes. They brought him down to Gaza and bound him with bronze shackles; and he ground at the mill in the prison.

Linked themes
John the Baptist was also a Nazirite (Lk 1:15).

Related works
Art: Rubens, *Samson Captured by the Philistines*, 1609–10 (National Gallery, London); Honthorst, *Samson and Delilah*, c.1615 (Cleveland Museum of Art, Cleveland); Matthias Stom, *Samson and Delilah*, 1630s (Galleria Nazionale d'Arte Antica, Rome); Rembrandt, *The Blinding of Samson*, 1636 (Frankfurt).

Literature: John Milton, *Areopagitica*, 1644; John Milton, *Samson Agonistes*, c.1671; D.H. Lawrence, 'Samson and Delilah', 1917.

Music: Handel, *Samson*, 1743; Saint-Saëns, *Samson et Dalila*, 1877; Michael Hurd (b.1931), *Samson*.

Ruth
The Book of **Ruth** tells the story of a foreigner whose loyalty to her widowed mother-in-law, Naomi, leads her to leave her own people and religion. This faithfulness is later rewarded when Ruth marries Naomi's kinsman Boaz and bears a child who becomes the father of **Jesse** and grandfather of King **David**.

Key concepts
Ruth's loyalty and faithfulness.

Ruth 1:1–2
In the days when the judges ruled, there was a famine in the land, and a certain man of Bethlehem in Judah went to live in the country of Moab, he and his wife and two sons. ² The name of the man was Elimelech and the name of his wife Naomi. [...]

Naomi's two sons marry Moabite women but, in time, both her sons and her husband die. Desolate, she decides to return home.

Ruth 1:7–8, 14–17
⁷ So [Naomi] set out from the place where she had been living, she and her two daughters-in-law, and they went on their way to go back to the land of Judah. ⁸ But Naomi said to her two daughters-in-law, "Go back each of you to your mother's house. May the LORD deal kindly with you, as you have dealt with the dead and with me. [...]
¹⁴ ... Orpah kissed her mother-in-law, but Ruth clung to her.
     ¹⁵ So she said, "See, your sister-in-law has gone back to her people and to her gods; return after your sister-in-law." ¹⁶ But Ruth said,
     "Do not press me to leave you
          or to turn back from following you!
     Where you go, I will go;
          where you lodge, I will lodge;
     your people shall be my people,
          and your God my God.
¹⁷ Where you die, I will die –
     there will I be buried. [...]"

Linked themes
Ruth is mentioned in the list of the ancestors of Jesus in Matthew 1:5.

Related works

Art: Rembrandt, *Ruth and Naomi*, c.1635–8 (Museum Boymans-van Beuningen, Rotterdam); Jean-Francois Millet, *Ruth and Boaz*, 1850–3 (Museum of Fine Arts, Boston); Marc Chagall, *Naomi and Her Daughters-in-Law*, 1960.

Literature: John Milton, 'Sonnet IX' ('Lady that in the prime'), 1642–5; John Keats, 'Ode to a Nightingale', 1819; Elizabeth Gaskell, *Ruth*, 1853.

Esther

The book of **Esther** shows a woman successfully defending her people against a conspiracy to destroy them. Esther, a Jew, becomes the wife of the Persian king after his former Queen, Vashti, had been executed for refusing to appear before the king and his officials to display her beauty. Challenged by her adopted father Mordecai to save the Jews, Esther bravely pleads with her all-powerful husband and outwits her chief adversary Haman.

Key concepts

Esther's courage; the conspiracy against the Jews is foiled.

Esther 8:3–8

³ Then Esther spoke again to the king; she fell at his feet, weeping and pleading with him to avert the evil design of Haman the Agagite and the plot that he had devised against the Jews. ⁴ The king held out the golden sceptre to Esther, ⁵ and Esther rose and stood before the king. She said, "If it pleases the king, and if I have won his favour, and if the thing seems right before the king, and I have his approval, let an order be written to revoke the letters devised by Haman ... which he wrote giving orders to destroy the Jews who are in all the provinces of the king. ⁶ For how can I bear to see the calamity that is coming on my people? Or how can I bear to see the destruction of my kindred?" ⁷ Then King Ahasuerus said to Queen Esther and to the Jew Mordecai, "See, I have given Esther the house of Haman, and they have hanged him on the gallows, because he plotted to lay hands on

the Jews. [8] You may write as you please with regard to the Jews, in the name of the king ..."

Related works

Art: Tintoretto, *Esther before Ahasuerus*, 1555 (Windsor Castle); Peter Paul Rubens, *Esther before Ahasuerus*, 1620; Cavallino, *Esther and Ahaseurus*, 1645–50 (Uffizi, Florence); Rembrandt, *Haman and Ahasuerus at the banquet with Esther*, 1660 (Pushkin Museum, Moscow).

Literature: Esther is cited as an example of a good woman by medieval and Renaissance writers e.g. Chaucer, *Book of the Duchess*; Vashti has been regarded as a feminist figure (see for example Charlotte Brontë, *Villette*, Ch 23). See also Charles Dickens, *Bleak House*, 1852; George Moore, *Esther Waters*, 1894.

Music: Handel, *Esther*, 1732.

Deborah and Jael

As a punishment for disobedience, God allows the **Israelites** to be oppressed by the King of **Canaan** and the commander of his army, Sisera. When the people pray for God's help, he uses two women to save them: **Deborah** the prophetess and judge (leader) of **Israel**, and Jael.

Key concepts

Deborah, a leader of Israel; God uses Deborah and Jael to deliver the Israelites from their enemies.

Judges 4:4–9

[4] At that time Deborah, a prophetess, wife of Lappidoth, was judging Israel. [5] She used to sit under the palm of Deborah between Ramah and Bethel in the hill country of Ephraim; and the Israelites came up to her for judgment. [6] She sent and summoned Barak son of Abinoam from Kedesh in Naphtali, and said to him, "The LORD, the God of Israel, commands you, 'Go, take position at Mount Tabor, bringing ten thousand from the

tribe of Naphtali and the tribe of Zebulun. [7] I will draw out Sisera, the general of Jabin's army, to meet you by the Wadi Kishon with his chariots and his troops; and I will give him into your hand.' " [8] Barak said to her, "If you will go with me, I will go; but if you will not go with me, I will not go." [9] And she said, "I will surely go with you; nevertheless, the road on which you are going will not lead to your glory, for the LORD will sell Sisera into the hand of a woman."

God gives Barak the victory and Sisera flees.

Judges 4:17–18, 21

[17] Now Sisera had fled away on foot to the tent of Jael wife of Heber the Kenite ... [18] Jael came out to meet Sisera, and said to him, "Turn aside, my lord, turn aside to me; have no fear." [...] [21] But Jael wife of Heber took a tent peg, and took a hammer in her hand, and went softly to him and drove the peg into his temple, until it went down into the ground – he was lying fast asleep from weariness – and he died.

Related works

Art: Artemisia Gentileschi, *Jael and Sisera*, 1620 (Szépmüvészeti Museum, Budapest); Rembrandt, *Jael Driving a Nail into the Head of Sisera*, c.1657–60.

Literature: Byron, *The Giaour*, 1812; Charlotte Brontë, *Villette*, 1853; Elizabeth Gaskell, *Cranford*, 1853.

3 POETRY AND WISDOM LITERATURE

Poetry is used to express worship of God and also to portray romantic love. Wisdom literature offers perspectives on human experience and guidance on practical issues of faith and daily life, such as how to respond to suffering, injustice and death. Wisdom is a quality which human beings need to seek and use if they are to live in obedient relationship to God.

PSALMS

SONG OF SOLOMON (SONG OF SONGS OR CANTICLES)

PROVERBS

ECCLESIASTES

JOB

PSALMS

A collection of one hundred and fifty poems or songs, many attributed to King **David**. They were used in the public worship of **Israel** and later by the Christian **Church**, but also express individual concerns. Themes include thanksgiving, laments or requests for God's help, songs of praise, and prayers for God's **forgiveness**.

Why have you forsaken me?

This Psalm of Lament, one of a number of similar psalms, expresses the speaker's suffering and appeals to God for help.

Key concepts

Feeling abandoned by God; mocked by enemies.

Psalm 22:1–2, 7–8, 16, 18–19

A Psalm of David.

¹ My God, my God, why have you forsaken me?

Why are you so far from helping me, from the words of my groaning?

² O my God, I cry by day, but you do not answer;

and by night, but find no rest. [...]

⁷ All who see me mock at me;

they make mouths at me, they shake their heads;

⁸ "Commit your cause to the LORD; let him deliver –

let him rescue the one in whom he delights!" [...]

¹⁶ For dogs are all around me;

a company of evildoers encircles me [...]

¹⁸ they divide my clothes among themselves,

and for my clothing they cast lots.

¹⁹ But you, O LORD, do not be far away!

O my help, come quickly to my aid!

Linked themes

A number of lines from this Psalm are quoted in the **Gospel** descriptions of the **Crucifixion** of **Jesus** and it has been seen by Christian commentators as prefiguring his experience on the **Cross** (see Chapter 7: Crucifixion and Burial).

Related works

Art: Tintoretto, *Crucifixion*, 1565 (Scuola di San Rocco, Venice); Pablo Picasso, *Crucifixion*, 1930 (Musée Picasso, Paris); Craig Aitchison, *Crucifixion*, 1997–8 (Private Collection).

Music: Handel, *The Messiah* ('All They That See Him Laugh Him to Scorn'; 'He Trusted in God').

The Lord is my shepherd

This is probably the best known of all the psalms. It has been read as reflecting **David**'s own experience as a shepherd and expressing his confidence in God's presence, protection and provision for all his needs.

Key concepts

God as a shepherd who provides rest, guidance, protection, blessing.

Psalm 23

A Psalm of David.
[1] The LORD is my shepherd, I shall not want.
[2]   He makes me lie down in green pastures;
he leads me beside still waters;
[3]   he restores my soul.
He leads me in right paths
   for his name's sake.

[4] Even though I walk through the darkest valley (**AV** 'valley of
      the shadow of death'),
   I fear no evil;
for you are with me;
   your rod and your staff –
   they comfort me.

[5] You prepare a table before me
   in the presence of my enemies;
you anoint my head with oil;
   my cup overflows.
[6] Surely goodness and mercy shall follow me
   all the days of my life,
   and I shall dwell in the house of the LORD
   my whole life long.

Linked themes
Jesus speaks of himself as the 'Good Shepherd' in John 10:14–18 (see Chapter 6:'I am the Good Shepherd').

Related works
Literature: Richard Crashaw, *Psalm 23*, 1648; John Bunyan, *Pilgrim's Progress*, 1678; Charlotte Brontë, *Jane Eyre*, 1848.

Music: Settings by Dvořák, Lennox Berkeley, Hubert Howells, Franz Liszt, John Rutter, Schubert, Stanford, Tchaikovsky, Telemann, Vaughan Williams and others; Leonard Bernstein, *Chichester Psalms*, 1965; Antonin Dvořák, *Biblical Songs*, 1894.

Have mercy on me, O God
This Psalm has traditionally been read as expressing **David**'s repentance after committing adultery with **Bathsheba** and murdering her husband.

Key concepts
God's mercy; acknowledgement of wrongdoing; the desire for God's cleansing and **forgiveness**.

Psalm 51:1–11
A Psalm of David, when the prophet Nathan came to him, after he had gone in to Bathsheba.
¹ Have mercy on me, O God,
      according to your steadfast love;
   according to your abundant mercy
      blot out my transgressions.
² Wash me thoroughly from my iniquity,
      and cleanse me from my sin.

³ For I know my transgressions,
      and my sin is ever before me.
⁴ Against you, you alone, have I sinned,

and done what is evil in your sight,
  so that you are justified in your sentence
  and blameless when you pass judgment.
[5] Indeed, I was born guilty,
  a sinner when my mother conceived me.

[6] You desire truth in the inward being;
  therefore teach me wisdom in my secret heart.
[7] Purge me with hyssop, and I shall be clean;
  wash me, and I shall be whiter than snow.
[8] Let me hear joy and gladness;
  let the bones that you have crushed rejoice.
[9] Hide your face from my sins,
  and blot out all my iniquities.

[10] Create in me a clean heart, O God,
  and put a new and right spirit within me.
[11] Do not cast me away from your presence,
  and do not take your holy spirit from me.

Linked themes
See Chapter 2 on David and Bathsheba. This Psalm was one of the Penitential Psalms used in the Medieval **Church**.

Related works
Literature: Thomas Wyatt, *Seven Penitential Psalms*, 1541.

Music: Gregorio Allegri, *Miserere Mei.*

SONG OF SOLOMON

This series of intimate and expressive love poems is also known as the Song of Songs or Canticles. The strongly erotic language, together with the absence of any overtly religious themes, has caused many to question its place in the **Bible** or to justify its inclusion by suggesting allegorical interpretations. In Jewish tradition, the Song has been treated as describing the love between God and **Israel**. A number of Christian commentators, from the **Fathers of the Church** onwards, have seen the male figure as representing **Christ** and the woman as his **Bride** the **Church**, or the individual believer.

Key concepts
The lover and his beloved.

Song of Solomon 2:1–6, 10–12, 16
I am a rose of Sharon,
   a lily of the valleys.

2 As a lily among brambles,
      so is my love among maidens.

3 As an apple tree among the trees of the wood,
      so is my beloved among young men.
   With great delight I sat in his shadow,
      and his fruit was sweet to my taste.
4 He brought me to the banqueting house,
      and his intention toward me was love.
5 Sustain me with raisins,
      refresh me with apples;
      for I am faint with love.
6 O that his left hand were under my head,
      and that his right hand embraced me! [...]
10 My beloved speaks and says to me:
   "Arise, my love, my fair one,
      and come away;
11 for now the winter is past,
      the rain is over and gone.
12 The flowers appear on the earth;
      the time of singing has come,
   and the voice of the turtle-dove

is heard in our land. [...]

[16] My beloved is mine and I am his;
   he pastures his flock among the lilies.

Song of Solomon 4:12
[12] A garden locked is my sister, my bride,
   a garden locked, a fountain sealed.

Linked themes
The concept of God as a lover or bridegroom wooing his people is expressed both in the **Old Testament**, for example in Hosea 2:14–20, and in the **New Testament**, where the Church is pictured as the **Bride of Christ** (Eph 5:32; Rev 19:7–9). Many images and phrases from the Song of Solomon are woven into the spirituality of the medieval Church and appear in the works of Richard Rolle and other **mystics**. Some phrases, such as the Rose of Sharon, were applied both to **Jesus** and to the **Virgin Mary**. The 'locked' or enclosed garden (Latin *Hortus conclusus*) symbolises purity and heaven. It is sometimes used as an attribute of Mary and appears in a number of images of the **Annunciation** and the Madonna and Child.

Related works
Art: Fra Filippo Lippi, *Annunciation*, c.1445 (National Gallery, London); Stephan Lochner, *Triptych with the Virgin and Child in an Enclosed Garden*, 1445–50; David Jones, *The Garden Enclosed*, 1924; Marc Chagall, *Song of Songs*; Salvador Dali, *Songs of King Solomon*, 1971.

Literature: Richard Rolle, c.1300, *Fire of Love*; Chaucer, 'Merchant's Tale'; Medieval lyrics ('In the Vale of Restless Mind', 'There is no Rose of such Virtue'); John Donne, 'Batter my heart', c.1609; Francis Quarles (1592–1644), 'My Beloved is Mine and I am his'; George Herbert, 'Paradise', published 1633; Andrew Marvell, 'The Garden', 1681; Byron, 'She Walks in Beauty like the Night', 1813; Toni Morrison, *Song of Solomon*, 1977; Toni Morrison, *Beloved*, 1988.

Music: Henry Purcell, *My Beloved Spake, c.*1680; Granville Bantock, *Song of Songs*; Benjamin Britten, *Canticle I: My Beloved is Mine*, 1947.

PROVERBS

Proverbs contains several collections of sayings, offering guidance on daily living, choices and relationships. Wisdom, here personified as a woman, is seen as a basic principle of life through which God's blessing can be found.

Key concepts
Wisdom springs from reverence for God; the need for humility and willingness to seek wisdom.

Proverbs 1:7–10, 20–3
[7] The fear of the LORD is the beginning of knowledge;
	fools despise wisdom and instruction.

[8] Hear, my child, your father's instruction,
	and do not reject your mother's teaching;
[9] for they are a fair garland for your head,
	and pendants for your neck.
[10] My child, if sinners entice you,
	do not consent. [...]

[20] Wisdom cries out in the street;
	in the squares she raises her voice.
[21] At the busiest corner she cries out;
	at the entrance of the city gates she speaks:
[22] "How long, O simple ones, will you love being simple?
	How long will scoffers delight in their scoffing
		and fools hate knowledge?
[23] Give heed to my reproof;
	I will pour out my thoughts to you;
		I will make my words known to you.

Linked themes

The Letter of James encourages its audience to ask God for wisdom (Jas 1:5).

Related works

Literature: Boethius, *Consolation of Philosophy*. Proverbs play a significant role in Old English literature (e.g. the Old English poem, *Precepts*, *Maxims*, *The Proverbs of Alfred*); William Shakespeare, *Winter's Tale*, c.1610; George Herbert, *Outlandish Proverbs*, 1640; Milton, *Paradise Regained*, 1667.

ECCLESIASTES

An enigmatic text which offers reflections on the meaning of existence, youth, old age and the value of human achievement. Although it claims to be written by **Solomon**, son of **David**, it is later in date.

Key concepts

The futility of human achievement; perspectives on human experience.

Ecclesiastes 1:1–2, 9

The words of the Teacher, the son of David, king in Jerusalem.
² Vanity of vanities, says the Teacher,
    vanity of vanities! All is vanity. [...]
⁹ What has been is what will be,
    and what has been done is what will be done;
    there is nothing new under the sun.

Ecclesiastes 3:1–11

For everything there is a season, and a time for every matter under heaven:
² a time to be born, and a time to die;
    a time to plant, and a time to pluck up what is planted;
³ a time to kill, and a time to heal;
    a time to break down, and a time to build up;

[4] a time to weep, and a time to laugh;
    a time to mourn, and a time to dance;
[5] a time to throw away stones, and a time to gather stones together;
    a time to embrace, and a time to refrain from embracing;
[6] a time to seek, and a time to lose;
    a time to keep, and a time to throw away;
[7] a time to tear, and a time to sew;
    a time to keep silence, and a time to speak;
[8] a time to love, and a time to hate;
    a time for war, and a time for peace.

[9] What gain have the workers from their toil? [10] I have seen the business that God has given to everyone to be busy with. [11] He has made everything suitable for its time; moreover, he has put a sense of past and future into their minds, yet they cannot find out what God has done from the beginning to the end.

Related works

Literature: William Dunbar (*c.*1460–*c.*1520), 'Of the World is Vanity'; Robert Browning, 'The Bishop Orders his Tomb at St Praxed's Church', 1845; William Makepeace Thackeray, *Vanity Fair*, 1847; Herman Melville, *Moby Dick*, 1851; T.S. Eliot, *The Waste Land*, 1922; Evelyn Waugh, *A Handful of Dust*, 1934.

Music: Granville Bantock, *Vanity of Vanities*, 1914.

JOB

The Book of **Job** addresses the mystery of undeserved suffering. God is shown allowing Satan to 'test' Job to see whether he will remain faithful in the face of loss, bereavement and personal affliction. Angered and protesting his innocence, Job engages in a lengthy dialogue with his 'comforters'. Eventually God intervenes to refute Job's complaints. Job repents and his prosperity is restored.

Key concepts
The problem of suffering; Job's trust in God is tested to the limit.

Job 1:8–12
[8] The LORD said to Satan, "Have you considered my servant Job? There is no one like him on the earth, a blameless and upright man who fears God and turns away from evil." [9] Then Satan answered the LORD, "Does Job fear God for nothing? [10] Have you not put a fence around him and his house and all that he has, on every side? You have blessed the work of his hands, and his possessions have increased in the land. [11] But stretch out your hand now, and touch all that he has, and he will curse you to your face." [12] The LORD said to Satan, "Very well, all that he has is in your power; only do not stretch out your hand against him!" So Satan went out from the presence of the LORD.

Verses 13–19 describe how Job learns that his oxen, donkeys, sheep and camels have been lost and a number of his servants killed. Finally, he is told that his sons and daughters have died in an accident.

Job 1:20–2
[20] Then Job arose, tore his robe, shaved his head, and fell on the ground and worshipped. [21] He said, "Naked I came from my mother's womb, and naked shall I return there; the LORD gave, and the LORD has taken away; blessed be the name of the LORD."
   [22] In all this Job did not sin or charge God with wrongdoing.

Job 2:3–8, 11
[3] The LORD said to Satan, "Have you considered my servant Job? … He still persists in his integrity, although you incited me against him, to destroy him for no reason." [4] Then Satan answered the LORD … [5] "stretch out your hand now and touch his bone and his flesh, and he will curse you to your face." [6] The LORD said to Satan, "Very well, he is in your power; only spare his life."
   [7] So Satan went out from the presence of the LORD, and

inflicted loathsome sores on Job from the sole of his foot to the crown of his head. [8]Job took a potsherd with which to scrape himself, and sat among the ashes. [...]

[11] Now when Job's three friends heard of all these troubles that had come upon him, each of them set out from his home – Eliphaz the Temanite, Bildad the Shuhite, and Zophar the Naamathite. They met together to go and console and comfort him.

Linked themes

The problem of undeserved suffering is raised in a number of **Psalms**. Christian commentators presented Job as a model of patient suffering.

Related works

Art: William Blake, *Satan Before the Throne of God*, 1821; William Blake, *Job's* Comforters, *c*.1805–6; Marc Chagall, *Job in Despair*, 1960; Dürer, *Job and His Wife*, 1504 (Städelsches Kunstinstitut, Frankfurt); La Tour, *Job Mocked by his Wife*, 1630s (Musée des Vosges, Épinal); Guido Reni, *The Triumph of Job*, 1636 (Nôtre Dame, Paris).

Literature: Milton, *Paradise Regained*, 1677; Daniel Defoe, *Roxana*, 1724; Archibald MacLeish, *J.B.*, 1958.

Music: Handel, *The Messiah* ('I Know That My Redeemer Liveth'), 1741–2; Ralph Vaughan Williams, *Job: A Masque for Dancing*, 1930.

4 THE PROPHETS

ELIJAH

ISAIAH

EZEKIEL

DANIEL

JONAH

Prophecy is a very important element within the **Old Testament** and can be found in a number of different contexts. Some books, such as **Isaiah**, Joel or Amos, are almost entirely composed of direct messages from God; others, such as **Daniel** and Ezekiel, combine messages and visions with the life story of the individual prophet. A third category comprises the historical books of Joshua, Judges, **Samuel** and Kings (known in Jewish tradition as 'former prophets') where the words and actions of figures such as **Elijah** and **Elisha** are embedded in the narrative.

A **prophet** was someone, male or female, who communicated God's message, sometimes through words alone, sometimes through dramatic actions. The task of prophets was to focus on what a relationship with God required of individuals and groups in terms of faith and worship, social issues, politics and family life. They warned of the need for **repentance**, they offered hope of **forgiveness** and they spoke of God's immediate and long-term plans for his people. Sometimes, as in the cases of **Moses**, Elijah and Elisha, they performed **miracles**.

ELIJAH

Elijah's uncompromising stance against evil brought him into conflict with King Ahab of **Israel** and his wife Jezebel, who killed a number of the prophets of God and promoted the worship of the Canaanite deity, **Baal.** In this story Elijah confronts the prophets of Baal single-handedly on **Mount Carmel** and proposes a trial of strength in order to win back the **Israelites** to serving God alone. Following the encounter, Elijah flees into the wilderness and is provided with food and drink by an angel.

Key concepts

Elijah's courage and trust in God; God proves his power.

1 Kings 18:22–7, 29

[22] Then Elijah said to the people, "I, even I only, am left a prophet of the LORD; but Baal's prophets number four hundred and fifty. [23] Let two bulls be given to us; let them choose one bull for themselves, cut it in pieces, and lay it on the wood, but put no fire to it; I will prepare the other bull and lay it on the wood, but put no fire to it. [24] Then you call on the name of your god and I will call on the name of the LORD; the god who answers by fire is indeed God." All the people answered, "Well spoken!" [25] Then Elijah said to the prophets of Baal, "Choose for yourselves one bull and prepare it first, for you are many; then call on the name of your god, but put no fire to it." [26] So they took the bull that was given them, prepared it, and called on the name of Baal from morning until noon, crying, "O Baal, answer us!" But there was no voice, and no answer …[27] At noon Elijah mocked them, saying, "Cry aloud! Surely he is a god; either he is meditating, or he has wandered away, or he is on a journey, or perhaps he is asleep and must be awakened." […] [29] As midday passed, they raved on until the time of the offering of the oblation, but there was no voice, no answer, and no response.

Elijah calls the people to him, builds an altar, places the wood and the bull upon it and drenches the whole sacrifice in water three times.

1 Kings 18:36–40

[36] At the time of the offering of the oblation, the prophet Elijah came near and said, "O LORD, God of Abraham, Isaac, and Israel, let it be known this day that you are God in Israel, that I am your servant, and that I have done all these things at your bidding. [37] Answer me, O LORD, answer me, so that this people may know that you, O LORD, are God, and that you have turned their hearts back." [38] Then the fire of the LORD fell and consumed the burnt offering, the wood, the stones, and the dust, and even licked up the water that was in the trench. [39] When all the people saw it, they fell on their faces and said, "The LORD indeed is God; the LORD indeed is God." [40] Elijah said to them, "Seize the prophets of Baal; do not let one of them escape." Then they seized them; and Elijah brought them down to the Wadi Kishon, and killed them there.

Linked themes

In the **New Testament** Elijah appears alongside **Jesus** at the **Transfiguration**.

Related works

Art: Rembrandt, *God's Judgement on Mount* Carmel, c.1645–50 (Städtische Wessenberg Gemäldegalerie, Constance); Rubens, *The Prophet Elijah Receiving Bread and Water from an Angel*, 1625–8 (Musée Bonnat, Bayonne); Juan Antonio Escalante, *An Angel Awakens the Prophet Elijah*, 1667 (Staatliche Museen, Berlin); William Blake, *Milton: Marriage of Heaven and Hell*, c.1793.

Literature: Herman Melville, *Moby Dick*, 1851.

Music: Mendelssohn, *Elijah*, 1846.

ISAIAH

The book of **Isaiah** is a collection of prophecies relating partly to the situation in **Judah** during the late eighth century BCE and partly to

the exile in **Babylon** during the sixth and fifth centuries BCE. It contains
a number of prophecies which speak both of God's judgement and of
hope for **forgiveness** and restoration.

This passage, one of several which describe a figure, God's 'servant',
who may represent an individual or the whole nation of **Israel**, was
later interpreted by Christians as foretelling the suffering and death of
Jesus.

Key concepts
The servant rejected by others yet providing forgiveness for those who
have turned away from God.

Isaiah 53:3–7, 9
[3] He was despised and rejected by others;
    a man of suffering and acquainted with infirmity;
  and as one from whom others hide their faces
    he was despised, and we held him of no account.

[4] Surely he has borne our infirmities
    and carried our diseases;
  yet we accounted him stricken,
    struck down by God, and afflicted.
[5] But he was wounded for our transgressions,
    crushed for our iniquities;
  upon him was the punishment that made us whole,
    and by his bruises we are healed.
[6] All we like sheep have gone astray;
    we have all turned to our own way,
  and the LORD has laid on him
    the iniquity of us all.

[7] He was oppressed, and he was afflicted,
    yet he did not open his mouth;
  like a lamb that is led to the slaughter,
    and like a sheep that before its shearers is silent,

so he did not open his mouth. [...]
⁹ They made his grave with the wicked
and his tomb with the rich ...

Linked themes

1 Peter 2:24–5 speaks of Jesus accepting suffering without retaliation and dying for the **sins** of others (see Chapter 8). The image of humankind as sheep who have gone astray is echoed in the **parable** of the Lost Sheep (see Chapter 6).

Related works

Art: Francisco de Zurbarán, *The Bound Lamb, c.* 1635–40 (Prado, Madrid).

Literature: Henry Vaughan (1622–95), 'Palm Sunday'.

Music: Handel, *The Messiah* ('He was despised'), 1741.

EZEKIEL

The Book of Ezekiel is set in the context of the **exile** in **Babylon**. It opens with this remarkable vision of God which is full of symbolism and suggestions of splendour and power. The living creatures and the moving wheels seem to imply that God is all-seeing and omnipresent.

Key concepts

The four living creatures; God enthroned in glory.

Ezekiel 1:4–10, 15–18, 22, 26–8

⁴ As I looked, a stormy wind came out of the north: a great cloud with brightness around it and fire flashing forth continually, and in the middle of the fire, something like gleaming amber. ⁵ In the middle of it was something like four living creatures. This was their appearance: they were of human form. ⁶ Each had four faces, and each of them had four wings. ⁷ Their legs were straight, and the soles of their feet were like the sole of a calf's foot; and they

sparkled like burnished bronze. [8] Under their wings on their four sides they had human hands. And the four had their faces and their wings thus: [9] their wings touched one another; each of them moved straight ahead, without turning as they moved. [10] As for the appearance of their faces: the four had the face of a human being, the face of a lion on the right side, the face of an ox on the left side, and the face of an eagle. [...]

[15] As I looked at the living creatures, I saw a wheel on the earth beside the living creatures, one for each of the four of them. [16] As for the appearance of the wheels and their construction: their appearance was like the gleaming of beryl; and the four had the same form, their construction being something like a wheel within a wheel. [17] When they moved, they moved in any of the four directions without veering as they moved. [18] Their rims were tall and awesome, for the rims of all four were full of eyes all around. [...]

[22] Over the heads of the living creatures there was something like a dome, shining like crystal, spread out above their heads. [...]

[26] And above the dome over their heads there was something like a throne, in appearance like sapphire; and seated above the likeness of a throne was something that seemed like a human form. [27] Upward from what appeared like the loins I saw something like gleaming amber, something that looked like fire enclosed all around; and downward from what looked like the loins I saw something that looked like fire, and there was a splendour all around. [28] Like the bow in a cloud on a rainy day, such was the appearance of the splendour all around. This was the appearance of the likeness of the glory of the LORD.

Linked themes

The four living creatures appear again in Revelation 4 and later became the symbols of the four **Evangelists**. **Christ** is often depicted seated on a rainbow in images of the **Last Judgement**.

Related works

Art: Fra Angelico, *Ezekiel's Vision of the Mystic Wheel*, c.1450 (Museo di San Marco, Florence); Raphael, *The Vision of Ezekiel*, 1516 (Pitti Palace, Florence); William Blake, *Ezekiel's Vision of the Cherubim and the Eyed Wheels*, 1803–5 (Museum of Fine Arts, Boston).

DANIEL

The Book of **Daniel** contains stories of life in exile in **Babylon** which illustrate the tensions of life for Jews living in an alien society, Daniel's visions and examples of his ability to interpret God's messages. This story emphasises that God's power is not limited to the land of **Israel** and that no ruler, however great, can disregard him with impunity.

Key concepts

The temple vessels are desecrated; God acts to punish; Daniel's gift of interpretation; God's sentence is carried out.

Daniel 5:1–6

King Belshazzar made a great festival for a thousand of his lords, and he was drinking wine in the presence of the thousand.

² Under the influence of the wine, Belshazzar commanded that they bring in the vessels of gold and silver that his father Nebuchadnezzar had taken out of the temple in Jerusalem, so that the king and his lords, his wives, and his concubines might drink from them. [...] ⁴ They drank the wine and praised the gods of gold and silver, bronze, iron, wood, and stone.

⁵ Immediately the fingers of a human hand appeared and began writing on the plaster of the wall of the royal palace, next to the lampstand. The king was watching the hand as it wrote. ⁶ Then the king's face turned pale, and his thoughts terrified him.

When the king's wise men fail to explain the meaning of the writing, Daniel, an exile from **Judah**, is brought in and offered a reward if he can provide an interpretation.

Daniel 5:17, 23–30

[17] Then Daniel answered in the presence of the king, "Let your gifts be for yourself, or give your rewards to someone else! Nevertheless I will read the writing to the king and let him know the interpretation. [...] [23] You have exalted yourself against the Lord of heaven! The vessels of his temple have been brought in before you, and you and your lords, your wives and your concubines have been drinking wine from them. You have praised the gods of silver and gold, of bronze, iron, wood, and stone, which do not see or hear or know; but the God in whose power is your very breath, and to whom belong all your ways, you have not honoured.

[24] "So from his presence the hand was sent and this writing was inscribed. [25] And this is the writing that was inscribed: MENE, MENE, TEKEL, and PARSIN. [26] This is the interpretation of the matter: MENE, God has numbered the days of your kingdom and brought it to an end; [27] TEKEL, you have been weighed on the scales and found wanting; [28] PERES, your kingdom is divided and given to the Medes and Persians."

[29] Then Belshazzar gave the command, and Daniel was clothed in purple, a chain of gold was put around his neck, and a proclamation was made concerning him that he should rank third in the kingdom.

[30] That very night Belshazzar, the Chaldean king, was killed.

Linked themes

Like **Joseph**, living in captivity in Egypt (see Chapter 2), Daniel is able to interpret God's messages to rulers and nations. Daniel is often depicted in the lions' den where he was placed for praying to God against a royal edict.

Related works

Art: Rembrandt, *Feast of Belshazzar*, c.1635 (National Gallery, London); Mattia Preti, *Belshazzar's Feast*, 1658.

Literature: Old English poem *Daniel*; late fourteenth-century poem *Cleanness*.

Music: William Walton, *Belshazzar's Feast*, 1930–1.

JONAH

Jonah, a very reluctant prophet, attempts to run away from God and ends up being swallowed and regurgitated by a whale. In a story which uses comedy and satire to make its points, he eventually agrees to preach repentance to the people of Nineveh and is very annoyed when they repent and win God's forgiveness.

Key concepts
Jonah's disobedience; God gives Jonah a second chance; God's love extends to other nations.

Jonah 1:1–4, 7
Now the word of the LORD came to Jonah son of Amittai, saying, ² "Go at once to Nineveh, that great city, and cry out against it; for their wickedness has come up before me." ³ But Jonah set out to flee to Tarshish from the presence of the LORD. He went down to Joppa and found a ship going to Tarshish; so he paid his fare and went on board, to go with them to Tarshish, away from the presence of the LORD.

⁴ But the LORD hurled a great wind upon the sea, and such a mighty storm came upon the sea that the ship threatened to break up. [...] ⁷ The sailors said to one another, "Come, let us cast lots, so that we may know on whose account this calamity has come upon us." So they cast lots, and the lot fell on Jonah.

Jonah advises the sailors to throw him overboard and they reluctantly comply. The sea becomes calm.

Jonah 1:17–2:1, 10
¹⁷ But the LORD provided a large fish to swallow up Jonah; and Jonah was in the belly of the fish three days and three nights.

Then Jonah prayed to the Lord his God from the belly of the fish [...] ¹⁰ Then the Lord spoke to the fish, and it spewed Jonah out upon the dry land.

Linked themes

In Matthew 12:38–42 Jesus is shown referring to the story of Jonah. Jonah's time in the belly of the whale was interpreted by Christian commentators as prefiguring the three days which Jesus spent in the tomb.

Related works

Art: Giotto, *Jonah Swallowed by the Whale,* 1304 (Scrovegni Chapel, Padua); Lorenzetto, *Jonah,* 1519 (S. Maria del Populo, Rome).

Literature: The late fourteenth-century poem *Patience.*

THE NEW TESTAMENT

The **New Testament** (NT) is the second part of the Christian **Bible**, written in Greek by the early Christian community between c.CE50–100. Like the **Old Testament**, it is an anthology of writings in different genres from many sources, but its focus is on one person, **Jesus** of **Nazareth**, and his followers.

The first four books of the New Testament, written between CE65 and CE100, recount the birth, **Ministry**, death and **Resurrection** of Jesus and are known as the **Gospels**, or 'good news'. The **Book of Acts**, also called 'The Acts of the **Apostles**', describes the **Ascension** of Jesus into heaven, the coming of the **Holy Spirit** to the **Disciples** and the initial growth of the Church, as the 'good news' about Jesus is preached firstly in **Jerusalem** and then throughout the eastern Mediterranean region. The twenty-one **Epistles** are letters sent c.CE50–100 by Christian leaders, particularly the **Apostle Paul**, to the communities of Jewish and **Gentile** believers which sprang up. The **Book of Revelation**, written to encourage Christians under threat of persecution, offers perspectives on the development of history and the end of time.

5 THE BIRTH AND CHILDHOOD OF JESUS

THE COMING OF THE WORD

THE BIRTH OF JOHN THE BAPTIST FORETOLD

THE ANGEL GABRIEL COMES TO MARY (THE ANNUNCIATION)

THE VISIT OF MARY TO ELIZABETH (THE VISITATION)

THE BIRTH OF JOHN THE BAPTIST

JOSEPH'S DOUBT

THE BIRTH OF JESUS AND THE VISIT OF THE SHEPHERDS

THE PRESENTATION IN THE TEMPLE

THE VISIT OF THE WISE MEN (MAGI)

THE FLIGHT INTO EGYPT AND THE MASSACRE OF THE INNOCENTS

THE CHILDHOOD OF JESUS

The birth of **Jesus Christ** is, not surprisingly, presented as a momentous event, with each **Gospel** writer emphasising particular aspects of its significance. **Luke** and **Matthew** focus on the conception of the child and his birth in ways which highlight his destiny as the **Christ** who is to be **Saviour** not only for the Jews but for all people. **John** offers a panoramic perspective, stating clearly that the one who came to earth is also the Creator, who has existed from before time began and is now uniquely made known in the person of Jesus.

THE COMING OF THE WORD

The opening verses of John's **Gospel**, often called 'the Prologue', are sometimes compared to the overture to an opera because of the way in which major themes of the Gospel, including the identity, significance and work of **Jesus Christ**, are anticipated and summarised. Jesus is presented as 'the **Word**' (Greek *logos*), who shared with God in the work of **creation** and whose coming brings life and light. These concepts are reinforced by deliberate echoes of the first chapter of the Book of Genesis: 'In the beginning God created …' (Gen 1:1); 'And God said "Let there be light and there was light"' (Gen 1:3). The writer, usually identified as **John the Evangelist**, also outlines the role of **John the Baptist**, the forerunner whose task was to point others to Christ. The summary of the **Incarnation**, 'The Word became flesh and lived among us,' indicates that in the person of Jesus, God has shown himself to humankind in the fullest possible way. The purpose is that all should have the opportunity to become 'children of God', a relationship offered as a gift which human beings have the freedom to accept or reject, rather than one which relies on their capacity to obey the **Law** given through **Moses**.

Key concepts
The identity, eternal existence and role of the **Word**; light in darkness; the role of **John the Baptist**; glory, **grace** and law, truth, **revelation**, the purpose and outcome of the **incarnation**.

John 1:1–18
In the beginning was the Word, and the Word was with God, and the Word was God. [2] He was in the beginning with God. [3] All things came into being through him, and without him not one thing came into being. What has come into being [4] in him was

life, and the life was the light of all people. [5] The light shines in the darkness, and the darkness did not overcome it.

[6] There was a man sent from God, whose name was John. [7] He came as a witness to testify to the light, so that all might believe through him. [8] He himself was not the light, but he came to testify to the light. [9] The true light, which enlightens everyone, was coming into the world.

[10] He was in the world, and the world came into being through him; yet the world did not know him. [11] He came to what was his own, and his own people did not accept him. [12] But to all who received him, who believed in his name, he gave power to become children of God, [13] who were born, not of blood or of the will of the flesh or of the will of man, but of God.

[14] And the Word became flesh and lived among us, and we have seen his glory, the glory as of a father's only son, full of grace and truth. [15] (John testified to him and cried out, "This was he of whom I said, 'He who comes after me ranks ahead of me because he was before me.'") [16] From his fullness we have all received, grace upon grace. [17] The law indeed was given through Moses; grace and truth came through Jesus Christ. [18] No one has ever seen God. It is God the only Son, who is close to the Father's heart, who has made him known.

Linked themes

Other **New Testament** writers also portray **Jesus** as the unique Son and **revelation** of God, as in Hebrews: 'Long ago God spoke to our ancestors in many and various ways by the prophets, [2] but in these last days he has spoken to us by a Son … through whom he also created the worlds. [3] He is the reflection of God's glory and the exact imprint of God's very being' (Heb 1:1–3). The concept of **Christ** as light coming into a dark world is also explored in Jn 3:19–21 and Jn 8:12 where Jesus claims: 'I am the light of the world. Whoever follows me will never walk in darkness but will have the light of life.' The implication that **salvation** now comes through the **grace** of God as a result of Christ's death on the **cross**, rather than through a requirement to keep **laws** contained in the **Old Testament**, is an important theme in the letters to the Romans, Galatians and Ephesians (Rom 3:21–8; Gal 2:16; Eph 2:8,9).

Related works

Literature: John Donne, *The Temple*, 1607; Milton, *Paradise Lost*, 1667; Edwin Muir, 'The Incarnate One', 1956.

Music: Carol, *This is the Truth Sent From Above*.

THE BIRTH OF JOHN THE BAPTIST FORETOLD

Luke opens his **Gospel** not with the birth of **Jesus** but with the linked narrative of the birth of his cousin, **John the Baptist**, some six months earlier. John appears early in each of the four Gospels as the messenger who is to prepare the way for the coming of Jesus, the **Messiah**. For this **ministry**, which forms a bridge between the **Old** and **New Testaments**, John is to be brought up as a **Nazirite** (Num 6:1–6), dedicated to **God** in the same way as Old Testament figures such as **Samuel** and **Samson**, and demonstrating the 'spirit and power' of another major prophet, **Elijah**. The child's name, John, means 'God has been gracious'. For his lack of faith, John's father **Zechariah** is struck dumb until the **prophecy** is fulfilled.

Key concepts

John as a link between the **prophecies** of the **Old Testament** and the coming of the **Messiah**; the importance of believing **God**'s promises; **angels** as divine messengers.

Luke 1:5–20, 24–5

[5] In the days of King Herod of Judea, there was a priest named Zechariah, who belonged to the priestly order of Abijah. His wife was a descendant of Aaron, and her name was Elizabeth. [6] Both of them were righteous before God, living blamelessly according to all the commandments and regulations of the Lord.

[7] But they had no children, because Elizabeth was barren, and both were getting on in years.

[8] Once when he was serving as priest before God and his section was on duty, [9] he was chosen by lot, according to the custom of the priesthood, to enter the sanctuary of the Lord and offer incense. [10] Now at the time of the incense offering, the whole assembly of the people was praying outside. [11] Then there appeared to him an angel of the Lord, standing at the right side of the altar of incense. [12] When Zechariah saw him, he was terrified; and fear overwhelmed him. [13] But the angel said to him, "Do not be afraid, Zechariah, for your prayer has been heard. Your wife Elizabeth will bear you a son, and you will name him John. [14] You will have joy and gladness, and many will rejoice at his birth, [15] for he will be great in the sight of the Lord. He must never drink wine or strong drink; even before his birth he will be filled with the Holy Spirit. [16] He will turn many of the people of Israel to the Lord their God. [17] With the spirit and power of Elijah he will go before him, to turn the hearts of parents to their children, and the disobedient to the wisdom of the righteous, to make ready a people prepared for the Lord." [18] Zechariah said to the angel, "How will I know that this is so? For I am an old man, and my wife is getting on in years." [19] The angel replied, "I am Gabriel. I stand in the presence of God, and I have been sent to speak to you and to bring you this good news. [20] But now, because you did not believe my words, which will be fulfilled in their time, you will become mute, unable to speak, until the day these things occur." [...]

[24] After those days his wife Elizabeth conceived, and for five months she remained in seclusion. She said, [25] "This is what the Lord has done for me when he looked favourably on me and took away the disgrace I have endured among my people."

Linked themes

The Bible contains a number of miraculous birth stories associated with significant figures, such as **Isaac**, son of **Abraham** and **Sarah**

(Gen 17:15–19), and the prophet **Samuel**, son of **Hannah** (1 Sam 1:1–20).

Hebrew tradition looked for the return of the prophet **Elijah** to make **Israel** acceptable to **God** (Mal 4:5–6) and re-establish righteousness and peace. When he begins his **ministry**, dressed as **Elijah** had been (Mk 1:6), John preaches **repentance** (Mt 3:1–17) and points to Jesus as 'the **Lamb of God** who takes away the **sin** of the world' (Jn 1:29).

Related works
Art: Giotto, *Annunciation to Zechariah*, *c*.1306 (Scrovegni Chapel, Padua).

THE ANGEL GABRIEL COMES TO MARY (THE ANNUNCIATION)

Six months after **Zechariah** is told of the forthcoming birth of **John the Baptist**, the angel **Gabriel** appears to **Mary** to announce that God has chosen her to be the mother of a child who will 'be Son of the most High' and whose **kingdom** will last forever. His name is to be **Jesus**, which means 'the Lord saves'. Mary is engaged, which at the time meant that a legal contract of marriage had been made, although the marriage would not be consummated until the bride left her father's house to live with her husband. Luke's account of the conversation between Mary and Gabriel stresses that the child is to be conceived through the action of the **Holy Spirit**. In contrast to Zechariah, Mary's response is one of wonder rather than disbelief and she commits herself to obedient co-operation with the will of **God**.

Key concepts
Virginal conception of Jesus; Jesus as coming **saviour** and king; Mary's obedient response.

Luke 1:26–38
[26] In the sixth month the angel Gabriel was sent by God to a town in Galilee called Nazareth, [27] to a virgin engaged to a man

whose name was Joseph, of the house of David. The virgin's name was Mary. [28] And he came to her and said, "Greetings, favoured one! The Lord is with you." [29] But she was much perplexed by his words and pondered what sort of greeting this might be. [30] The angel said to her, "Do not be afraid, Mary, for you have found favour with God. [31] And now, you will conceive in your womb and bear a son, and you will name him Jesus. [32] He will be great, and will be called the Son of the Most High, and the Lord God will give to him the throne of his ancestor David. [33] He will reign over the house of Jacob forever, and of his kingdom there will be no end." [34] Mary said to the angel, "How can this be, since I am a virgin?" [35] The angel said to her, "The Holy Spirit will come upon you, and the power of the Most High will overshadow you; therefore the child to be born will be holy; he will be called Son of God. [36] And now, your relative Elizabeth in her old age has also conceived a son; and this is the sixth month for her who was said to be barren. [37] For nothing will be impossible with God." [38] Then Mary said, "Here am I, the servant of the Lord; let it be with me according to your word." Then the angel departed from her.

Linked themes

Luke's account tells the story of the conception of Jesus from the perspective of Mary, whereas Matthew focuses on the response of **Joseph** (Mt 1:18–25). The intention of both narratives is to emphasise that Mary remains a virgin and that the child is conceived, not as in the stories of **Isaac**, **Samuel** and John the Baptist through God enabling the barren to conceive, nor, as in the case of contemporary Greco-Roman myths, through a lustful god impregnating a human woman, but through the work of the Holy Spirit. Paintings of the **Annunciation** often show the Holy Spirit present as a dove, with the conception effected through a beam of light.

Gabriel's greeting was later incorporated into the short prayer *Ave Maria* (**Hail Mary**).

Related works

Art: Fra Angelico, *Annunciation*, c.1440; (S. Marco, Florence); Filippo Lippi, *The Annunciation*, c.1455–60 (National Gallery, London); Botticelli, *Annunciation*, 1485 (Metropolitan Museum, New York); Leonardo da Vinci, *Annunciation*, c.1472, (Uffizi, Florence); Philippe de Champaigne, *Annunciation*, 1645 (Wallace Collection, London); Dante Gabriel Rossetti, *Annunciation*, 1850 (Tate Gallery, London); Edward Burne-Jones, *Annunciation*, 1879 (Lady Lever Art Gallery, Liverpool); Oskar Kokoscha, *Annunciation*, 1911 (Museum am Ostwall, Dortmund); Salvador Dali, *Annunciation*, 1960 (Vatican, Rome); Andy Warhol, *Annunciation*, 1984 (Andy Warhol Museum, Pittsburgh).

Literature: Chaucer parodies the Annunciation in the *Miller's Tale*; *The Annunciation* (Coventry, N-town, Towneley and York Mystery Play Cycles); John Donne, 'Annunciation', 1607; Milton describes Mary as a 'second Eve' in *Paradise Lost*, Bk 5, 1667.

Music: *Angelus ad Virginem*; Hans Leo Hassler (1564–1612), *Dixit Maria*.

THE VISIT OF MARY TO ELIZABETH (THE VISITATION)

Luke's interwoven stories meet when **Mary** goes to stay with her cousin, **Elizabeth**, who is pregnant with **John the Baptist**. At the sound of Mary's voice, John leaps in his mother's womb, recognising **Jesus** even before birth. In response, Mary is given a song of praise (sometimes called the *Magnificat* from its opening in Latin: '*Magnificat anima mea Dominum*') in which she gives thanks for God's faithful keeping of his promises to his people and the coming of **salvation** to the oppressed, the poor and the weak.

Key concepts

John's recognition of **Jesus**; **Mary**'s song of praise; **God**'s mercy to the lowly; God keeping his promises.

Luke 1:39–56

[39] In those days Mary set out and went with haste to a Judean town in the hill country, [40] where she entered the house of Zechariah and greeted Elizabeth. [41] When Elizabeth heard Mary's greeting, the child leaped in her womb. And Elizabeth was filled with the Holy Spirit [42] and exclaimed with a loud cry, "Blessed are you among women, and blessed is the fruit of your womb. [43] And why has this happened to me, that the mother of my Lord comes to me? [44] For as soon as I heard the sound of your greeting, the child in my womb leaped for joy. [45] And blessed is she who believed that there would be a fulfillment of what was spoken to her by the Lord."

[46] And Mary said,

"My soul magnifies the Lord,
[47]   and my spirit rejoices in God my Saviour,
[48] for he has looked with favour on the lowliness of his servant.
    Surely, from now on all generations will call me blessed;
[49] for the Mighty One has done great things for me,
    and holy is his name.
[50] His mercy is for those who fear him
    from generation to generation.
[51] He has shown strength with his arm;
    he has scattered the proud in the thoughts of their hearts.
[52] He has brought down the powerful from their thrones,
    and lifted up the lowly;
[53] he has filled the hungry with good things,
    and sent the rich away empty.
[54] He has helped his servant Israel,
    in remembrance of his mercy,
[55] according to the promise he made to our ancestors,
    to Abraham and to his descendants forever."

[56] And Mary remained with her about three months and then returned to her home.

Linked themes

Mary's song is woven from a number of **Old Testament** passages and echoes the words of **Hannah** (1 Sam 2:1–10), celebrating the miraculous birth of her son, the prophet **Samuel**, a key figure in the history of **Israel**. Here, as elsewhere in his **Gospel**, **Luke's** narrative emphasises the role of women and depicts God choosing to work through the humble rather than the mighty. The **Magnificat** has often been taken as a charter for social justice and its theme of reversal is extended throughout the Gospel of Luke, with **Jesus** shown socialising with the marginalised rather than with the wealthy or successful. **Elizabeth's** words, 'Blessed are you among women,' were also later incorporated into the *Ave Maria*.

Related works

Art: Giotto, *Visitation*, 1306 (Scrovegni Chapel, Padua): Ghirlandaio, *Visitation*, 1486–90 (S. Maria Novella, Florence); Luca della Robbia, *Meeting of Mary and Elisabeth*, 1450 (San Giovanni Fuorcivitas, Pistoia); Jacopo Pontormo, *Visitation*, 1528–9 (S. Annunziata, Florence); Ghislaine Howard, *Visitation*, 2001 (Hope University, Liverpool).

Literature: Gerard Manley Hopkins, *May Magnificat*.

Music: Settings of the *Magnificat* including Monteverdi, *Magnificat*, 1610; Johann Sebastian Bach, *Magnificat*, 1727–35.

THE BIRTH OF JOHN THE BAPTIST

The birth of **John the Baptist**, already remarkable because of the age of his parents, is followed by the dramatic events during his **circumcision** and naming. As he confirms the child's name, **Zechariah's** speech is restored and he utters a song of praise for God's faithfulness which foretells the coming and work of the promised **Saviour** and the role which John himself will play. This song (later known as the *Benedictus*, from the Latin for 'Blessed') later became a **canticle** used in the daily worship of the **Church**.

Key concepts

Fulfilment of **Old Testament prophecy**; role of **John the Baptist** in preparing the way for the coming of the **Messiah**; **Jesus** as light in darkness.

Luke 1:57–60, 62–3, 67–79

⁵⁷ Now the time came for Elizabeth to give birth, and she bore a son. ⁵⁸ Her neighbours and relatives heard that the Lord had shown his great mercy to her, and they rejoiced with her.

⁵⁹ On the eighth day they came to circumcise the child, and they were going to name him Zechariah after his father. ⁶⁰ But his mother said, "No; he is to be called John." […] ⁶²Then they began motioning to his father to find out what name he wanted to give him. ⁶³ He asked for a writing tablet and wrote, "His name is John." And all of them were amazed. […]

⁶⁷ Then his father Zechariah was filled with the Holy Spirit and spoke this prophecy:

⁶⁸ "Blessed be the Lord God of Israel,

for he has looked favourably on his people and redeemed them.

⁶⁹ He has raised up a mighty saviour for us

in the house of his servant David,

⁷⁰ as he spoke through the mouth of his holy prophets from of old,

⁷¹   that we would be saved from our enemies and from the hand of all who hate us.

⁷² Thus he has shown the mercy promised to our ancestors,

and has remembered his holy covenant,

⁷³ the oath that he swore to our ancestor Abraham,

to grant us ⁷⁴ that we, being rescued from the hands of our enemies,

might serve him without fear, ⁷⁵ in holiness and righteousness before him all our days.

⁷⁶ And you, child, will be called the prophet of the Most High;

for you will go before the Lord to prepare his ways,

[77] to give knowledge of salvation to his people
    by the forgiveness of their sins.
[78] By the tender mercy of our God,
    the dawn from on high will break upon us,
[79] to give light to those who sit in darkness and in the shadow of
        death,
    to guide our feet into the way of peace."

Linked themes

The coming **Messiah** will be a descendant of **David**, Israel's greatest king, and his coming fulfils promises made to Abraham. The role of Zechariah's son John the Baptist in preaching **repentance** (turning away from sin) and pointing others to **Jesus** is outlined in all the **Gospels** (Mt 3; Mk 1:1–11; Lk 3:1–22; Jn 1:6–9, 19–37).

Related works

Art: Fra Angelico, *The Naming of St John the Baptist* (S. Marco, Florence); Tintoretto, *The Birth of St John the Baptist,* 1540s. The closeness of the relationship between Elizabeth, Mary and their sons is often portrayed by artists as in Leonardo da Vinci, *The Virgin and Child with St Anne and the Young St John the Baptist,* c.1501 (National Gallery, London); Raphael's *Virgin and Child with St John the Baptist,* 1507 (Louvre, Paris) and Murillo's, *The Holy Family and the Infant Baptist,* c.1670 (Wallace Collection).

Music: Settings of the *Benedictus* including those by Byrd, Haydn, Mozart, Rossini and Britten.

JOSEPH'S DOUBT

Matthew portrays the conception and birth of **Jesus** through the eyes of **Joseph**, **Mary**'s fiancé. Joseph is, according to Matthew, a righteous man who takes God's **law** seriously and therefore faces a moral dilemma when confronted with Mary's pregnancy. His decision to withdraw from the relationship quietly and thus protect Mary from public humiliation and punishment is overtaken by the appearance of an angel who reassures him of Mary's purity and outlines the unique nature and role of the child who will be born.

Key concepts

Guidance or **revelation** through dreams; virginal conception of Jesus; fulfilment of **prophecy**; Jesus as **saviour** from **sin**; **Emmanuel**: God with us.

Matthew 1:18–25

[18] Now the birth of Jesus the Messiah took place in this way. When his mother Mary had been engaged to Joseph, but before they lived together, she was found to be with child from the Holy Spirit. [19] Her husband Joseph, being a righteous man and unwilling to expose her to public disgrace, planned to dismiss her quietly. [20] But just when he had resolved to do this, an angel of the Lord appeared to him in a dream and said, "Joseph, son of David, do not be afraid to take Mary as your wife, for the child conceived in her is from the Holy Spirit. [21] She will bear a son, and you are to name him Jesus, for he will save his people from their sins." [22] All this took place to fulfil what had been spoken by the Lord through the prophet:
[23] "Look, the virgin shall conceive and bear a son,
     and they shall name him Emmanuel,"
which means, "God is with us." [24] When Joseph awoke from sleep, he did as the angel of the Lord commanded him; he took her as his wife, [25] but had no marital relations with her until she had borne a son; and he named him Jesus.

Linked themes

The description 'Emmanuel, which means God with us' describes the **Incarnation**, which the Prologue to **John's Gospel** defines as 'the Word became flesh and lived among us' (Jn 1:14).

The virginal conception of **Jesus** is presented by **Matthew** as the fulfilment of the words of the **Old Testament** prophet, **Isaiah** (Isa 7:14).

Later writers identified many additional **Old Testament** incidents and prophecies as foreshadowing this event and revealing its miraculous nature.

Related works
Literature: The Old English poem *Christ I*; *Joseph's Trouble about Mary* (York Mystery Play Cycle).

Music: *Cherry-tree Carol*.

THE BIRTH OF JESUS AND THE VISIT OF THE SHEPHERDS

Luke sets the **Nativity** (birth) of **Jesus** within both the wider context of world history and specifically Jewish expectations of the coming of the **Messiah. Bethlehem**, the city of **King David**, one of the greatest figures in the **Old Testament**, was the predicted birthplace of the **Saviour** (Mic 5:2). The mention of a manger (feeding trough) has led to the assumption that the event took place in a stable or cave. It is more likely that the delivery took place in an ordinary home, at one end of the family living quarters where animals would have been kept at night. The simplicity of the birth narrative and the apparent ordinariness of the human cast are strikingly juxtaposed with the account of **angels**, bringing an awareness of the presence and glory of God and proclaiming the deeper significance of the event.

Key concepts
Jesus born in the city of David; no room in the inn; baby laid in a manger; the message of the angels coming first to ordinary people.

Luke 2:1–20

In those days a decree went out from Emperor Augustus that all the world should be registered. [2] This was the first registration and was taken while Quirinius was governor of Syria. [3] All went to their own towns to be registered. [4] Joseph also went from the town of Nazareth in Galilee to Judea, to the city of David called Bethlehem, because he was descended from the house and family of David. [5] He went to be registered with Mary, to whom he was engaged and who was expecting a child. [6] While they were there, the time came for her to deliver her child. [7] And she gave birth to her firstborn son and wrapped him in bands of cloth, and laid him in a manger, because there was no place for them in the inn.

[8] In that region there were shepherds living in the fields, keeping watch over their flock by night. [9] Then an angel of the Lord stood before them, and the glory of the Lord shone around them, and they were terrified. [10] But the angel said to them, "Do not be afraid; for see – I am bringing you good news of great joy for all the people: [11] to you is born this day in the city of David a Saviour, who is the Messiah, the Lord. [12] This will be a sign for you: you will find a child wrapped in bands of cloth and lying in a manger." [13] And suddenly there was with the angel a multitude of the heavenly host, praising God and saying,

[14] "Glory to God in the highest heaven,
and on earth peace among those whom he favours!"

[15] When the angels had left them and gone into heaven, the shepherds said to one another, "Let us go now to Bethlehem and see this thing that has taken place, which the Lord has made known to us." [16] So they went with haste and found Mary and Joseph, and the child lying in the manger. [17] When they saw this, they made known what had been told them about this child; [18] and all who heard it were amazed at what the shepherds told them. [19] But Mary treasured all these words and pondered them in her heart. [20] The shepherds returned, glorifying and praising God for all they had heard and seen, as it had been told them.

Linked themes

This account was amplified by later writers. The ox and the ass, not mentioned in the **canonical** Gospels, appear in the **apocryphal *Gospel of Pseudo-Matthew*** (*c.* eighth or ninth century): 'On the third day after the nativity of our Lord Jesus Christ, the most blessed Mary went out of the cave, and entering a stable, put her child in a manger and the ox and ass adored him. Then was fulfilled that which was spoken by Isaiah the prophet, who said, "The ox hath known his master, and the ass his master's crib" (Isa 1:3) … [and] by Habakkuk the prophet, who said, "Between two animals thou art known"' (Hab 3:2). The words quoted from Habakkuk are in fact based on a misreading of the Latin text in which *in medio animalium* (in the midst of the animals) had been substituted for *in medio annorum* (in the midst of the years). The second-century **Book of James** (the **Protevangelium**) adds the presence of midwives to attest to the **Virgin birth.** 'The glory of the Lord' witnessed by the shepherds recalls the experience of **Moses**, also a shepherd, when confronted by the **Burning Bush** (see Chapter 2). The words of the **angels** later formed the opening lines of the *Gloria*, a **canticle** (song of praise) used in Christian worship.

Related works

The popularity of the nativity as a topic grew rapidly from the thirteenth century onwards. St Francis is said to have created the first 'crib scene' in 1223. The amplified story appears in medieval mystery plays, poetry and carols, stained glass, sculpture and manuscript illumination as well as innumerable paintings.

Art: Hugo van der Goes, *The Adoration of the Shepherds*, 1476–9 (Uffizi, Florence); Botticelli, *Mystic Nativity*, 1501 (National Gallery, London); Giorgione, *Adoration of the Shepherds*, 1505–10 (National Gallery, Washington); Francisco de Zurbarán, *The Adoration of the Shepherds*, 1638–9 (Musée des Beaux Arts, Grenoble); Rembrandt, *Adoration of the Shepherds*, 1646 (National Gallery, London); Paul Gauguin, *Christmas Night*, c.1894 (Indianapolis Museum of Art); Henry Moore, *Mother and Child*, 1983 (St Paul's Cathedral, London); Beryl Cook, *Nativity Scene*, 1990.

Literature: Medieval lyrics ('I sing of a Maiden', 'There is no Rose'); *Birth of Christ* (York Mystery Cycle); *Second Shepherds' Play* (Towneley Cycle); Robert Southwell (1561–95), 'New Heaven, New Warre'; Milton: 'Hymn on the Morning of Christ's Nativity', 1629; Richard Crashaw, 'In the Holy Nativity of our Lord', 1646; Gerard Manley Hopkins, 'Rosa Mystica', 1989;

Thomas Hardy, 'The Oxen', 1915; Edwin Muir, 'The Christmas', 1956; R.S. Thomas, 'Pietà', 1966.

Music: Corelli, *Christmas*, Concerto, 1712; Johann Sebastian Bach, *Christmas*, Oratorio, 1734; Handel, *The Messiah* ('There were shepherds abiding in the fields', 'Glory to God'), 1741; Hector Berlioz, *L'Enfance du Christ*, 1850–4; Olivier Messiaen, *La Nativité du Seigneur*, 1935.

THE PRESENTATION IN THE TEMPLE

Every Jewish boy was **circumcised** on the eighth day after his birth and was formally named. After childbirth a woman was considered ritually unclean for forty days if the child was a boy (eighty days if it was a girl). **Jesus** and his family are clearly shown conforming to the requirements of the Jewish **law**. The fact that **Mary** and **Joseph** brought two pigeons to the **temple** for their **sacrifice**, an option called the offering of the poor, indicates their limited means. **Simeon** and **Anna**, representatives of those in **Israel** who were faithfully waiting for the appearance of the **Messiah**, now recognise him in the child brought to the **temple** to be dedicated to God. **Simeon**'s song of praise became part of the daily worship of the **Church** as the *Nunc Dimittis*. **Simeon** predicts the impact of the coming of the child and the opposition that he will face, and speaks of **salvation** for both **Gentiles** and Jews.

Key concepts
The naming of Jesus; recognition of the Messiah by Simeon and Anna; fulfilment of **prophecy**; Simeon's **canticle** of praise; Jesus as a 'light to the Gentiles' and the glory of **Israel**.

Luke 2:21–40
[21] After eight days had passed, it was time to circumcise the child; and he was called Jesus, the name given by the angel before he was conceived in the womb.

[22] When the time came for their purification according to the law of Moses, they brought him up to Jerusalem to present him

to the Lord [23] (as it is written in the law of the Lord, "Every firstborn male shall be designated as holy to the Lord"), [24] and they offered a sacrifice according to what is stated in the law of the Lord, "a pair of turtle-doves or two young pigeons."

[25] Now there was a man in Jerusalem whose name was Simeon; this man was righteous and devout, looking forward to the consolation of Israel, and the Holy Spirit rested on him. [26] It had been revealed to him by the Holy Spirit that he would not see death before he had seen the Lord's Messiah. [27] Guided by the Spirit, Simeon came into the temple; and when the parents brought in the child Jesus, to do for him what was customary under the law, [28] Simeon took him in his arms and praised God, saying,

[29] "Master, now you are dismissing your servant in peace,
    according to your word;
[30] for my eyes have seen your salvation,
[31] which you have prepared in the presence of all peoples,
[32] a light for revelation to the Gentiles
    and for glory to your people Israel."

[33] And the child's father and mother were amazed at what was being said about him. [34] Then Simeon blessed them and said to his mother Mary, "This child is destined for the falling and the rising of many in Israel, and to be a sign that will be opposed [35] so that the inner thoughts of many will be revealed – and a sword will pierce your own soul too."

[36] There was also a prophet, Anna the daughter of Phanuel, of the tribe of Asher. She was of a great age, having lived with her husband seven years after her marriage, [37] then as a widow to the age of eighty-four. She never left the temple but worshipped there with fasting and prayer night and day. [38] At that moment she came, and began to praise God and to speak about the child to all who were looking for the redemption of Jerusalem.

[39] When they had finished everything required by the law of the Lord, they returned to Galilee, to their own town of Nazareth. [40] The child grew and became strong, filled with wisdom; and the favour of God was upon him.

Linked themes

Once again, **Christ** is pictured as light in darkness (compare Jn 1:3–9; Jn 3:19–21; Jn 8:12). The Western **Church** later celebrated this event in the festival of **Candlemas** (February 2) when candles were carried in procession to symbolise Christ, 'a light for **revelation** to the Gentiles' (Lk 2:32). Simeon's warning to Mary that 'a sword will pierce your own soul' was later interpreted as foreshadowing the grief which she would experience at Christ's **Crucifixion**.

Related works

Art: Hans Memling, *Presentation in the Temple*, 1463 (National Gallery of Art, Washington); Fra Bartolomeo, *Presentation of Jesus in the Temple*, 1488 (Vienna); Carpaccio, *Presentation of Christ in the Temple*, 1510 (Galeria dell'Accademia, Venice); Rembrandt, *Nunc Dimittis* (*Simeon Holding the Christ Child*), c.1669.

Literature: T.S. Eliot, *A Song for Simeon*, 1928.

Music: Settings of the *Nunc Dimittis*.

THE VISIT OF THE WISE MEN (MAGI)

Matthew places the birth of Jesus in the reign of **Herod the Great** (d.4BCE) which means that it probably occurred in 5BCE. Once again Matthew emphasises fulfilment of **Old Testament prophecy**. The belief that stars and other astronomical phenomena could indicate significant events was widespread. Matthew may have had in mind the words of the **Old Testament** prophet **Balaam:** 'a star shall come out of **Jacob**' (Num 24:17). The visit of the **Magi**, who are **Gentiles** from the East (possibly Persia, Babylon or Arabia) and in search of the new 'king of the Jews', indicates that the birth is relevant to those beyond **Israel**. Their gifts, suitable for offering to a king or god, have been interpreted as symbolic of the child's future: gold (kingship), frankincense (royal priesthood) and myrrh (future suffering and death).

Key concepts

Universal significance of **Christ**'s birth (**Jesus** worshipped by **Gentiles**); symbolic gifts; antagonism of King Herod and threat to the existing order; **revelation** through a dream.

Matthew 2:1–12

In the time of King Herod, after Jesus was born in Bethlehem of Judea, wise men from the East came to Jerusalem, [2] asking, "Where is the child who has been born king of the Jews? For we observed his star at its rising, and have come to pay him homage." [3] When King Herod heard this, he was frightened, and all Jerusalem with him; [4] and calling together all the chief priests and scribes of the people, he inquired of them where the Messiah was to be born. [5] They told him, "In Bethlehem of Judea; for so it has been written by the prophet:

[6] 'And you, Bethlehem, in the land of Judah,
   are by no means least among the rulers of Judah;
for from you shall come a ruler
   who is to shepherd my people Israel.'"

[7] Then Herod secretly called for the wise men and learned from them the exact time when the star had appeared. [8] Then he sent them to Bethlehem, saying, "Go and search diligently for the child; and when you have found him, bring me word so that I may also go and pay him homage." [9] When they had heard the king, they set out; and there, ahead of them, went the star that they had seen at its rising, until it stopped over the place where the child was. [10] When they saw that the star had stopped, they were overwhelmed with joy. [11] On entering the house, they saw the child with Mary his mother; and they knelt down and paid him homage. Then, opening their treasure chests, they offered him gifts of gold, frankincense, and myrrh. [12] And having been warned in a dream not to return to Herod, they left for their own country by another road.

Linked themes

The **New Testament** says nothing of the status, number or names of the Magi. It was **Tertullian** (*c.*160–*c.*225) who described them as kings, probably influenced by Old Testament passages such as Isa 60:3,6: 'Nations shall come to your light and kings to the brightness of your dawn … all those from Sheba shall come … they shall bring gold and frankincense.' **Origen** (b.*c.*185) gave their number as three (an inference from the gifts offered) and a sixth-century work names them as Gaspar, Melchior and Balthasar. The homage offered to Jesus is in tune with other episodes in the **Gospels** in which Gentiles seek him out (e.g. Jn 12:20–1) and **prefigures** the command that his followers should 'make **disciples** of all nations' (Mt 28:19). The festival of **Epiphany** (6 January) celebrates the manifestation (Greek *epiphaneia*) of Jesus to the Magi and hence to the Gentiles.

Related works

Art: Andrea Mantegna, *Adoration of the Magi*, 1495–1505 (J. Paul Getty Museum, Los Angeles); Bramantino, *Adoration of the Magi*, 1498, (National Gallery, London); Dürer, *Adoration of the Magi*, 1504 (Uffizi, Florence); Rubens, *Adoration of the Magi*, 1624 (King's College, Cambridge).

Literature: *Herod* and *The Magi* (York Mystery Cycle); John Donne, 'Nativitie', 1607; T.S. Eliot, *The Journey of the Magi*, 1927.

Music: Peter Cornelius (1824–74), *Die Könige*; Gian Carlo Menotti, *Amahl and the Night Visitors*, 1951; Benjamin Britten, *Canticle IV: Journey of the Magi*, 1971.

THE FLIGHT INTO EGYPT AND THE MASSACRE OF THE INNOCENTS

The brutality of **Herod's** response to the birth of a perceived rival is consistent with his wider reputation as a tyrant who did not hesitate to murder members of his own family. The **flight into Egypt** which makes the family into refugees and their eventual move to **Nazareth**, away from the threat of Herod's son, are seen by **Matthew** as further fulfilments of **Old Testament prophecy**.

Key concepts

Christ born into a context of hatred, danger and human suffering; fulfilment of Old Testament prophecy.

Matthew 2:13–23

[13] Now after they had left, an angel of the Lord appeared to Joseph in a dream and said, "Get up, take the child and his mother, and flee to Egypt, and remain there until I tell you; for Herod is about to search for the child, to destroy him." [14] Then Joseph got up, took the child and his mother by night, and went to Egypt, [15] and remained there until the death of Herod. This was to fulfil what had been spoken by the Lord through the prophet, "Out of Egypt I have called my son."

[16] When Herod saw that he had been tricked by the wise men, he was infuriated, and he sent and killed all the children in and around Bethlehem who were two years old or under, according to the time that he had learned from the wise men. [17] Then was fulfilled what had been spoken through the prophet Jeremiah:
[18] "A voice was heard in Ramah,

wailing and loud lamentation,

Rachel weeping for her children;

she refused to be consoled, because they are no more."

[19] When Herod died, an angel of the Lord suddenly appeared in a dream to Joseph in Egypt and said, [20] "Get up, take the child and his mother, and go to the land of Israel, for those who were seeking the child's life are dead." [21] Then Joseph got up, took the child and his mother, and went to the land of Israel. [22] But when he heard that Archelaus was ruling over Judea in place of his father Herod, he was afraid to go there. And after being warned in a dream, he went away to the district of Galilee. [23] There he made his home in a town called Nazareth, so that what had been

spoken through the prophets might be fulfilled, "He will be called a Nazorean."

Linked themes

There may be a perceived parallel in the mind of the writer with the story of **Moses**, who led the Israelites out of Egypt in the **Exodus** and whose life was threatened by the determination of the Egyptian Pharaoh to kill all male Jewish babies born at the time. The story of the flight into Egypt was expanded in the **apocryphal** *Gospel of Pseudo-Matthew* to include the miracle of the date palm (or cherry tree in North European versions) which miraculously bowed down to offer its fruit to the **Virgin Mary**.

Related works

Art: Rembrandt, *The Dream of St Joseph*, 1650–5 (Museum of Fine Arts, Budapest); Fra Angelico, *Massacre of the Innocents*, 1451–3 (Museo di San Marco, Florence); Altdorfer, *Rest on the Flight into Egypt,* 1510 (Staatliches Museum, Berlin); David, *Rest on the Flight into Egypt,* 1510 (National Gallery, Washington); Murillo, *Flight into Egypt*, 1655–60 (Museum of Fine Arts, Budapest).

Literature: *Slaughter of the Innocents* (Coventry Mystery Cycle); Richard Crashaw, 'To the Infant Martyrs', 1656; Carol Ann Duffy, 'Mrs Herod', 1999.

Music: *Coventry Carol*; Hector Berlioz, *L'Enfance du Christ*, 1850–4.

THE CHILDHOOD OF JESUS

Luke sums up **Jesus'** boyhood in one sentence: 'The child grew and became strong, filled with wisdom; and the favour of God was upon him' (Lk 2:40). The only additional information comes from this further episode set in the **temple** in Jerusalem (compare the **Presentation** above). Jesus had probably travelled to **Jerusalem** with his parents to celebrate the annual **Passover** a number of times before but this incident, as he moves towards adulthood, serves to mark out his unusual degree of understanding and emphasises once more his unique relationship with God.

Key concepts
The wisdom of Jesus; Jesus at home in the temple.

Luke 2:41–52

[41] Now every year his parents went to Jerusalem for the festival of the Passover. [42] And when he was twelve years old, they went up as usual for the festival. [43] When the festival was ended and they started to return, the boy Jesus stayed behind in Jerusalem, but his parents did not know it. [44] Assuming that he was in the group of travellers, they went a day's journey. Then they started to look for him among their relatives and friends. [45] When they did not find him, they returned to Jerusalem to search for him. [46] After three days they found him in the temple, sitting among the teachers, listening to them and asking them questions. [47] And all who heard him were amazed at his understanding and his answers. [48] When his parents saw him they were astonished; and his mother said to him, "Child, why have you treated us like this? Look, your father and I have been searching for you in great anxiety." [49] He said to them, "Why were you searching for me? Did you not know that I must be in my Father's house?" [50] But they did not understand what he said to them. [51] Then he went down with them and came to Nazareth, and was obedient to them. His mother treasured all these things in her heart.

[52] And Jesus increased in wisdom and in years, and in divine and human favour.

Linked themes
Luke may be suggesting a link between this second episode in the temple and the story of the prophet **Samuel** (1 Sam 3:1–14) whose miraculous birth, home in the temple and later ministry in some ways foreshadow the life of Jesus. Jesus' description of the temple as his

Father's house is later restated in Lk 19:45–6, by which time he is teaching there on a daily basis.

While the **canonical Gospels** are relatively silent about Jesus' childhood, the **apocryphal** 'infancy' *Gospel of Thomas* and *Gospel of Pseudo-Matthew* introduce a number of stories about **miracles** he is said to have performed as a boy, including bringing to life twelve sparrows he had made from clay.

Related works

Art: Duccio, *Disputation with the Doctors* [teachers], 1308–11 (Museo dell'Opera del Duomo, Siena); Paolo Caliari Veronese, *Jesus with the Doctors in the Temple*, sixteenth century (Museo Prado, Madrid); Gerrit van Honthorst, *The Childhood of Christ*, 1650; Holman Hunt, *The Finding of the Saviour in the Temple*, 1854–5 (Birmingham Museum and Art Gallery).

Literature: John Donne, *La Corona*, Sonnet 4, 1607; Christopher Smart, 'Christ Disputing among the Doctors', *The Parables of our Lord and Saviour Christ*, 1768.

Music: Henry Purcell, *Blessed Virgin's Expostulation*, 1693; Johannes Brahms (1833–97), 'Marias Wallfart', *Marienlieder*.

6 THE MINISTRY AND TEACHING OF JESUS

THE BAPTISM OF JESUS

THE TEMPTATION OF JESUS IN THE DESERT

THE CALLING OF THE DISCIPLES

NICODEMUS VISITS JESUS

THE WOMAN AT THE WELL

THE DEATH OF JOHN THE BAPTIST

THE TRANSFIGURATION

THE TEACHING OF JESUS: THE SERMON ON THE MOUNT

THE TEACHING OF JESUS: PARABLES

THE TEACHING OF JESUS: THE 'I AM' SAYINGS

THE TEACHING OF JESUS: JUDGEMENT

MIRACLES

>THE FEEDING OF THE FIVE THOUSAND

>THE RAISING OF LAZARUS

>THE PARALYSED MAN

THE TRIUMPHAL ENTRY INTO JERUSALEM

THE LAST SUPPER

JESUS WASHES HIS DISCIPLES' FEET

Luke's Gospel states that **Jesus** was about thirty years old when he began to teach and preach. The beginning of his **ministry** is marked in the Gospel narratives by his encounter with **John the Baptist**, his **baptism** and the period of temptation in the desert. There followed a period of some three years during which he travelled through the towns and countryside of **Galilee** and later to **Jerusalem**. Jesus is shown gathering a group of close followers whom he taught and trained, teaching about the **Kingdom of God**, performing **miracles** and confronting various religious leaders who raise objections to his words and actions. Eventually in Jerusalem the growing opposition to Jesus culminates in his arrest and execution. The Gospel writers frequently suggest connections between the key figures, stories and promises of the **Old Testament** and the events of Jesus' life.

THE BAPTISM OF JESUS

John the Baptist now fulfils the role foretold before his birth (see Chapter 5) and the prophecy of Isaiah 40:3–5 as he appears in the desert to prepare the people for the arrival of God's **Messiah**, a long-hoped-for event promised in the **Old Testament**. He announces that the time of God's coming to rule (and of his judgement on wrongdoing) is near and that all must be baptised in the River Jordan as a sign of cleansing and willingness to change both attitudes and behaviour. To John's surprise, Jesus himself comes to ask for **baptism**, as a sign of identification with the people he has come to save. As Jesus emerges from the river, the **Holy Spirit** appears from heaven in the form of a dove. Jesus is empowered for his task and affirmed as the Son of God in words from the Old Testament (Ps 2:7; Isa 42:1).

Key concepts
John the Baptist; preparing the way; **repentance**; the kingdom of heaven; fulfilment of Old Testament **prophecy**; baptism; God's judgement on **sin**; the Holy Spirit; Jesus as Son of God and Messiah.

Matthew 3:1–17

In those days John the Baptist appeared in the wilderness of Judea, proclaiming, [2] "Repent, for the kingdom of heaven has come near." [3] This is the one of whom the prophet Isaiah spoke when he said,

"The voice of one crying out in the wilderness:
'Prepare the way of the Lord,
    make his paths straight.' "

[4] Now John wore clothing of camel's hair with a leather belt around his waist, and his food was locusts and wild honey. [5] Then the people of Jerusalem and all Judea were going out to him, and all the region along the Jordan, [6] and they were baptized by him in the river Jordan, confessing their sins.

[7] But when he saw many Pharisees and Sadducees coming for baptism, he said to them, "You brood of vipers! Who warned you to flee from the wrath to come? [8] Bear fruit worthy of repentance. [9] Do not presume to say to yourselves, 'We have Abraham as our ancestor'; for I tell you, God is able from these stones to raise up children to Abraham. [10] Even now the axe is lying at the root of the trees; every tree therefore that does not bear good fruit is cut down and thrown into the fire.

[11] "I baptize you with water for repentance, but one who is more powerful than I is coming after me; I am not worthy to carry his sandals. He will baptise you with the Holy Spirit and fire. [12] His winnowing fork is in his hand, and he will clear his threshing floor and will gather his wheat into the granary; but the chaff he will burn with unquenchable fire."

[13] Then Jesus came from Galilee to John at the Jordan, to be baptised by him. [14] John would have prevented him, saying, "I need to be baptized by you, and do you come to me?" [15] But Jesus answered him, "Let it be so now; for it is proper for us in this way to fulfil all righteousness." Then he consented. [16] And when Jesus had been baptized, just as he came up from the water, suddenly the heavens were opened to him and he saw the Spirit of God descending like a dove and alighting on him. [17] And a

voice from heaven said, "This is my Son, the Beloved, with whom I am well pleased."

Linked themes

The desert or wilderness, which forms a considerable part of the terrain of the Middle East, is a common setting for important events in the Bible. It is seen both as a place of testing and a place where God speaks to his people. The Jordan had particular significance as the river which the Israelites crossed to enter the 'Promised Land' (Josh 3:7–4:9). In Acts 1:5 Jesus is shown promising his Disciples baptism 'with the Holy Spirit', a promise fulfilled on the Day of Pentecost (Acts 2:1–4). Jesus also speaks frequently of the coming of God's judgement.

Related works

Art: Hieronymus Bosch, St John in the Wilderness, c.1450–1516 (Museo Lázaro Galdiano, Madrid); Piero della Francesca, Baptism of Christ, 1448–50 (National Gallery, London); Geertgen tot Sint Jans, Saint John the Baptist in the Wilderness, c.1495 (Staatliche Museen, Berlin); Leonardo da Vinci, St John the Baptist, 1508–13; Tintoretto, Baptism of Christ, 1579–81 (Scuola di S. Rocco, Venice); Piero della Carracci, Baptism of Christ, 1584 (S. Gregorio, Bologna); Nicholas Poussin, The Baptist Baptises the Crowds, 1632 (National Gallery of Art, Washington); Henri-Georges Roualt, Baptism of Christ, 1911 (Museum of Modern Art, Paris).

Literature: Edmund Spenser, Faerie Queene, I. xi, 1590; George Herbert, 'Holy Baptism', 1633; John Milton, Paradise Regained, 1671; Charles Dickens, Dombey and Son, Ch 5, 1846–50; Flannery O'Connor, 'The River', A Good Man is Hard to Find, 1955; Camus, The Fall, 1956.

THE TEMPTATION OF JESUS IN THE DESERT

The beginning of Jesus' ministry is marked not only by the high point of his baptism and affirmation as the Son of God but also by a period of severe testing of his identity, call and obedience. He fasts for forty days and nights in the desert, as did two key Old Testament figures:

Moses, when receiving the **Ten Commandments** on **Mount Sinai** (Ex 34:28), and **Elijah**, in the wilderness after defeating the prophets of **Baal** (1 Kings 19:8). Jesus' obedience to God is tested in ways which recall both the temptation of humankind in the **Garden of Eden** (see Chapter 1) and the forty years which the **Israelites** spent in the wilderness on their way from **Egypt** to **Canaan** (see Chapter 2).

Confronted by the **Devil**, Jesus is tempted to use his power to meet his own needs, to test God's protection by a spectacular stunt and to trade allegiance to his father for untold earthly influence and wealth. In this battle of words, Jesus quotes three times from sayings attributed to Moses (Deut 6–8) from the story of Israel in the wilderness. Unlike **Adam** and **Eve** and unlike the Israelites during the **Exodus**, Jesus consistently chooses obedience to God's will.

Key concepts

Temptation; the identity of **Jesus**; obedience to God; the **Devil**.

Matthew 4:1–11

Then Jesus was led up by the Spirit into the wilderness to be tempted by the devil. [2] He fasted forty days and forty nights, and afterwards he was famished. [3] The tempter came and said to him, "If you are the Son of God, command these stones to become loaves of bread." [4] But he answered, "It is written,

'One does not live by bread alone,

but by every word that comes from the mouth of God.'"

[5] Then the devil took him to the holy city and placed him on the pinnacle of the temple, [6] saying to him, "If you are the Son of God, throw yourself down; for it is written,

'He will command his angels concerning you,'

and 'On their hands they will bear you up,

so that you will not dash your foot against a stone.'"

[7] Jesus said to him, "Again it is written, 'Do not put the Lord your God to the test.'"

[8] Again, the devil took him to a very high mountain and showed him all the kingdoms of the world and their splendour; [9] and he

said to him, "All these I will give you, if you will fall down and worship me." ¹⁰ Jesus said to him, "Away with you, Satan! for it is written,

'Worship the Lord your God,
    and serve only him.'"

¹¹ Then the devil left him, and suddenly angels came and waited on him.

Linked themes

In Genesis 3 **Adam** and **Eve** are shown succumbing to the temptation to eat the fruit of the forbidden tree. Their disobedience was understood to have caused alienation from God and a predisposition to **sin**, called **original sin**, a condition which they passed on to all humankind. During the **Exodus** from Egypt, God is said to have led **Israel** into the wilderness to test whether or not they would keep his commandments (Deut 8:2).

Related works

Art: Juan de Flandes, *Temptation of Christ*, 1496–9 (National Gallery, Washington); Moretto da Brescia, *Christ in the Wilderness*, c.1540; Botticelli, *Temptation of Christ*, 1581–2 (Sistine Chapel, Vatican, Rome); Gustave van de Woestyne, *Christ in the Desert*, 1939 (Museum of Fine Arts, Ghent); Stanley Spencer, *Christ in the Wilderness series*, 1939–54.

Literature: Old English poem *Christ and Satan*; *The Temptation* (York, N-town and Chester Mystery Cycles); Milton, *Paradise Regained*, 1667; Dostoevsky, 'The Grand Inquisitor', *The Brothers Karamasov*, 1886; T.S. Eliot, *Murder in the Cathedral*, 1935; Jim Crace, *Quarantine*, 1997.

THE CALLING OF THE DISCIPLES

It was customary for Jewish **rabbis** to have groups of **disciples** or followers and many people were drawn to **Jesus** because of his teaching and actions. The **Gospels** indicate that one of Jesus' priorities is to select a group of twelve men who will accompany, work with and learn from him and in due course take his message to others. Jesus does not choose religious leaders but ordinary people, including fishermen and a tax collector. Within the group Simon **Peter**, and **James** and **John**, the sons of Zebedee, emerge as an inner circle, present at the **Transfiguration** and in the **Garden of Gethsemane**. Peter, who denies Jesus after his arrest and is later forgiven, becomes a key leader in the early years of the **Church**. James is the first of the **Twelve** to be executed. John is often identified as 'the beloved disciple', and the writer of John's Gospel. All of the 'Twelve', except **Judas**, are later regarded as **apostles** and **saints**.

Key concepts
Calling; following Jesus.

Mark 1:16–20
[16] As Jesus passed along the Sea of Galilee, he saw Simon and his brother Andrew casting a net into the sea – for they were fishermen. [17] And Jesus said to them, "Follow me and I will make you fish for people." [18] And immediately they left their nets and followed him. [19] As he went a little farther, he saw James son of Zebedee and his brother John, who were in their boat mending the nets. [20] Immediately he called them; and they left their father Zebedee in the boat with the hired men, and followed him.

Mark 3:13–19
[13] [Jesus] went up the mountain and called to him those whom he wanted, and they came to him. [14] And he appointed twelve, whom he also named apostles, to be with him, and to be sent out to proclaim the message, [15] and to have authority to cast out demons. [16] So he appointed the twelve: Simon (to whom he gave the name Peter); [17] James son of Zebedee and John the brother of James (to whom he gave the name Boanerges, that is, Sons of Thunder); [18] and Andrew, and Philip, and Bartholomew, and Matthew, and Thomas, and James son of Alphaeus, and Thaddaeus, and Simon the Cananaean, [19] and Judas Iscariot, who betrayed him.

Linked themes

The challenge and cost of becoming a disciple of Jesus is emphasised elsewhere in the Gospels (see Lk 9:18–27). The twelve disciples do not find travelling with and learning from Jesus easy. They frequently misunderstand his teaching and make mistakes. However, with the exception of Judas who eventually betrays Jesus and commits suicide, they go on to form the core leadership of the **Early Church** in the **Book of Acts**. A number of others, including women, are portrayed in the Gospels accompanying Jesus and witnessing his work and preaching.

Related works

Art: Duccio, *Calling of Peter and Andrew*, 1308–11 (National Gallery of Art, Washington); Ghirlandaio, *Calling of the First Disciples*, 1481 (Sistine Chapel, Vatican, Rome); Marco Basaiti, *The Calling of Zebedee's Sons*, 1510.

Music: Edward Elgar, *The Apostles*, 1903.

NICODEMUS VISITS JESUS

Nicodemus, a **Pharisee** and Jewish leader, comes under cover of darkness to discover more about **Jesus**. He acknowledges the signs performed by Jesus but is challenged about his ability to comprehend the **Kingdom of God**, which the signs represent. Understanding and membership of that kingdom depend not on Jewish birth but on a second birth or birth from above, a gift from God which all must experience. **Baptism** in water (a sign of cleansing and of death and new life) needs to be accompanied by this inner spiritual rebirth. This is the work of the **Holy Spirit** who, like the wind (the same word in Greek and Hebrew), is invisible yet clearly powerful.

Although he is a teacher of the Jewish law, Nicodemus finds Jesus' words hard to understand. Jesus therefore uses a familiar story from the **Exodus** narrative (see Chapter 2: The bronze serpent) in which the **Israelites** grumbled and were punished by an invasion of poisonous snakes. God told **Moses** to place a bronze serpent on a pole (Num 21:6–9). All who looked at it would be healed. John's narrative indicates a parallel with the lifting up of Jesus on the **cross** to bring **forgiveness** and **eternal life** to all who will receive it. In his love for a sinful world God has sent his Son to offer forgiveness but his coming requires human beings to make a choice: to respond to the 'Light of the World' (Jn 8:12) or to remain in darkness, rather than risk exposure and change.

Key concepts

The kingdom of God; the second birth; Moses and the serpent in the wilderness; the gift of eternal life; light and darkness.

John 3:1–21

Now there was a Pharisee named Nicodemus, a leader of the Jews. [2] He came to Jesus by night and said to him, "Rabbi, we know that you are a teacher who has come from God; for no one can do these signs that you do apart from the presence of God." [3] Jesus answered him, "Very truly, I tell you, no one can see the kingdom of God without being born from above." [4] Nicodemus said to him, "How can anyone be born after having grown old? Can one enter a second time into the mother's womb and be born?" [5] Jesus answered, "Very truly, I tell you, no one can enter the kingdom of God without being born of water and Spirit. [6] What is born of the flesh is flesh, and what is born of the Spirit is spirit. [7] Do not be astonished that I said to you, 'You must be born from above.' [8] The wind blows where it chooses, and you hear the sound of it, but you do not know where it comes from or where it goes. So it is with everyone who is born of the Spirit." [9] Nicodemus said to him, "How can these things be?" [10] Jesus answered him, "Are you a teacher of Israel, and yet you do not understand these things?

[11] "Very truly, I tell you, we speak of what we know and testify to what we have seen; yet you do not receive our testimony. [12] If I have told you about earthly things and you do not believe, how can you believe if I tell you about heavenly things? [13] No one has ascended into heaven except the one who descended from heaven,

the Son of Man. [14] And just as Moses lifted up the serpent in the wilderness, so must the Son of Man be lifted up, [15] that whoever believes in him may have eternal life.

[16] "For God so loved the world that he gave his only Son, so that everyone who believes in him may not perish but may have eternal life.

[17] "Indeed, God did not send the Son into the world to condemn the world, but in order that the world might be saved through him. [18] Those who believe in him are not condemned; but those who do not believe are condemned already, because they have not believed in the name of the only Son of God. [19] And this is the judgment, that the light has come into the world, and people loved darkness rather than light because their deeds were evil. [20] For all who do evil hate the light and do not come to the light, so that their deeds may not be exposed. [21] But those who do what is true come to the light, so that it may be clearly seen that their deeds have been done in God."

Linked themes

The beginning of **John's Gospel** refers to those who become 'children of God ... born, not of the will of the flesh ... but of God' (Jn 1:12–13). The concept of **Christ** coming as a light in a dark world also appears in Jn 1:1–11 and Jn 8:12 where Jesus claims: 'Whoever follows me will never walk in darkness but will have the light of life.' The Holy Spirit comes to the **Disciples** in Acts 2 with 'a sound like the rush of violent wind' (see Chapter 8: The Birth of the Church (Pentecost)). Nicodemus appears twice again in the Gospels: he challenges the Pharisees (Jn 7:50–2) who wish to arrest Jesus, and after the **Crucifixion** he and **Joseph of Arimathea** take Jesus' body for burial (Jn 19:38–42).

Related works

Art: Michelangelo, *Christ Crucified between the Virgin and Nicodemus*, c.1552–4 (Louvre, Paris); William Holman Hunt, *The Light of the World*, 1853 (Keble College, Oxford); John La Farge, *Visit of Nicodemus to Christ*, 1880 (Smithsonian American Art Museum).

Literature: Light is an important image in the medieval poem *Pearl*, the *Cloud of Unknowing*, Spenser's *Faerie Queene* and Milton's *Paradise Lost*. See also Henry Vaughan, 'The Night', 1655.

THE WOMAN AT THE WELL

This encounter between **Jesus** and a **Samaritan** woman crosses traditional boundaries of culture, gender, race and religion, as he deliberately engages with someone most Jews would have regarded as an outcast. Strictly religious male Jews did not speak to any woman in public, let alone one whose reputation is so damaged that she has to visit the well alone at noon when others are resting. Moreover, the Samaritans were regarded with distrust and hostility by Jews. Originally worshippers of many gods, the Samaritans later adopted the worship of **Jehovah** but only accepted part of the Jewish scriptures and built their own temple close to where this conversation is set.

Jesus asks the surprised woman for a drink, drawing her into a conversation which challenges both her expectations and her behaviour. Water, wells and fountains were particularly powerful images in this dry region, appearing frequently in the Bible as symbols of the new life and power offered by God. Intrigued by the offer of 'living' (fresh, running) water, the woman finds herself discussing her lifestyle and the meaning of true worship of God.

Key themes

Water as a symbol of spiritual life; the gift of **eternal life** for all; the nature of true worship; Jesus as **Messiah**.

John 4:5–30

[Jesus] came to a Samaritan city called Sychar, near the plot of ground that Jacob had given to his son Joseph. [6] Jacob's well was there, and Jesus, tired out by his journey, was sitting by the well. It was about noon.

[7] A Samaritan woman came to draw water, and Jesus said to her, "Give me a drink." [8] (His disciples had gone to the city to buy food.) [9] The Samaritan woman said to him, "How is it that

you, a Jew, ask a drink of me, a woman of Samaria?" (Jews do not share things in common with Samaritans.) [10] Jesus answered her, "If you knew the gift of God, and who it is that is saying to you, 'Give me a drink,' you would have asked him, and he would have given you living water." [11] The woman said to him, "Sir, you have no bucket, and the well is deep. Where do you get that living water? [12] Are you greater than our ancestor Jacob, who gave us the well, and with his sons and his flocks drank from it?" [13] Jesus said to her, "Everyone who drinks of this water will be thirsty again, [14] but those who drink of the water that I will give them will never be thirsty. The water that I will give will become in them a spring of water gushing up to eternal life." [15] The woman said to him, "Sir, give me this water, so that I may never be thirsty or have to keep coming here to draw water."

[16] Jesus said to her, "Go, call your husband, and come back." [17] The woman answered him, "I have no husband." Jesus said to her, "You are right in saying, 'I have no husband'; [18] for you have had five husbands, and the one you have now is not your husband. What you have said is true!" [19] The woman said to him, "Sir, I see that you are a prophet. [20] Our ancestors worshipped on this mountain, but you say that the place where people must worship is in Jerusalem." [21] Jesus said to her, "Woman, believe me, the hour is coming when you will worship the Father neither on this mountain nor in Jerusalem. [22] You worship what you do not know; we worship what we know, for salvation is from the Jews. [23] But the hour is coming, and is now here, when the true worshippers will worship the Father in spirit and truth, for the Father seeks such as these to worship him. [24] God is spirit, and those who worship him must worship in spirit and truth." [25] The woman said to him, "I know that Messiah is coming" (who is called Christ). "When he comes, he will proclaim all things to us." [26] Jesus said to her, "I am he, the one who is speaking to you."

[27] Just then his disciples came. They were astonished that he was speaking with a woman, but no one said, "What do you want?" or, "Why are you speaking with her?" [28] Then the woman

left her water jar and went back to the city. She said to the people, [29] "Come and see a man who told me everything I have ever done! He cannot be the Messiah, can he?" [30] They left the city and were on their way to him.

Linked themes

In Jn 7:37–8 Jesus declares: 'Let anyone who is thirsty come to me' (echoing Isa 55:1) and promises 'Out of the believer's heart shall flow rivers of living water', an allusion to the **prophet** Ezekiel's vision of a life-giving river flowing out from the Temple in Jerusalem (Ezek 47). In the Book of **Revelation**, the 'water of life' flows from the throne of God (Rev 22:1) and all are invited to 'take the water of life as a gift' (Rev 22:17).

One of the most famous stories told by Jesus features one of the despised Samaritans caring for a wounded traveller (Lk 10:25–37). In Acts 1 Jesus is shown commanding his **Disciples** to share his message with those in **Jerusalem**, Judea, Samaria and beyond (Acts 1:8).

Related works

Art: Juan de Flande, *Christ and the Woman of Samaria*, 1496–9 (Louvre, Paris); Annibale Carracci, *Christ and the Woman of Samaria*, 1563–94; William Turner, *Landscape: Christ and the Woman of Samaria, c.*1825 (Tate Gallery, London); Mario Sironi, *Christ and the Samaritan Woman*, 1947 (Vatican, Rome).

Literature: Chaucer, *Wife of Bath's Prologue, Canterbury Tales*; *Jacob's Well* (fifteenth century); Edmund Spenser, *The Faerie Queene*, Bk I, xi, 1590; Henry Vaughan, 'The Search' and 'Religion' in *Silex Scintilans*, 1655; Emily Dickinson, 'I Know Where Wells Grow – Droughtless Wells', c.1862.

THE DEATH OF JOHN THE BAPTIST

The account of **John's** execution by **Herod Antipas**, ruler of the region of **Galilee**, apparently at the instigation of his wife Herodias and her daughter Salome, highlights the threat posed by the ruthless Herodian dynasty and the inevitability of confrontation between the forces of reform and corruption. The death of John, **Jesus'** cousin and the one who proclaimed his coming as **Messiah**, also looks forward to Jesus' own suffering and death. The placing of this sombre story, midway through **Matthew's Gospel**, recalls the **Massacre of the Innocents**, the attempt by Antipas' father, **Herod the Great**, to remove the infant Jesus, and foreshadows Jesus' eventual death at the hands of weak and corrupt rulers.

Key concepts
John the Baptist challenges immorality; parallels between Jesus and John.

Matthew 14:1–12
At that time Herod the ruler heard reports about Jesus; [2] and he said to his servants, "This is John the Baptist; he has been raised from the dead, and for this reason these powers are at work in him." [3] For Herod had arrested John, bound him, and put him in prison on account of Herodias, his brother Philip's wife, [4] because John had been telling him, "It is not lawful for you to have her." [5] Though Herod wanted to put him to death, he feared the crowd, because they regarded him as a prophet. [6] But when Herod's birthday came, the daughter of Herodias danced before the company, and she pleased Herod [7] so much that he promised on oath to grant her whatever she might ask. [8] Prompted by her mother, she said, "Give me the head of John the Baptist here on a platter." [9] The king was grieved, yet out of regard for his oaths and for the guests, he commanded it to be given; [10] he sent and had John beheaded in the prison. [11] The head was brought on a platter and given to the girl, who brought it to her mother. [12] His disciples came and took the body and buried it; then they went and told Jesus.

Linked themes

Luke records that Jesus is taken before Herod Antipas for questioning during his own trial (Lk 23:6–12).

Related works

Art: Fra Filippo Lippi, *Feast of Herod, Salome's Dance*, c.1452–64 (Prato, Duomo); Hans Memling, *Beheading of the Baptist*, 1474–9 (Memling-museum, Bruges); Caravaggio, *Salome with the Head of John the Baptist*, 1607 (National Gallery, London); Peter Paul Rubens, *Feast of Herod*, 1630; Guido Reni, *Salome with the Head of John the Baptist*, 1639–40 (Art Institute, Chicago); Gustave Moreau, *The Apparition (Dance of Salomé)*, c.1876; Gustav Klimt, *Salome*, 1909 (Galleria d'Arte Moderna, Venice).

Literature: Chaucer's *Pardoner's Tale;* Oscar Wilde, *Salome*, 1893; Browning, 'Fra Lippo Lippi', 1855; Joris-Karl Huysman, *A Rebours*, 1903; Carol Ann Duffy, *Salome*.

Music: Jules Massenet, *Herodiade*, 1881; Richard Strauss, *Salome*, 1905.

THE TRANSFIGURATION

Mountains are often the setting for special experiences of God in the Bible and God's presence is frequently signified by a cloud descending on the place of encounter. **Moses** entered the cloud which rested on **Mount Sinai** to receive the tablets of stone bearing the **Ten Commandments** (Ex 24:12–18). **Jesus** was tempted on a mountain top and preached from a mountain side. Here he is shown with his whole physical being transformed, his face and his clothing shining. The mountain is unnamed but may be Mount Tabor or Mount Hermon.

The episode is placed between two warnings from Jesus to his disciples that he must suffer and die before being raised from the dead (Mt 16:21, 17:22). The inner circle, **Peter, James** and **John**, are shown witnessing a vision of Jesus revealed in glory and accompanied by **Moses** and **Elijah**, who represent the **Law** and **Prophets** of the **Old Testament**. Luke's **Gospel** notes that they 'were speaking of [Jesus'] departure (death), which he was about to accomplish at Jerusalem'

(Lk 9:31). Glory and suffering are thus clearly linked together. Once again, as at Jesus' **baptism**, a voice from heaven affirms that Jesus is God's beloved son, the promised **Messiah**.

Key concepts
Jesus revealed in glory; **Moses** and **Elijah** (the **Law** and the **Prophets**).

Matthew 17:1–8
Six days later, Jesus took with him Peter and James and his brother John and led them up a high mountain, by themselves. [2] And he was transfigured before them, and his face shone like the sun, and his clothes became dazzling white. [3] Suddenly there appeared to them Moses and Elijah, talking with him. [4] Then Peter said to Jesus, "Lord, it is good for us to be here; if you wish, I will make three dwellings here, one for you, one for Moses, and one for Elijah." [5] While he was still speaking, suddenly a bright cloud overshadowed them, and from the cloud a voice said, "This is my Son, the Beloved; with him I am well pleased; listen to him!" [6] When the disciples heard this, they fell to the ground and were overcome by fear. [7] But Jesus came and touched them, saying, "Get up and do not be afraid." [8] And when they looked up, they saw no one except Jesus himself alone.

Linked themes
This vision of Jesus recalls Moses descending from Mount Sinai with his face 'shining' after speaking with God (Ex 34:29). It also looks forward to visions of Jesus in heaven: 'I saw one like the Son of Man … his face was like the sun shining with full force' (Rev 1:13, 16).

Related works
Art: Duccio, *Transfiguration*, 1311 (National Gallery, London); Andrei Rublev, *Transfiguration*, 1405; Giovanni Bellini, *Transfiguration of Christ*, c.1487 (Correr Museum, Venice); Gerard David, *Transfiguration of Christ*, 1520 (O.L. Vrouwekerk, Bruges).

Literature: Edwin Muir (1887–1959), *The Transfiguration*.

THE TEACHING OF JESUS: THE SERMON ON THE MOUNT

Chapters 5–7 of **Matthew's Gospel**, known as the **Sermon on the Mount** from the setting, present a collection of the teachings of Jesus portraying the coming of the **Kingdom of God** as a catalyst which must transform not only belief but also behaviour. **Luke** gathers much of the same ethical teaching into what is known as 'the Sermon on the Plain' (Lk 6:20–49).

The definitions of blessing or happiness in Matthew 5:3–12 are traditionally known as **'The Beatitudes'** (from Latin *beatus*, 'blessed'). They demonstrate the difference between the values of the kingdom of heaven (Mt 4:17) and those of the world. Jesus emphasises that his teaching is not a replacement for the **Law** but a fulfilment of it (Mt 5:17), and gives practical examples of the way his followers are to live. The teaching of the Law and the **prophets** is summed up in Matthew 7:12, '… do to others as you would have them do to you', the 'Golden Rule' well known to the Jewish tradition before this time. In Matthew 6:9–13, now known as the **'Lord's Prayer'** or the 'Our Father' (Latin *Paternoster*), followers of Jesus are encouraged to pray simply and directly, addressing God as their father. The Sermon concludes with illustrations of the choices that Jesus' teaching presents.

Key concepts

The nature of blessing; the fulfilment of the **Law** of **Moses** and of the prophets; the demands and rewards of following Jesus' teaching; directions on prayer and daily living; God as Father.

Matthew 5:1–18, 27–30, 38–45; 6:7–15, 19–21, 24–9, 33–4; 7:1–7, 12–14

When Jesus saw the crowds, he went up the mountain; and after he sat down, his disciples came to him. [2] Then he began to speak, and taught them, saying:

[3] "Blessed are the poor in spirit, for theirs is the kingdom of heaven.

[4] "Blessed are those who mourn, for they will be comforted.

[5] "Blessed are the meek, for they will inherit the earth.

[6] "Blessed are those who hunger and thirst for righteousness, for they will be filled.

[7] "Blessed are the merciful, for they will receive mercy.

[8] "Blessed are the pure in heart, for they will see God.

[9] "Blessed are the peacemakers, for they will be called children of God.

[10] "Blessed are those who are persecuted for righteousness' sake, for theirs is the kingdom of heaven.

[11] "Blessed are you when people revile you and persecute you and utter all kinds of evil against you falsely on my account. [12] Rejoice and be glad, for your reward is great in heaven, for in the same way they persecuted the prophets who were before you.

[13] "You are the salt of the earth; but if salt has lost its taste, how can its saltiness be restored? It is no longer good for anything, but is thrown out and trampled under foot.

[14] "You are the light of the world. A city built on a hill cannot be hid. [15] No one after lighting a lamp puts it under the bushel basket, but on the lampstand, and it gives light to all in the house. [16] In the same way, let your light shine before others, so that they may see your good works and give glory to your Father in heaven.

[17] "Do not think that I have come to abolish the law or the prophets; I have come not to abolish but to fulfil. [18] For truly I tell you, until heaven and earth pass away, not one letter, not one stroke of a letter, will pass from the law until all is accomplished. [...]

[27] "You have heard that it was said, 'You shall not commit adultery.' [28] But I say to you that everyone who looks at a woman with lust has already committed adultery with her in his heart. [29] If your right eye causes you to sin, tear it out and throw it away; it is better for you to lose one of your members than for your whole body to be thrown into hell. [30] And if your right hand causes you to sin, cut it off and throw it away; it is better for you to lose one of your members than for your whole body to go into hell. [...]

[38] "You have heard that it was said, 'An eye for an eye and a tooth for a tooth.' [39] But I say to you, Do not resist an evildoer. But if anyone strikes you on the right cheek, turn the other also; [40] and if anyone wants to sue you and take your coat, give your cloak as well; [41] and if anyone forces you to go one mile, go also the second mile. [42] Give to everyone who begs from you, and do not refuse anyone who wants to borrow from you.

[43] "You have heard that it was said, 'You shall love your neighbour and hate your enemy.' [44] But I say to you, Love your enemies and pray for those who persecute you, [45] so that you may be children of your Father in heaven. [...]

[7] "When you are praying, do not heap up empty phrases as the Gentiles do; for they think that they will be heard because of their many words. [8] Do not be like them, for your Father knows what you need before you ask him.

[9] "Pray then in this way:
   Our Father in heaven,
      hallowed be your name.
[10]   Your kingdom come.
      Your will be done,
         on earth as it is in heaven.
[11]   Give us this day our daily bread.
[12]   And forgive us our debts,
         as we also have forgiven our debtors.
[13]   And do not bring us to the time of trial,
         but rescue us from the evil one.

[14] For if you forgive others their trespasses, your heavenly Father will also forgive you; [15] but if you do not forgive others, neither will your Father forgive your trespasses. [...]

[19] "Do not store up for yourselves treasures on earth, where moth and rust consume and where thieves break in and steal; [20] but store up for yourselves treasures in heaven, where neither moth nor rust consumes and where thieves do not break in and steal. [21] For where your treasure is, there your heart will be also. [...]

[24] "No one can serve two masters; for a slave will either hate the one and love the other, or be devoted to the one and despise the other. You cannot serve God and wealth (**AV** 'God and Mammon').

[25] "Therefore I tell you, do not worry about your life, what you will eat or what you will drink, or about your body, what you will wear. Is not life more than food, and the body more than clothing? [26] Look at the birds of the air; they neither sow nor reap nor gather into barns, and yet your heavenly Father feeds them. Are you not of more value than they? [27] And can any of you by worrying add a single hour to your span of life? [28] And why do you worry about clothing? Consider the lilies of the field, how they grow; they neither toil nor spin, [29] yet I tell you, even Solomon in all his glory was not clothed like one of these. [...] [33] But strive first for the kingdom of God and his righteousness, and all these things will be given to you as well.

[34] "So do not worry about tomorrow, for tomorrow will bring worries of its own. Today's trouble is enough for today.

"Do not judge, so that you may not be judged. [2] For with the judgment you make you will be judged, and the measure you give will be the measure you get. [3] Why do you see the speck (**AV** 'mote') in your neighbour's eye, but do not notice the log (**AV** 'beam') in your own eye? [4] Or how can you say to your neighbour, 'Let me take the speck out of your eye,' while the log is in your own eye? [5] You hypocrite, first take the log out of your own eye, and then you will see clearly to take the speck out of your neighbour's eye.

[6] "Do not give what is holy to dogs; and do not throw your pearls before swine, or they will trample them under foot and turn and maul you.

[7] "Ask, and it will be given you; search, and you will find; knock, and the door will be opened for you. [...]

[12] "In everything do to others as you would have them do to you; for this is the law and the prophets.

[13] "Enter through the narrow gate; for the gate is wide and the

road is easy that leads to destruction, and there are many who take it. [14] For the gate is narrow and the road is hard that leads to life, and there are few who find it.

Linked themes

Matthew may be suggesting a parallel between Jesus and **Moses**, who received the Law on **Mount Sinai**, so that Mt 5–7 is to be understood in the context of Ex 20–4. For example, the Beatitudes (Mt 5:3–11) can be read as corresponding to the **Ten Commandments** (Ex 20:1–17). This Moses **typology** continues elsewhere in Matthew's **Gospel** and gives a strong Jewish context to his presentation of Jesus. The first four beatitudes can be seen to be linked to Isaiah 61:1–2, verses believed to apply to the expected **Messiah** who is pictured bringing good news to the oppressed, binding up the broken-hearted, proclaiming release to captives and comforting all who mourn.

Related works

Art: Fra Angelico, *Sermon on the Mount*, c.1450 (Museo di S. Marco, Florence); Piero di Cosimo (1462–1521), *Sermon on the Mount and Healing of the Leper* (Sistine Chapel, Vatican, Rome); Claude Lorrain, *Sermon on the Mount*, 1656 (Frick Collection, New York).

Literature: in Tolstoy's *Resurrection* (1899), the Sermon on the Mount is described as: 'not beautiful abstract thoughts, presenting for the most part exaggerated and impossible demands, but simple, clear, practical commandments, which if obeyed (and this was quite feasible) would establish a completely new order of human society'. On the Beatitudes, see Herman Melville, *The Confidence Man*, 1857 and *Billy Budd*, 1885–91.

Music: Settings of the Lord's Prayer.

THE TEACHING OF JESUS: PARABLES

Following the Jewish tradition of teaching by illustration and indirect methods, much of **Jesus'** teaching is in the form of **parables**, a Greek term that covers many literary devices including simile, metaphor and aphorism. These stories draw on familiar details of everyday life but carry added levels of meaning for the audience to discover. Some of Jesus' parables were difficult to understand and required explanation. This may have been intentional, either to draw in the listeners or to deflect the attention of the authorities. Many of these narratives and the characters in them, such as the **Prodigal Son** and the **Good Samaritan**, have been absorbed into everyday language. The parable has remained a popular form in literature, as in 'The Parable of the Doorkeeper' in Franz Kafka's *The Trial* (1925), and Jorge Luis Borges' 'Inferno, I, 32' in *Labyrinths: Selected Stories and Other Writings* (1970).

The Parable of the Sower

The Parable of the Sower is an extended **allegory** with an agricultural theme, for which **Mark** offers an interpretation that emphasises the need to respond to the preaching of God's word. Mark's warning against rejecting the word highlights the threat posed by difficulties, persecution, worry and worldliness – concerns that may reflect the situation of the early Christian community for which he was writing.

Key concepts

The seed as the word of God; different kinds of ground represent different responses to God's word.

Mark 4:2–20

[2] [Jesus] began to teach them many things in parables, and in his teaching he said to them: [3] "Listen! A sower went out to sow. [4] And as he sowed, some seed fell on the path, and the birds came and ate it up. [5] Other seed fell on rocky ground, where it did not have much soil, and it sprang up quickly, since it had no depth of soil. [6] And when the sun rose, it was scorched; and since it had no root, it withered away. [7] Other seed fell among thorns, and the thorns grew up and choked it, and it yielded no grain. [8] Other seed fell into good soil and brought forth grain, growing up and increasing and yielding thirty and sixty and a hundredfold." [9] And he said, "Let anyone with ears to hear listen!"

[10] When he was alone, those who were around him along with the twelve asked him about the parables. [11] And he said to them, "To you has been given the secret of the kingdom of God, but for those outside, everything comes in parables; [12] in order that

'they may indeed look, but not perceive,
and may indeed listen, but not understand;
so that they may not turn again and be forgiven.' "

[13] And he said to them, "Do you not understand this parable? Then how will you understand all the parables? [14] The sower sows the word. [15] These are the ones on the path where the word is sown: when they hear, Satan immediately comes and takes away the word that is sown in them. [16] And these are the ones sown on rocky ground: when they hear the word, they immediately receive it with joy. [17] But they have no root, and endure only for a while; then, when trouble or persecution arises on account of the word, immediately they fall away. [18] And others are those sown among the thorns: these are the ones who hear the word, [19] but the cares of the world, and the lure of wealth, and the desire for other things come in and choke the word, and it yields nothing. [20] And these are the ones sown on the good soil: they hear the word and accept it and bear fruit, thirty and sixty and a hundredfold."

Linked themes

Verses 11–12 refer to Isaiah 6:9–10. There is an implied link here to the theme of harvest, used elsewhere by Jesus as an image for the **Last Judgement**.

Related works

Art: Pieter Bruegel the Elder, *Parable of the Sower*, 1557; Domenico Feti, *Parable of the Good Samaritan*, c.1623 (Gallerie dell'Accademia, Venice).

Literature: Geoffrey Chaucer's 'Parson's Tale' in *The Canterbury Tales*, c.1400; John Milton, Sonnet XVIII, 'On the Late Massacre in Piedmont', 1655; William Cowper, 'The Sower', from *Olney Hymns*, 1779; Kafka,

'Parable of the Doorkeeper' *The Trial*, 1925; Flannery O'Connor, *The Violent Bear it Away*, 1960.

Parables of the Kingdom of Heaven

The first and second of these brief **parables** are concerned with responding to the **Kingdom of Heaven**, a discovery so valuable that it is worth any price. The third parable presents a vivid image of selection, exclusion and punishment at the **Last Judgement**.

Key concepts

The need to choose the kingdom of heaven above everything else; the coming Last Judgement.

Matthew 13:44–50

[44] "The kingdom of heaven is like treasure hidden in a field, which someone found and hid; then in his joy he goes and sells all that he has and buys that field.

[45] "Again, the kingdom of heaven is like a merchant in search of fine pearls; [46] on finding one pearl of great value, he went and sold all that he had and bought it.

[47] "Again, the kingdom of heaven is like a net that was thrown into the sea and caught fish of every kind; [48] when it was full, they drew it ashore, sat down, and put the good into baskets but threw out the bad. [49] So it will be at the end of the age. The angels will come out and separate the evil from the righteous [50] and throw them into the furnace of fire, where there will be weeping and gnashing of teeth.

Linked themes

The separation of evil from good and destruction of the evil while a **remnant** of the good are saved also occurs in the story of the **Flood**, and at **Sodom and Gomorrah**.

Related works

Art: John Everett Millais, *The Hidden Treasure*, 1864; Domenico Feti, *Parable of the Lost Drachma*, 1618–22 (Gemäldegalerie, Dresden).

Literature: The late fourteenth-century poem *Pearl*; George Herbert, *The Pearl*; R.S. Thomas, 'The Bright Field', *Laboratories of the Spirit*, 1975.

The parable of the Good Samaritan

The context of this story is a conversation designed not to elicit truth but to put **Jesus** on the spot. The question 'Who is my neighbour?' could, in the contemporary context, have been an attempt to justify the speaker restricting care to his own racial or religious group. The **parable**, however, shifts the focus. The question Jesus seems to ask is: 'Are *you* a good neighbour, offering love to all, regardless of religious, traditional and racial boundaries?' The devout Jewish **priest** and **Levite** could not risk contact with what might have been a dead body in case they were rendered ritually unclean so they failed to care. Instead it is a **Samaritan**, a member of a group despised by Jews, who responds in love and thus poses a challenge to all who would claim to live by God's standards.

Key concepts

Importance of love for others; rejection of prejudices and stereotypes.

Luke 10:25–37

[25] Just then a lawyer stood up to test Jesus. "Teacher," he said, "what must I do to inherit eternal life?" [26] He said to him, "What is written in the law? What do you read there?" [27] He answered, "You shall love the Lord your God with all your heart, and with all your soul, and with all your strength, and with all your mind; and your neighbour as yourself." [28] And he said to him, "You have given the right answer; do this, and you will live."

[29] But wanting to justify himself, he asked Jesus, "And who is my neighbour?" [30] Jesus replied, "A man was going down from Jerusalem to Jericho, and fell into the hands of robbers, who stripped him, beat him, and went away, leaving him half dead. [31] Now by chance a priest was going down that road; and when he saw him, he passed by on the other side. [32] So likewise a Levite, when he came to the place and saw him, passed by on

the other side. [33] But a Samaritan while travelling came near him; and when he saw him, he was moved with pity. [34] He went to him and bandaged his wounds, having poured oil and wine on them. Then he put him on his own animal, brought him to an inn, and took care of him. [35] The next day he took out two denarii, gave them to the innkeeper, and said, 'Take care of him; and when I come back, I will repay you whatever more you spend.' [36] Which of these three, do you think, was a neighbour to the man who fell into the hands of the robbers?" [37] He said, "The one who showed him mercy." Jesus said to him, "Go and do likewise."

Linked themes
Christian commentators, such as **Origen** and **Ambrose**, developed a complex allegorical interpretation of The Good Samaritan in which the man going to Jericho is **Adam**, the Good Samaritan is Jesus, the robbers are the **Devil**, the priest represents the **Law**, the Levite represents the **Prophets**, and the Inn is the **Church**, etc.

Related works
Art: Jacopo Bassano, *The Good Samaritan*, c.1550–70; Govaert Flinck (from an engraving by Rembrandt), *The Good Samaritan*, 1640; Vincent Van Gogh, *Good Samaritan*, 1890 (Rijksmuseum Kröller-Müller, Otterlo, Netherlands); Paula Modersohn-Becker, *The Good Samaritan*, 1906.

Literature: The late fourteenth-century poem, *Piers Plowman*, links Jesus and the Good Samaritan (Passus 17, 18); Henry Fielding, *Joseph Andrews*, 1742.

The parables of the Lost Sheep and the Prodigal Son
The Lost Sheep and the **Prodigal Son** are both parables that illustrate the unconditional love of God for those who are willing to return to God. **Jesus** himself extends this love to 'tax collectors and sinners' by eating with them, anticipating their inclusion in the **Kingdom of God**.

Key concepts

God's love in seeking out those who turn away from him; God's willingness to accept those who return to him.

Luke 15:1–7, 11–32

Now all the tax collectors and sinners were coming near to listen to him. [2] And the Pharisees and the scribes were grumbling and saying, "This fellow welcomes sinners and eats with them."

[3] So he told them this parable: [4] "Which one of you, having a hundred sheep and losing one of them, does not leave the ninety-nine in the wilderness and go after the one that is lost until he finds it? [5] When he has found it, he lays it on his shoulders and rejoices. [6] And when he comes home, he calls together his friends and neighbours, saying to them, 'Rejoice with me, for I have found my sheep that was lost.' [7] Just so, I tell you, there will be more joy in heaven over one sinner who repents than over ninety-nine righteous persons who need no repentance. [...]

[11] Then Jesus said, "There was a man who had two sons. [12] The younger of them said to his father, 'Father, give me the share of the property that will belong to me.' So he divided his property between them. [13] A few days later the younger son gathered all he had and travelled to a distant country, and there he squandered his property in dissolute living. [14] When he had spent everything, a severe famine took place throughout that country, and he began to be in need. [15] So he went and hired himself out to one of the citizens of that country, who sent him to his fields to feed the pigs. [16] He would gladly have filled himself with the pods that the pigs were eating; and no one gave him anything. [17] But when he came to himself he said, 'How many of my father's hired hands have bread enough and to spare, but here I am dying of hunger! [18] I will get up and go to my father, and I will say to him, "Father, I have sinned against heaven and before you; [19] I am no longer worthy to be called your son; treat me like one of your hired hands."' [20] So he set off and went to his father. But while he was still far off, his father saw him and

was filled with compassion; he ran and put his arms around him and kissed him. [21] Then the son said to him, 'Father, I have sinned against heaven and before you; I am no longer worthy to be called your son.' [22] But the father said to his slaves, 'Quickly, bring out a robe – the best one – and put it on him; put a ring on his finger and sandals on his feet. [23] And get the fatted calf and kill it, and let us eat and celebrate; [24] for this son of mine was dead and is alive again; he was lost and is found!' And they began to celebrate.

[25] "Now his elder son was in the field; and when he came and approached the house, he heard music and dancing. [26] He called one of the slaves and asked what was going on. [27] He replied, 'Your brother has come, and your father has killed the fatted calf, because he has got him back safe and sound.' [28] Then he became angry and refused to go in. His father came out and began to plead with him. [29] But he answered his father, 'Listen! For all these years I have been working like a slave for you, and I have never disobeyed your command; yet you have never given me even a young goat so that I might celebrate with my friends. [30] But when this son of yours came back, who has devoured your property with prostitutes, you killed the fatted calf for him!' [31] Then the father said to him, 'Son, you are always with me, and all that is mine is yours. [32] But we had to celebrate and rejoice, because this brother of yours was dead and has come to life; he was lost and has been found.'"

Linked themes

Throughout his ministry, Jesus was criticised by religious leaders of the time for associating with those considered to be 'sinners' and outcasts. He sought out tax collectors such as **Matthew** and Zaccheus and challenged those who wished to kill a woman accused of adultery, thus demonstrating the desire of God to rescue and restore human beings depicted in these stories.

Related works

Art: Guercino, *Return of the Prodigal Son*, 1619 (Kunsthistorisches Museum, Vienna); G. van Honthorst, *The Prodigal Son*, 1622 (Alte Pinakothek, Munich); Rembrandt, *The Return of the Prodigal Son*, 1668–9 (The Hermitage, St Petersberg); Murillo, *The Return of the Prodigal Son*, c.1670–4 (National Gallery of Art, Washington); Pierre Puvis de Chavannes, *The Prodigal Son*, c.1879 (National Gallery of Art, Washington); Girogio De Chiroco, *Prodigal Son*, 1922 (Civic Modern Art Gallery, Milan).

Literature: William Shakespeare, *Merchant of Venice*, 2:6, 1596–8; *As You Like It*, 1.1, 1598–9; and *Winter's Tale*, 4:3, 1610; Ben Jonson, *Cynthia's Revels*, 1600.

THE TEACHING OF JESUS: THE 'I AM' SAYINGS

Questions about who **Jesus** is dominate the first part of **John**'s **Gospel**. In conversations with both the **Pharisees** and his **Disciples**, Jesus repeatedly uses the form 'I am ...', often drawing on images and incidents from the **Old Testament**. In some cases Jesus underlines his claims with an accompanying **miracle**.

By using the words 'I am', Jesus appears to be claiming to be God, for in Ex 3:13–14 God reveals his divine name for the first time in a phrase which can be translated, 'I AM' (see Chapter 2: Moses and the Exodus). The potentially blasphemous implications of Jesus using God's name to refer to himself, coupled with his evocative metaphors, would have caused offence to many of his audience.

Key concepts

Jesus as 'the Bread of Life', 'the Light of the World', 'the **Good Shepherd**', 'the Way, the Truth and the Life' and 'the True Vine'.

'I am the bread of life'

After **Jesus** miraculously feeds a crowd of 5,000 from five loaves of bread and two fish (Jn 6:1–13), his **Disciples** draw comparisons with the miraculous bread, or 'manna' from heaven, which God fed the **Israelites** while they were in the desert (Ex 16:1–15) hundreds of years earlier. Jesus directs their attention to spiritual rather than physical needs.

John 6:35, 48–51

[35] Jesus said to them, "I am the bread of life. Whoever comes to me will never be hungry, and whoever believes in me will never be thirsty." […]

[48] I am the bread of life. [49] Your ancestors ate the manna in the wilderness, and they died. [50] This is the bread that comes down from heaven, so that one may eat of it and not die. [51] I am the living bread that came down from heaven. Whoever eats of this bread will live forever; and the bread that I will give for the life of the world is my flesh."

Linked themes

At the **Last Supper** Jesus breaks the bread and the identification of Jesus' flesh with bread is the basis of the **Eucharist**, instituted by Jesus in Lk 22:19: 'Then he took a loaf of bread, and when he had given thanks, he broke it and gave it to them, saying, "This is my body, which is given for you. Do this in remembrance of me."'

'I am the light of the world'

In his Prologue **John** refers to **Jesus** as 'the light' (Jn 1:4–5). Here Jesus uses the same metaphor for himself as part of a dispute with the **Pharisees** about his identity.

John 8:12

[12] Again Jesus spoke to them, saying, "I am the light of the world. Whoever follows me will never walk in darkness but will have the light of life."

Linked themes

In Jewish tradition light was a metaphor for **salvation**, with darkness or blindness a sign of **sin**. In the **Old Testament**, light often indicated the presence of God, as in Ex 13:21 where the **Israelites** are guided through the desert by a pillar of cloud by day and a pillar of fire by night to give them light. Jesus illustrates his claim to be the light in Jn 9:1–9 by giving sight to a man who had been born blind.

Related works
Art: William Holman Hunt, *The Light of the World*, c.1900–4.

'I am the good shepherd'
Throughout the Gospels Jesus uses sheep metaphors to refer generally to the crowds of lost and helpless people who follow him, and refers specifically to the 'the lost sheep of the house of **Israel**' (Mt 10:6). In John 10 Jesus extends the metaphor, describing himself as the **Good Shepherd** who cares for the sheep.

John 10:14–18
[14] I am the good shepherd. I know my own and my own know me, [15] just as the Father knows me and I know the Father. And I lay down my life for the sheep. [16] I have other sheep that do not belong to this fold. I must bring them also, and they will listen to my voice. So there will be one flock, one shepherd. [17] For this reason the Father loves me, because I lay down my life in order to take it up again. [18] No one takes it from me, but I lay it down of my own accord. I have power to lay it down, and I have power to take it up again. I have received this command from my Father."

Linked themes
In Ezekiel 34:12 God uses the shepherd metaphor of himself: 'As shepherds seek out their flocks when they are among their scattered sheep, so I will seek out my sheep.' The sheep image is also used in the Parable of the Lost Sheep (Lk 15:1–7).

Related works

Art: Bartolomé Esteban Murillo, *The Good Shepherd*, c.1660 (Getty Museum); Bartolomé Esteban Murillo, *The Christ Child as the Good Shepherd*, 1675–70 (Prado, Madrid).

Literature: There is a strong pastoral tradition in English Literature e.g. Spenser, *Shepheard's Calendar*, 1579; John Milton, *Lycidas*, 1638.

Music: Handel, *The Messiah* ('He shall feed His Flock'), 1741.

'I am the way, the truth and the life'

As his death approaches, **Jesus** reassures his **Disciples** that he is going to be with God, his Father, and that through their relationship with him his disciples can join him.

Key concepts

Trusting in Jesus and his promises; Jesus as the way, the truth and the life; to know Jesus is to know God the Father.

John 14:1–7

"Do not let your hearts be troubled. Believe in God, believe also in me. [2] In my Father's house there are many dwelling places. If it were not so, would I have told you that I go to prepare a place for you? [3] And if I go and prepare a place for you, I will come again and will take you to myself, so that where I am, there you may be also. [4] And you know the way to the place where I am going." [5] Thomas said to him, "Lord, we do not know where you are going. How can we know the way?" [6] Jesus said to him, "I am the way, and the truth, and the life. No one comes to the Father except through me. [7] If you know me, you will know my Father also. From now on you do know him and have seen him."

Linked themes

Jesus' similar earlier claim, 'I am the resurrection and the life', is demonstrated when he raises **Lazarus** from the dead (Jn 11:25).

Related works
Literature: Bernard Malamud, *God's Grace*, 1982.

'I am the true vine'
Here **Jesus** uses another extended metaphor, speaking of himself as a vine; his Father, God, as the vinegrower; and those who believe in him as fruitful branches. Those who do not believe are to be burned, possibly a reference to the **Last Judgement**.

Key concepts
Cleansing, growth and acceptance by God all depend on a close relationship with Jesus.

John 15:1–8
"I am the true vine, and my Father is the vinegrower. [2] He removes every branch in me that bears no fruit. Every branch that bears fruit he prunes to make it bear more fruit. [3] You have already been cleansed by the word that I have spoken to you. [4] Abide in me as I abide in you. Just as the branch cannot bear fruit by itself unless it abides in the vine, neither can you unless you abide in me. [5] I am the vine, you are the branches. Those who abide in me and I in them bear much fruit, because apart from me you can do nothing. [6] Whoever does not abide in me is thrown away like a branch and withers; such branches are gathered, thrown into the fire, and burned. [7] If you abide in me, and my words abide in you, ask for whatever you wish, and it will be done for you. [8] My Father is glorified by this, that you bear much fruit and become my disciples."

Linked themes
In Jeremiah 2:21–2 God speaks about **Israel** as a vine that does not bear good fruit. The vine metaphor recalls Jesus' first miracle, turning water into wine (Jn 2:1–11). There may also be a suggestion of the central role of wine, the fruit of the vine, in the **Eucharist**.

Related works
Literature: George Herbert, 'The Sacrifice', 'Bunch of Grapes', 'The Church Militant', 1633.

THE TEACHING OF JESUS: JUDGEMENT

Passages in the **Gospels** which refer to the linked themes of the **Second Coming** of **Jesus Christ** and the **Last Judgement** have been subject to a wide range of interpretations from the earliest days of the **Church**. In Matthew 24 and 25 Jesus is shown describing future events, including his own return, and speaking of the need for human beings to be ready to account for their lives. The passage below pictures the **Son of Man**, a term Jesus uses of himself, separating humankind like a shepherd dividing sheep from goats. Those accepted by God will be placed in honour at his right hand and enjoy **eternal life**. Those who fall short will be placed at his left hand and sent away into eternal punishment.

Matthew 25:31–46

[31] "When the Son of Man comes in his glory, and all the angels with him, then he will sit on the throne of his glory. [32] All the nations will be gathered before him, and he will separate people one from another as a shepherd separates the sheep from the goats, [33] and he will put the sheep at his right hand and the goats at the left. [34] Then the king will say to those at his right hand, 'Come, you that are blessed by my Father, inherit the kingdom prepared for you from the foundation of the world; [35] for I was hungry and you gave me food, I was thirsty and you gave me something to drink, I was a stranger and you welcomed me, [36] I was naked and you gave me clothing, I was sick and you took care of me, I was in prison and you visited me.' [37] Then the righteous will answer him, 'Lord, when was it that we saw you hungry and gave you food, or thirsty and gave you something to drink? [38] And when was it that we saw you a stranger and welcomed you, or naked and gave you clothing? [39] And when

was it that we saw you sick or in prison and visited you?' [40] And the king will answer them, 'Truly I tell you, just as you did it to one of the least of these who are members of my family, you did it to me.' [41] Then he will say to those at his left hand, 'You that are accursed, depart from me into the eternal fire prepared for the devil and his angels; [42] for I was hungry and you gave me no food, I was thirsty and you gave me nothing to drink, [43] I was a stranger and you did not welcome me, naked and you did not give me clothing, sick and in prison and you did not visit me.' [44] Then they also will answer, 'Lord, when was it that we saw you hungry or thirsty or a stranger or naked or sick or in prison, and did not take care of you?' [45] Then he will answer them, 'Truly I tell you, just as you did not do it to one of the least of these, you did not do it to me.' [46] And these will go away into eternal punishment, but the righteous into eternal life."

Linked themes

God's judgement is a theme which runs through the **Bible** from the story of **Adam** and **Eve** onwards. Some examples of God's judgement on **sin**, such as the story of the **Flood** (see Chapter 1: Noah and the Flood) and the destruction of **Sodom and Gomorrah**, acquired particular significance and form the backdrop to **New Testament** warnings about the consequences of sin. The Book of **Revelation** describes not only the **Last Judgement** but also the creation of a **new heaven and a new earth**.

Related works

Art: Judgement: Seven Corporal works of Mercy, English wall paintings.

MIRACLES

Jesus, like some **Old Testament** prophets such as **Moses** and **Elijah**, is shown performing miraculous deeds, described in the **Gospels** as 'signs', 'deeds of power' and 'marvels'. These acts are presented as evidence that Jesus is the promised **Messiah** and the Son of God. They can be divided into three main categories: nature miracles (including the provision of food and drink and controlling the forces of nature), healing, and raising the dead to life. The Gospel accounts have been subject to a wide range of interpretation by commentators through the centuries.

The feeding of the five thousand

The feeding of the five thousand, in which Jesus takes what is offered to him and a large crowd is fed, is the only miracle to occur in all four Gospels.

Key concepts

Jesus provides for the needs of his followers.

John 6:3, 5–13

[3] Jesus went up the mountain and sat down there with his disciples. [...] [5] When he looked up and saw a large crowd coming toward him, Jesus said to Philip, "Where are we to buy bread for these people to eat?" [6] He said this to test him, for he himself knew what he was going to do. [7] Philip answered him, "Six months' wages would not buy enough bread for each of them to get a little." [8] One of his disciples, Andrew, Simon Peter's brother, said to him, [9] "There is a boy here who has five barley loaves and two fish. But what are they among so many people?" [10] Jesus said, "Make the people sit down." Now there was a great deal of grass in the place; so they sat down, about five thousand in all. [11] Then Jesus took the loaves, and when he had given thanks, he distributed them to those who were seated; so also the fish, as much as they wanted. [12] When they were satisfied, he told his disciples, "Gather up the fragments left over, so that nothing may be lost." [13] So they gathered them up, and from the fragments of the five barley loaves, left by those who had eaten, they filled twelve baskets.

Linked themes
Some **Old Testament** miracles, including the provision of **manna** in the desert (see Chapter 2: Moses and the Exodus), have been seen as prefiguring this event. Jesus' breaking of bread in this miracle has also been seen as foreshadowing his institution of the **Holy Communion** or **Mass** at the **Last Supper** and can also be linked to Christ's description of himself as the Bread of Life (Jn 6:35, 41).

Related works
Art: Albrecht Dürer, *The Feeding of the Five Thousand, c.*1503; Tintoretto, *The Miracle of the Loaves and* Fishes, *c.*1545–50.

Literature: Anthony Trollope, *Barchester Towers,* 1857.

The raising of Lazarus
Lazarus and his sisters **Mary** and **Martha** were close friends of **Jesus**. This account of the death and raising of Lazarus to life by Jesus emphasises the trust which the two sisters place in Jesus and may look forward to Jesus' own **Resurrection**.

Key concepts
Mary and Martha trust Jesus in the face of bereavement; the power of Jesus over death.

John 11:1–3, 17, 20–27, 32–44
Now a certain man was ill, Lazarus of Bethany, the village of Mary and her sister Martha. [2] Mary was the one who anointed the Lord with perfume and wiped his feet with her hair; her brother Lazarus was ill. [3] So the sisters sent a message to Jesus, "Lord, he whom you love is ill." [...]

[17] When Jesus arrived, he found that Lazarus had already been in the tomb four days. [...] [20] When Martha heard that Jesus was coming, she went and met him, while Mary stayed at home. [21] Martha said to Jesus, "Lord, if you had been here, my brother would not have died. [22] But even now I know that God will give

you whatever you ask of him." [23] Jesus said to her, "Your brother will rise again." [24] Martha said to him, "I know that he will rise again in the resurrection on the last day." [25] Jesus said to her, "I am the resurrection and the life. Those who believe in me, even though they die, will live, [26] and everyone who lives and believes in me will never die. Do you believe this?" [27] She said to him, "Yes, Lord, I believe that you are the Messiah, the Son of God, the one coming into the world." [...]

[32] When Mary came where Jesus was and saw him, she knelt at his feet and said to him, "Lord, if you had been here, my brother would not have died." [33] When Jesus saw her weeping, and the Jews who came with her also weeping, he was greatly disturbed in spirit and deeply moved. [34] He said, "Where have you laid him?" They said to him, "Lord, come and see." [35] Jesus began to weep. [36] So the Jews said, "See how he loved him!" [37] But some of them said, "Could not he who opened the eyes of the blind man have kept this man from dying?"

[38] Then Jesus, again greatly disturbed, came to the tomb. It was a cave, and a stone was lying against it. [39] Jesus said, "Take away the stone." Martha, the sister of the dead man, said to him, "Lord, already there is a stench because he has been dead four days." [40] Jesus said to her, "Did I not tell you that if you believed, you would see the glory of God?" [41] So they took away the stone. And Jesus looked upward and said, "Father, I thank you for having heard me. [42] I knew that you always hear me, but I have said this for the sake of the crowd standing here, so that they may believe that you sent me." [43] When he had said this, he cried with a loud voice, "Lazarus, come out!" [44] The dead man came out, his hands and feet bound with strips of cloth, and his face wrapped in a cloth. Jesus said to them, "Unbind him, and let him go."

Linked themes

The raising of Lazarus has been seen as foreshadowing the resurrection of Jesus (see Chapter 7).

Related works

Art: Giotto, *Raising of Lazarus*, 1304–6 (Scrovegni Chapel, Padua); Geertgen tot Sint Jans, *Raising of Lazarus*, 1480s (Louvre, Paris); Rembrandt, *Raising of Lazarus*, c.1630 (County Art Museum, Los Angeles); Sebastiano del Piombo, *Raising of Lazarus*, 1517–19 (National Gallery, London); Vincent Van Gogh, *The Raising of Lazarus* (after Rembrandt), 1890; Caravaggio, *The Raising of Lazarus*, 1608–9 (Museo Nazionale, Messina); Pietro Annigoni, *Resurrection of Lazarus*, 1946 (Vatican, Rome).

Literature: Charles Dickens, *David Copperfield*, Ch 2, 1849; Leo Tolstoy, *Resurrection*, 1899; Sylvia Plath, 'Lady Lazarus', 1962; Eugene O'Neil, *Lazarus Laughed*, 1927; Thom Gunn (1929–2004), 'Lazarus Not Raised'; Carol Ann Duffy, *Mrs Lazarus*, 1999.

The paralysed man

Key concepts
The power of **Jesus** to forgive **sin**; the power of Jesus to heal.

Mark 2:3–12
[3] Then some people came, bringing to him a paralysed man, carried by four of them. [4] And when they could not bring him to Jesus because of the crowd, they removed the roof above him; and after having dug through it, they let down the mat on which the paralytic lay. [5] When Jesus saw their faith, he said to the paralytic, "Son, your sins are forgiven." [6] Now some of the scribes were sitting there, questioning in their hearts, [7] "Why does this fellow speak in this way? It is blasphemy! Who can forgive sins but God alone?" [8] At once Jesus perceived in his spirit that they were discussing these questions among themselves; and he said to them, "Why do you raise such questions in your hearts? [9] Which is easier, to say to the paralytic, 'Your sins are forgiven,' or to say, 'Stand up and take your mat and walk'? [10] But so that you may know that the Son of Man has authority on earth to forgive sins" – he said to the paralytic – [11] "I say to you, stand up, take your

mat and go to your home." [12] And he stood up, and immediately took the mat and went out before all of them; so that they were all amazed and glorified God, saying, "We have never seen anything like this!"

Linked themes
Jesus is shown performing a number of other healing miracles including the healing of the Blind Man (Mk 8:22–6) and the Ten Lepers (Lk 17:11–19).

Related works
Art: Jan van Hemessen, *Arise, Take Up Thy Bed, and Walk*, mid-sixteenth century (National Gallery of Art, Washington); Bartolomé Esteban Murillo, *Christ healing the Paralytic at the Pool of Bethesda*, 1667–70 (National Gallery, London).

THE TRIUMPHAL ENTRY INTO JERUSALEM

All four **Gospels** describe this event, an occasion of rejoicing and popular acclaim which can also be read as introducing the **Passion** narrative and leading inexorably towards the death of **Jesus** on the **Cross**. The behaviour of the crowds, including pilgrims gathered to celebrate the festival of the **Passover,** seems to show that Jesus is greeted both as a spiritual and a political deliverer. Many at the time expected the **Messiah** to bring liberation from Roman occupation. Jesus, however, is not riding a war horse but a donkey. Matthew presents this as fulfilment of a **prophecy** in Zechariah 9:9: 'Behold your king…humble, and mounted on an ass,' suggesting that Jesus offers spiritual rather than political liberation.

The context of this passage reveals tensions which will lead to the death of Jesus. **Luke** describes how Jesus, drawing near to **Jerusalem**, weeps over the lack of understanding of its people, and the suffering which lies ahead for the city. He then moves into the **Temple** where he drives out the money changers who exploit the poor. Within a few days, some hailing Jesus as the coming king will be calling for his death.

This event is celebrated on the Sunday before **Easter**, known as **Palm Sunday** from the palm branches described in Jn 12:13.

Key concepts

Marks the beginning of the **Passion** narrative; the response of the crowds; recognition of the **Messiah**; Jesus fulfilling **prophecy**.

Luke 19:28–40

[28] After he had said this, he went on ahead, going up to Jerusalem.

[29] When he had come near Bethphage and Bethany, at the place called the Mount of Olives, he sent two of the disciples, [30] saying, "Go into the village ahead of you, and as you enter it you will find tied there a colt that has never been ridden. Untie it and bring it here. [31] If anyone asks you, 'Why are you untying it?' just say this, 'The Lord needs it.'" [32] So those who were sent departed and found it as he had told them. [33] As they were untying the colt, its owners asked them, "Why are you untying the colt?" [34] They said, "The Lord needs it." [35] Then they brought it to Jesus; and after throwing their cloaks on the colt, they set Jesus on it. [36] As he rode along, people kept spreading their cloaks on the road. [37] As he was now approaching the path down from the Mount of Olives, the whole multitude of the disciples began to praise God joyfully with a loud voice for all the deeds of power that they had seen, [38] saying,

"Blessed is the king who comes in the name of the Lord!
Peace in heaven, and glory in the highest heaven!"

[39] Some of the Pharisees in the crowd said to him, "Teacher, order your disciples to stop." [40] He answered, "I tell you, if these were silent, the stones would shout out."

Linked themes

The shouts of 'Blessed is he who comes in the name of the Lord' echo Psalm 118:26–7, indicating that Jesus is seen as the promised **Messiah**. The cries of 'Hosanna' ('Save [us]') come from the same **psalm**. Jesus is greeted as the 'Son of **David**', entering the city where David was king.

Spreading of garments on the road was also a sign of welcome to a ruler.

Related works

Art: Giotto, *Entry of Christ into Jerusalem*, 1304–6; Duccio, *Entry into Jerusalem*, 1308–11 (Cathedral, Siena); Fra Angelico, *Entry into Jerusalem*, 1448–55 (San Marco, Florence).

Literature: George Herbert, 'The Altar', 1633; Henry Vaughan (1622–95), 'Palm Sunday'; William Faulkner, *A Fable*, 1955.

Music: Thomas Weelkes (1575–1623), *Hozanna to the Son of David*.

THE LAST SUPPER

The **Gospels** set the death of **Jesus** during the annual **Passover** festival, which commemorated the deliverance of the **Israelites** from **Egypt** (see **Exodus**). New Testament writers saw key parallels between these two events, describing Jesus as the '**Lamb of God**', whose death for humankind was prefigured by the sacrificial lambs whose blood marked out Israelite homes and saved them from destruction: 'our paschal (**Passover**) lamb, **Christ**, has been sacrificed' (1 Corinthians 5:7). The **synoptic** gospels (**Matthew**, **Mark** and **Luke**) present Jesus' last supper with his **Disciples** before his death as a Passover meal in which his words and actions give new meaning to the existing ritual and explain the significance of his approaching death.

The **synoptic** Gospels all place the **Last Supper** in an 'Upper Room'. The order of events and form of words differ slightly but during the meal Jesus is described as taking bread, blessing and breaking it and giving it to his disciples with the words: 'Take, eat; this is my body' (Mt 26:26). Luke adds, 'Do this in remembrance of me' (Lk 22:19). Jesus also takes the cup of wine and, after giving thanks, says 'Drink from it, all of you, for this is my blood of the covenant, which is poured out for many for the forgiveness of sins' (Mt 26:27). Luke has: 'This cup … is the new covenant in my blood' (Lk 22:20). These words and actions form the heart of the commemoration which **St Paul** describes in 1 Corinthians as 'the Lord's Supper', later called the **Eucharist**, **Holy Communion** or **Mass**.

Key concepts
Context of a **Passover** Meal; the sacrificial death of **Jesus**; the new significance of bread and wine; the new covenant; the institution of the **Eucharist**, **Holy Communion** or **Mass**.

Matthew 26:17–30
[17] On the first day of Unleavened Bread the disciples came to Jesus, saying, "Where do you want us to make the preparations for you to eat the Passover?" [18] He said, "Go into the city to a certain man, and say to him, 'The Teacher says, My time is near; I will keep the Passover at your house with my disciples.'" [19] So the disciples did as Jesus had directed them, and they prepared the Passover meal.

[20] When it was evening, he took his place with the twelve; [21] and while they were eating, he said, "Truly I tell you, one of you will betray me." [22] And they became greatly distressed and began to say to him one after another, "Surely not I, Lord?" [23] He answered, "The one who has dipped his hand into the bowl with me will betray me. [24] The Son of Man goes as it is written of him, but woe to that one by whom the Son of Man is betrayed! It would have been better for that one not to have been born." [25] Judas, who betrayed him, said, "Surely not I, Rabbi?" He replied, "You have said so."

[26] While they were eating, Jesus took a loaf of bread, and after blessing it he broke it, gave it to the disciples, and said, "Take, eat; this is my body." [27] Then he took a cup, and after giving thanks he gave it to them, saying, "Drink from it, all of you; [28] for this is my blood of the covenant, which is poured out for many for the forgiveness of sins. [29] I tell you, I will never again drink of this fruit of the vine until that day when I drink it new with you in my Father's kingdom."

[30] When they had sung the hymn, they went out to the Mount of Olives.

Linked themes

St Paul's commentary on the Last Supper can be found in 1 Cor 11:23–6.

Related works

Art: Leonardo da Vinci, *Last Supper*, 1495–7 (S. Maria delle Grazie, Milan); Bassano, *Last Supper*, 1542 (Borghese Gallery, Rome); Jacopo Tintoretto, *Last Supper*, 1556–8 (S. Trovaso, Venice); Peter Paul Rubens, *Last Supper*, 1630 (Pushkin Museum of Fine Arts, Moscow); William Blake, *Last Supper*, 1799 (National Gallery of Art, Washington); Emil Nolde, *Last Supper*, 1909; Salvador Dali, *Last Supper*, 1955; Andy Warhol, *The Last Supper Paintings*, 1986.

Literature: *Corpus Christi Carol* (sixteenth century); Henry Vaughan (1622–95), 'The Feast'; George Herbert, 'Holy Communion', 1633; Edward Taylor (1642–1729), *Preparatory Meditations*; T.S. Eliot, 'East Coker', *Four Quartets*, 1944.

Music: Eric Thiman, *The Last Supper*, 1930.

JESUS WASHES HIS DISCIPLES' FEET

John's Gospel does not describe the giving of the bread and wine but instead shows **Jesus** washing the feet of the **Disciples**, a menial task usually carried out by a slave. **Peter** objects but is told that unless he allows himself to be washed in this way he will no longer be a Disciple of Jesus. Jesus explains that, as their Lord and Teacher, he has offered a model of service, an example of care which they should give to one another. The Last Supper, and in particular the washing of the Disciples' feet, is commemorated on **Maundy Thursday**.

Key concepts

Washing of the **Disciples'** feet; symbolic cleansing; **Jesus** models servant-hood; prediction of betrayal by **Judas**; a new commandment to love.

John 13:1–15, 34–5

Now before the festival of the Passover, Jesus knew that his hour had come to depart from this world and go to the Father. Having loved his own who were in the world, he loved them to the end. [2] The devil had already put it into the heart of Judas son of Simon Iscariot to betray him. And during supper [3] Jesus, knowing that the Father had given all things into his hands, and that he had come from God and was going to God, [4] got up from the table, took off his outer robe, and tied a towel around himself. [5] Then he poured water into a basin and began to wash the disciples' feet and to wipe them with the towel that was tied around him. [6] He came to Simon Peter, who said to him, "Lord, are you going to wash my feet?" [7] Jesus answered, "You do not know now what I am doing, but later you will understand." [8] Peter said to him, "You will never wash my feet." Jesus answered, "Unless I wash you, you have no share with me." [9] Simon Peter said to him, "Lord, not my feet only but also my hands and my head!" [10] Jesus said to him, "One who has bathed does not need to wash, except for the feet, but is entirely clean. And you are clean, though not all of you." [11] For he knew who was to betray him; for this reason he said, "Not all of you are clean."

[12] After he had washed their feet, had put on his robe, and had returned to the table, he said to them, "Do you know what I have done to you? [13] You call me Teacher and Lord – and you are right, for that is what I am. [14] So if I, your Lord and Teacher, have washed your feet, you also ought to wash one another's feet. [15] For I have set you an example, that you also should do as I have done to you. [...]

[34] I give you a new commandment, that you love one another. Just as I have loved you, you also should love one another. [35] By this everyone will know that you are my disciples, if you have love for one another."

Linked themes

In Mark 10:42–5 **Jesus** tells his **disciples** that whoever wishes to be great must serve others and that he came into the world 'not to be served but to serve and give his life as a ransom for many'.

Related works

Art: Duccio, *Washing of the Feet*, 1308–11; Tintoretto, *Christ Washing the Feet of the Disciples*, 1557 (National Gallery, London); Ford Madox Brown, *Jesus washing Peter's feet at the Last Supper*, c.1851 (Tate Gallery, London); Hans Feibusch, *The Footwashing*, 1990.

7 THE DEATH AND RESURRECTION OF JESUS

BETRAYAL AND ARREST

JESUS INTERROGATED AND CONDEMNED

CRUCIFIXION AND BURIAL

RESURRECTION

The final stages of the life of **Jesus** are often described as 'The **Passion**', a term derived from the Latin *passio* meaning 'to suffer'. Some cycles of Passion imagery begin with Jesus' entry into **Jerusalem** and cover the whole of his last week in the city; others focus on his final twenty-four hours starting with the **Last Supper** or the 'Betrayal and Arrest'. All follow the **Gospel** accounts in emphasising the willingness of Jesus to bear pain, abuse, misunderstanding and eventually death in order to win **forgiveness** for sinful humankind. Depictions of the symbols of the suffering endured by Jesus are known as the *Arma Christi* or **Instruments of the Passion**. The three **Synoptic Gospels** give largely similar accounts of the betrayal, trial and **crucifixion** of Jesus, while **John's** Gospel provides some additional material. The passages below have been selected to give as many aspects of these accounts as possible in a limited space.

BETRAYAL AND ARREST

The Gospel accounts make it clear that **Judas Iscariot** is the human agent of betrayal while also emphasising that Jesus submits voluntarily to events, including his arrest, as part of God's plan foretold in **Old Testament** prophecy. The episode in the **Garden of Gethsemane** stresses the humanity of Jesus, as he faces and accepts the suffering which lies ahead. **Peter**'s self-confident boast of complete loyalty is soon challenged; like his companions he falls asleep and, in the end, he too deserts Jesus.

Key concepts

Betrayal by Judas; fulfilment of **prophecy**; Jesus predicts Peter's denial; Jesus prays in agony but accepts his coming suffering as God's will; Jesus forbids the use of violence to defend him.

Matthew 26:14–16, 31–52, 56

[14] Then one of the twelve, who was called Judas Iscariot, went to the chief priests [15] and said, "What will you give me if I betray him to you?" They paid him thirty pieces of silver. [16] And from that moment he began to look for an opportunity to betray him. [...]

[31] Then Jesus said to them, "You will all become deserters because of me this night; for it is written,

'I will strike the shepherd,

and the sheep of the flock will be scattered.'

[32] But after I am raised up, I will go ahead of you to Galilee." [33] Peter said to him, "Though all become deserters because of you, I will never desert you." [34] Jesus said to him, "Truly I tell you, this very night, before the cock crows, you will deny me three times." [35] Peter said to him, "Even though I must die with you, I will not deny you." And so said all the disciples.

[36] Then Jesus went with them to a place called Gethsemane; and he said to his disciples, "Sit here while I go over there and pray." [37] He took with him Peter and the two sons of Zebedee, and began to be grieved and agitated. [38] Then he said to them, "I am deeply grieved, even to death; remain here, and stay awake with me." [39] And going a little farther, he threw himself on the ground and prayed, "My Father, if it is possible, let this cup

pass from me; yet not what I want but what you want." [40] Then he came to the disciples and found them sleeping; and he said to Peter, "So, could you not stay awake with me one hour? [41] Stay awake and pray that you may not come into the time of trial; the spirit indeed is willing, but the flesh is weak." [42] Again he went away for the second time and prayed, "My Father, if this cannot pass unless I drink it, your will be done." [43] Again he came and found them sleeping, for their eyes were heavy. [44] So leaving them again, he went away and prayed for the third time, saying the same words. [45] Then he came to the disciples and said to them, "Are you still sleeping and taking your rest? See, the hour is at hand, and the Son of Man is betrayed into the hands of sinners. [46] Get up, let us be going. See, my betrayer is at hand."

[47] While he was still speaking, Judas, one of the twelve, arrived; with him was a large crowd with swords and clubs, from the chief priests and the elders of the people. [48] Now the betrayer had given them a sign, saying, "The one I will kiss is the man; arrest him." [49] At once he came up to Jesus and said, "Greetings, Rabbi!" and kissed him. [50] Jesus said to him, "Friend, do what you are here to do." Then they came and laid hands on Jesus and arrested him. [51] Suddenly, one of those with Jesus put his hand on his sword, drew it, and struck the slave of the high priest, cutting off his ear. [52] Then Jesus said to him, "Put your sword back into its place; for all who take the sword will perish by the sword. [...] [56] Then all the disciples deserted him and fled.

Linked themes

Matthew relates that Judas repented of his betrayal and attempted to return the money to the chief priests. He then hanged himself and the money was used to buy an area called 'the Potter's Field' as a place of burial for strangers (Mt 27:3–10). In Acts 1:15–26, Peter refers to Judas' act of betrayal and death and a replacement is chosen to join the other apostles.

Related works

Art: Giovanni Bellini, *Agony in the Garden*, c.1459 (National Gallery, London); Andrea Mantegna, *Agony in the Garden*, c.1459 (National Gallery, London); El Greco, *Agony in the Garden*, c.1588 (Toledo, Ohio); Giotto di Bondone, *Kiss of Judas*, 1304–6; Caravaggio, *The Taking of Christ*, 1602; Rembrandt, *Judas Returns the Thirty Pieces*, 1629; Jacob Smits, *Kiss of Judas*, 1908 (Antwerp Royal Museum).

Literature: *The Agony and Betrayal* (York Mystery Cycle); George Herbert, 'The Sacrifice', 1633; Nikos Kazantzakis, *Last Temptation of Christ*, 1960; Brendan Kennelly, *The Book of Judas*, 1991.

Music: John Henry Maunder (1858–1920), *Olivet to Calvary*.

JESUS INTERROGATED AND CONDEMNED

Jesus was taken in turn before Caiaphas the High Priest, **Pilate** the Roman Governor and **Herod Antipas** (Lk 23:6–12). During this period he was subjected not only to questioning but to flogging and humiliation. The narratives bring out not only the religious tensions which lie behind Jesus' arrest but also the political complexities of a country under Roman occupation.

Jesus before the High Priest and Peter's denial

Jesus stands alone before the high priest, his Disciples scattered. He is accused of threatening to destroy the **Temple**, and of blasphemy for claiming equality with God; he is beaten and mocked as a false **prophet**. Meanwhile Peter fulfils Jesus' prediction by denying his relationship with him.

Key concepts

The enmity of the religious leaders; false witnesses testify against Jesus; Jesus claims to be the **Messiah**; Jesus is condemned to death and beaten; Peter denies knowing Jesus.

Mark 14:53–72

[53] They took Jesus to the high priest; and all the chief priests, the elders, and the scribes were assembled. [54] Peter had followed him at a distance, right into the courtyard of the high priest; and he was sitting with the guards, warming himself at the fire. [55] Now the chief priests and the whole council were looking for testimony against Jesus to put him to death; but they found none. [56] For many gave false testimony against him, and their testimony did not agree. [57] Some stood up and gave false testimony against him, saying, [58] "We heard him say, 'I will destroy this temple that is made with hands, and in three days I will build another, not made with hands.'" [59] But even on this point their testimony did not agree. [60] Then the high priest stood up before them and asked Jesus, "Have you no answer? What is it that they testify against you?" [61] But he was silent and did not answer. Again the high priest asked him, "Are you the Messiah, the Son of the Blessed One?" [62] Jesus said, "I am; and

'you will see the Son of Man

seated at the right hand of the Power,'

and 'coming with the clouds of heaven.'"

[63] Then the high priest tore his clothes and said, "Why do we still need witnesses? [64] You have heard his blasphemy! What is your decision?" All of them condemned him as deserving death. [65] Some began to spit on him, to blindfold him, and to strike him, saying to him, "Prophesy!" The guards also took him over and beat him.

[66] While Peter was below in the courtyard, one of the servant-girls of the high priest came by. [67] When she saw Peter warming himself, she stared at him and said, "You also were with Jesus, the man from Nazareth." [68] But he denied it, saying, "I do not know or understand what you are talking about." And he went out into the forecourt. Then the cock crowed. [69] And the servant-girl, on seeing him, began again to say to the bystanders, "This man is one of them." [70] But again he denied it. Then after a little while the bystanders again said to Peter, "Certainly you are one

of them; for you are a Galilean." [71] But he began to curse, and he swore an oath, "I do not know this man you are talking about." [72] At that moment the cock crowed for the second time. Then Peter remembered that Jesus had said to him, "Before the cock crows twice, you will deny me three times." And he broke down and wept.

Linked themes
Peter is forgiven and re-commissioned by Jesus after the **Resurrection** (Jn 21:15–19).

Related works
Art: Duccio, *Christ before Annas and Peter Denying Jesus*, 1308–11 (Duomo, Siena); Caravaggio, *The Denial of St Peter*, 1610; Gerrit van Honthurst, *Christ before Caiaphas* (National Gallery, London), c.1618; Rembrandt, *Peter Denying Christ*, c.1620–5 (Minneapolis Institute of Arts); Georges Rouault, *Christ and the High Priest* (Philips Collection, Washington).

Literature: *Christ before Annas and Caiaphas* (York Mystery Cycle).

Jesus appears before Pilate
Because the Jewish authorities did not have the power to carry out executions, it was necessary for **Jesus** to appear before **Pilate**, the Roman governor. All the **Gospel** accounts suggest that Pilate sought to save Jesus but eventually gave in to the will of the religious authorities and the hostile crowd.

Key concepts
Pilate willing to release Jesus; the crowd choose Barabbas; Pilate 'washes his hands' of the matter and submits to the crowd's wishes; Jesus is mocked and stripped.

Matthew 27:11–31
[11] Now Jesus stood before the governor; and the governor asked him, "Are you the King of the Jews?" Jesus said, "You say so." [12] But when he was accused by the chief priests and elders, he

did not answer. [13] Then Pilate said to him, "Do you not hear how many accusations they make against you?" [14] But he gave him no answer, not even to a single charge, so that the governor was greatly amazed.

[15] Now at the festival the governor was accustomed to release a prisoner for the crowd, anyone whom they wanted. [16] At that time they had a notorious prisoner, called Jesus Barabbas. [17] So after they had gathered, Pilate said to them, "Whom do you want me to release for you, Jesus Barabbas or Jesus who is called the Messiah?" [18] For he realised that it was out of jealousy that they had handed him over. [19] While he was sitting on the judgment seat, his wife sent word to him, "Have nothing to do with that innocent man, for today I have suffered a great deal because of a dream about him." [20] Now the chief priests and the elders persuaded the crowds to ask for Barabbas and to have Jesus killed. [21] The governor again said to them, "Which of the two do you want me to release for you?" And they said, "Barabbas." [22] Pilate said to them, "Then what should I do with Jesus who is called the Messiah?" All of them said, "Let him be crucified!" [23] Then he asked, "Why, what evil has he done?" But they shouted all the more, "Let him be crucified!"

[24] So when Pilate saw that he could do nothing, but rather that a riot was beginning, he took some water and washed his hands before the crowd, saying, "I am innocent of this man's blood; see to it yourselves." [25] Then the people as a whole answered, "His blood be on us and on our children!" [26] So he released Barabbas for them; and after flogging Jesus, he handed him over to be crucified.

[27] Then the soldiers of the governor took Jesus into the governor's headquarters, and they gathered the whole cohort around him. [28] They stripped him and put a scarlet robe on him, [29] and after twisting some thorns into a crown, they put it on his head. They put a reed in his right hand and knelt before him and mocked him, saying, "Hail, King of the Jews!" [30] They spat on him, and took the reed and struck him on the head. [31] After

mocking him, they stripped him of the robe and put his own clothes on him. Then they led him away to crucify him.

Linked themes
All the Gospel accounts emphasise that Jesus did not defend himself against accusation, remaining silent during much of his interrogation. This quiet acceptance was later seen as recalling the prophecy of **Isaiah**: 'He was oppressed and afflicted, yet he did not open his mouth; like a lamb that is led to the slaughter' (Isa 53:7).

Related works
Art: Tintoretto, *Christ Before Pilate*, 1566–7 (Scuola di San Rocco, Venice); Diego Rodriguez de Silva y Velázquez, *Christ after the Flagellation*, 1632 (National Gallery, London); Anthony van Dyck, *Flagellation*, 1620 (Museo del Prado, Madrid); Caravaggio, *Flagellation*, 1606 (Capodimonte Museum, Naples).

Literature: *Christ before Pilate* (York Mystery Cycle); William Shakespeare, *Macbeth*, 1601; Francis Bacon, 'Of Truth', *Essays*, 1612; Mikhail Bulgakov, *The Master and Margarita*, 1939; Carol Ann Duffy, *Pilate's Wife*, 1999.

CRUCIFIXION AND BURIAL

The death of **Jesus Christ** on the **Cross** is a central event in Christian teaching and, along with the **Nativity**, the most frequently depicted in art and literature. Jesus is crucified, a form of execution reserved by the Romans for slaves, foreigners and violent criminals, and the most painful and degrading of deaths. He is mocked by many of those who watch, and challenged to show his power by setting himself free.

For the **Gospel** authors, however, the death of Jesus is not a brutal end to a promising career but the central component of God's plan to save humankind from the consequences of **sin**. Jesus is portrayed as a willing **sacrifice**, sinless yet prepared to bear the guilt of sinful humankind and even praying for **forgiveness** for those who nail him to the **Cross**. His words at the **Last Supper**, together with the timing of his execution, taking place as it does during **Passover** week, link his sacrifice with the **Exodus** narrative in which the blood of sacrificed lambs marked out the **Israelites** for deliverance from God's judgement (see Chapter 2: Moses and the Exodus).

Particular significance has been attached to the seven utterances made by Jesus while he hung on the Cross (see **Seven Last Words from the Cross**). The day upon which Jesus died later became known as **Good Friday**.

The road to Calvary

Executions were not allowed within the city walls of **Jerusalem**. Instead, Jesus is taken to **Golgotha** (also called **Calvary**), meaning 'the place of the skull', a term which may refer to the shape of the hill or to its function as a site of execution. Condemned men usually carried their own cross, but it appears that Jesus, who had already undergone flogging, was unable to do this alone. Jesus refuses the wine which probably contained a narcotic to help ease the pain.

Key concepts

The journey to Calvary; Jesus refuses drugged wine.

Matthew 27:32–4

[32] As they went out, they came upon a man from Cyrene named Simon; they compelled this man to carry his cross. [33] And when they came to a place called Golgotha (which means Place of a Skull), [34] they offered him wine to drink, mixed with gall; but when he tasted it, he would not drink it.

Linked themes

Later interpreters drew a parallel between this scene and **Isaac** carrying the wood to the place where he was to be sacrificed (see Chapter 2: The Sacrifice of Isaac). The Gospel accounts were subsequently ampli-fied in devotional texts to include descriptions of the suffering of Jesus as he made his way to Calvary. His route was later recreated as the *Via Crucis* or *Via Dolorosa* and is still re-enacted by pilgrims to Jerusalem.

Related works

Art: Hieronymous Bosch, *The Road to Calvary*, 1490 (Kunsthistorisches Museum, Vienna); Ridolpho Ghirlandaio, *The Procession to Calvary*, c.1505; Jacopo Bassano, *The Way to Calvary*, c.1545 (National Gallery, London); Pieter Bruegel the Elder, *The Road to Calvary*, 1564 (Kunsthistorisches Museum, Vienna); El Greco, *Christ Carrying the Cross*, 1587–96 (Museo Nacional, Barcelona); Peter Paul Rubens, *Ascent to Calvary*, 1636–7 (Museum of Fine Arts, Brussels).

Literature: World War I poets, especially Wilfred Owen and Siegfried Sassoon, liken the ordinary soldier to Christ carrying his Cross.

Jesus is crucified (Luke's gospel)

The **Gospel** writers do not dwell on the brutal details of the **crucifixion** process. What they do emphasise is the attitude of **Jesus** to those around him: his prayer for **forgiveness** for those who are crucifying him; his silence when mocked; his acceptance of the robber who **repents**.

Key concepts

Jesus crucified alongside two robbers; soldiers cast lots for his clothes; the inscription on the Cross; Jesus derided by bystanders; one robber reviles Jesus, the other repents.

Luke 23:32–43, 46

[32] Two others also, who were criminals, were led away to be put to death with him. [33] When they came to the place that is called The Skull, they crucified Jesus there with the criminals, one on his right and one on his left. [[[34] Then Jesus said, "Father, forgive them; for they do not know what they are doing."]] And they cast lots to divide his clothing. [35] And the people stood by, watching; but the leaders scoffed at him, saying, "He saved others; let him save himself if he is the Messiah of God, his chosen one!" [36] The soldiers also mocked him, coming up and offering him sour wine, [37] and saying, "If you are the King of the Jews, save yourself!" [38] There was also an inscription over him, "This is the King of the Jews."

[39] One of the criminals who were hanged there kept deriding him and saying, "Are you not the Messiah? Save yourself and us!" [40] But the other rebuked him, saying, "Do you not fear God, since you are under the same sentence of condemnation? [41] And we indeed have been condemned justly, for we are getting what we deserve for our deeds, but this man has done nothing wrong." [42] Then he said, "Jesus, remember me when you come into your kingdom." [43] He replied, "Truly I tell you, today you will be with me in Paradise." [...]
[46] Then Jesus, crying with a loud voice, said, "Father, into your hands I commend my spirit." Having said this, he breathed his last.

Linked themes
This account contains a number of echoes of Psalm 22, a **psalm** interpreted by Christian writers as foreshadowing the sufferings of **Christ** (see Chapter 3: Psalms).

Related works
Art: Agnolo Gaddi, *Crucifixion*, c.1393–6 (Uffizi, Florence); Andrea del Castagno, *Crucifixion*, 1455 (S. Appollonia, Florence); Brueghel the younger, *Crucifixion*, 1617 (Museum of Fine Arts, Budapest); Tintoretto, *The Crucifixion of Christ*, 1566; Peter Paul Rubens, *Crucifixion*, 1635.

Literature: The Old English poem *Dream of the Rood*; Medieval English lyrics ('Whanne ic se on rode', 'Woefully araide'); *The Crucifixion* and *Death of Christ* (York Mystery Cycle).

Music: Handel, *The Messiah*, 1741; Haydn, *The Seven Last Words of our Saviour from the Cross*, 1785; John Stainer, *The Crucifixion*, 1887; Penderecki, *St Luke Passion*, 1963–6.

Jesus is crucified (Matthew's gospel)
Matthew, like **Mark**, describes the sense of abandonment and separation from **God** experienced by **Jesus** as he hung on the **Cross**, cut off from his Father as he bore the punishment for human **sin**.

Matthew's account also presents details which indicate the far-reaching implications of this event: the sun is darkened and the earth shakes; the curtain in the **Temple**, which separated off the Holy of Holies, was torn from top to bottom suggesting the beginning of a new spiritual era; a watching **Gentile**, the Roman centurion, is among those who recognise Jesus as Son of God, suggesting that his death is for all peoples.

Key concepts

Darkness falls; Jesus cries out to God and dies; the curtain of the **Temple** is torn in two; the earthquake; a Roman centurion acknowledges Jesus' significance.

Matthew 27:45–54

[45] From noon on, darkness came over the whole land until three in the afternoon. [46] And about three o'clock Jesus cried with a loud voice, "Eli, Eli, lema sabachthani?" that is, "My God, my God, why have you forsaken me?" [47] When some of the bystanders heard it, they said, "This man is calling for Elijah." [48] At once one of them ran and got a sponge, filled it with sour wine, put it on a stick, and gave it to him to drink. [49] But the others said, "Wait, let us see whether Elijah will come to save him." [50] Then Jesus cried again with a loud voice and breathed his last. [51] At that moment the curtain of the temple was torn in two, from top to bottom. The earth shook, and the rocks were split. [52] The tombs also were opened, and many bodies of the saints who had fallen asleep were raised. [53] After his resurrection they came out of the tombs and entered the holy city and appeared to many. [54] Now when the centurion and those with him, who were keeping watch over Jesus, saw the earthquake and what took place, they were terrified and said, "Truly this man was God's Son!"

Linked themes

Jesus' cry of desolation is a quotation from Psalm 22:1, a **psalm** interpreted by Christian writers as foreshadowing the sufferings of **Christ** (see Chapter 3: Psalm 22). The description of the dead rising from their tombs was later woven into the doctrine of the **Harrowing of Hell**, a concept which was very influential in the medieval **Church**.

Related works
Art: El Greco, *Christ on the Cross*, 1600–10; Rembrandt (etching), *The Crucifixion*, 1653; Velázquez, *Christ on the Cross*, c.1632 (Prado, Madrid); Craig Aitchison, *Crucifixion*, 1997–8.

Literature: John Donne, 'Good Friday, 1613. Riding Westward', 'The Cross'; George Herbert, 'Redemption', 1633; John Bunyan, *The Pilgrim's Progress*, 1678; Christina Rossetti (1830–94), 'Good Friday morning'; W.B. Yeats, *Calvary*, 1920; James Joyce, *Portrait of the Artist*, 1915; David Jones, 'Anathemata', 1952; David Gascoyne (1916–2001), 'Ecce Homo', *Miserere*; Geoffrey Hill, 'Canticle for Good Friday', 'Lacrimae', 1978.

Music: Bach, *St Matthew Passion*, 1729.

Jesus is crucified (John's gospel)
John's account emphasises the faithfulness of the women who remain close to **Jesus** till the end and the concern of Jesus for his mother's well being after his death.

Key concepts
The women witness the crucifixion; Jesus entrusts his mother to John's care; Jesus dies; a soldier pierces Jesus' side; fulfilment of **Old Testament prophecy**.

John 19:25–37
[25] ... Meanwhile, standing near the cross of Jesus were his mother, and his mother's sister, Mary the wife of Clopas, and Mary Magdalene. [26] When Jesus saw his mother and the disciple whom he loved standing beside her, he said to his mother, "Woman, here is your son." [27] Then he said to the disciple, "Here is your mother." And from that hour the disciple took her into his own home.

[28] After this, when Jesus knew that all was now finished, he said (in order to fulfil the scripture), "I am thirsty." [29] A jar full of sour wine was standing there. So they put a sponge full of the wine on a branch of hyssop and held it to his mouth. [30] When Jesus had received the wine, he said, "It is finished." Then he bowed his head and gave up his spirit.

[31] Since it was the day of Preparation, the Jews did not want the bodies left on the cross during the sabbath, especially because that sabbath was a day of great solemnity. So they asked Pilate to have the legs of the crucified men broken and the bodies removed. [32] Then the soldiers came and broke the legs of the first and of the other who had been crucified with him. [33] But when they came to Jesus and saw that he was already dead, they did not break his legs. [34] Instead, one of the soldiers pierced his side with a spear, and at once blood and water came out. [35] (He who saw this has testified so that you also may believe. His testimony is true, and he knows that he tells the truth.) [36] These things occurred so that the scripture might be fulfilled, "None of his bones shall be broken." [37] And again another passage of scripture says, "They will look on the one whom they have pierced."

Linked themes

John 19:28 seems to echo Psalm 69:21: 'For my thirst they gave me vinegar to drink.' John 19:36 may refer to Exodus 12:46 which says that none of the bones of the **Passover** lamb must be broken, or to Psalm 34:20 which describes God's care for the innocent sufferer. John 19:37 refers to Zechariah 12:10.

Related works

Art: Master of Rimini, *Crucifixion, c.*1350; Peter Paul Rubens, *Crucifixion*, 1620; Paul Gauguin, *Crucifixion*, 1889; Stanley Spencer, *Crucifixion*, 1934; Salvador Dali, *Christ of St John of the Cross*, 1951.

Literature: Medieval lyrics ('Stond well, moder, under Rode'); *Death of Christ* (York Mystery Cycle).

Music: Antonio Vivaldi, *Stabat Mater*, 1717; Bach, *St John Passion*, 1723; Giovanni Battista Pergolesi, *Stabat Mater*, 1729; Gioachino Antonio Rossini, *Stabat Mater*, 1842.

The burial

Immediate burial is required before the **Sabbath**, the Jewish day of rest, which on this occasion also coincides with the beginning of the **Passover**. Somewhat surprisingly, a member of the Jewish religious council, **Joseph of Arimathea**, claims the body of **Jesus** and places it in his own tomb, while the faithful women wait nearby. John 19:39 records that **Nicodemus**, another high-ranking Jewish figure who had talked with Jesus (see Chapter 6: Nicodemus visits Jesus) helps in the task. The still wary Jewish authorities insist that the tomb is securely sealed.

Key concepts

Joseph of Arimathea arranges burial; the women wait nearby; the tomb is made secure.

Matthew 27:57–66

57 When it was evening, there came a rich man from Arimathea, named Joseph, who was also a disciple of Jesus. 58 He went to Pilate and asked for the body of Jesus; then Pilate ordered it to be given to him. 59 So Joseph took the body and wrapped it in a clean linen cloth 60 and laid it in his own new tomb, which he had hewn in the rock. He then rolled a great stone to the door of the tomb and went away. 61 Mary Magdalene and the other Mary were there, sitting opposite the tomb.

62 The next day, that is, after the day of Preparation, the chief priests and the Pharisees gathered before Pilate 63 and said, "Sir, we remember what that impostor said while he was still alive, 'After three days I will rise again.' 64 Therefore command the tomb to be made secure until the third day; otherwise his disciples may go and steal him away, and tell the people, 'He has been raised from the dead,' and the last deception would be worse than the first." 65 Pilate said to them, "You have a guard of soldiers;

go, make it as secure as you can." [66] So they went with the guard and made the tomb secure by sealing the stone.

Linked themes

The removal of the body of Jesus from the **Cross** is only briefly described in the **Gospels** but later became an important topic in art and devotion. In particular **Mary** was depicted holding her dead son in her arms in a scene known as the Pietà, which forms an emotive parallel to many **Nativity** images.

Related works

Art: Rogier Van der Weyden, *Deposition from the Cross*, c.1439–43 (Museo del Prado, Madrid); Peter Paul Rubens, *Deposition of Christ*, 1602 (Borghese, Rome); Sandro Botticelli, *Pietà*, after 1490; Michelangelo, *Pietà*, 1498–9 (Vatican, Rome); Giovanni Bellini, *Pietà*, c.1500 (Accademia, Venice); Titian, *Pietà*, 1570–6 (Gallerie dell'Accademia, Venice); Fra Angelico, *The Entombment*, c.1445 (Alte Pinakothek, Munich); Caravaggio, *Entombment*, 1602 (Vatican, Rome); Rogier van der Weyden, *Entombment*, c.1450 (Uffizi, Florence); Titian, *Entombment*, c.1525; Peter Paul Rubens, *Entombment*, c.1612 (J. Paul Getty Museum, Los Angeles); Andrea Mantegna, *The Dead Christ*, c.1500 (Brera, Milan).

Literature: *Death of Christ* (York Mystery Cycle); David Gascoyne (1916–2001), 'Pietà'.

RESURRECTION

The **Gospel** writers relate that on the third day after the **Crucifixion**, now known as **Easter Sunday**, the tomb in which **Jesus'** body had been placed was found to be empty. They also describe a number of subsequent encounters between Jesus and his followers in which the despair the disciples had experienced at his death is gradually transmuted through doubt, confusion and bewilderment into a conviction that he has indeed risen from the dead. The accounts given here suggest that recognition of the risen Jesus is not always immediate but emerges slowly as he speaks and acts in ways which are familiar. The process of recognition also becomes a process of learning and recommissioning.

The empty tomb

According to the **Gospels**, the women are the first to return to the tomb as soon as the **Sabbath** is over. **Mary Magdalene** discovers that the stone has been removed and, fearing that enemies or grave robbers have removed the body, summons **Peter** and the beloved **Disciple** (**John the Evangelist**) who find that the linen wrappings remain but that the body has gone. Inconsolable with grief, Mary is shown encountering two angelic figures and then a man she takes to be the gardener. As he speaks her name, Mary recognises the figure as **Jesus**. Jesus tells her not to touch him (in Latin *Noli me tangere*), but to tell his disciples that he is risen and coming to meet them. Jesus speaks of God as his father and the father of the **Disciples**.

Key concepts

Mary Magdalene; Peter and John discover the empty tomb; Mary encounters Jesus; Jesus foretells his ascension.

John 20:1–18

Early on the first day of the week, while it was still dark, Mary Magdalene came to the tomb and saw that the stone had been removed from the tomb. [2] So she ran and went to Simon Peter and the other disciple, the one whom Jesus loved, and said to them, "They have taken the Lord out of the tomb, and we do not know where they have laid him." [3] Then Peter and the other disciple set out and went toward the tomb. [4] The two were running together, but the other disciple outran Peter and reached the tomb first. [5] He bent down to look in and saw the linen wrappings lying there, but he did not go in. [6] Then Simon Peter came, following him, and went into the tomb. He saw the linen wrappings lying there, [7] and the cloth that had been on Jesus' head, not lying with the linen wrappings but rolled up in a place by itself. [8] Then the other disciple, who reached the tomb first, also went in, and he saw and believed; [9] for as yet they did not understand the scripture, that he must rise from the dead. [10] Then the disciples returned to their homes.

[11] But Mary stood weeping outside the tomb. As she wept, she bent over to look into the tomb; [12] and she saw two angels in white, sitting where the body of Jesus had been lying, one at the head and the other at the feet. [13] They said to her, "Woman, why are you weeping?" She said to them, "They have taken away my Lord, and I do not know where they have laid him." [14] When she had said this, she turned around and saw Jesus standing there, but she did not know that it was Jesus. [15] Jesus said to her, "Woman, why are you weeping? Whom are you looking for?" Supposing him to be the gardener, she said to him, "Sir, if you have carried him away, tell me where you have laid him, and I will take him away." [16] Jesus said to her, "Mary!" She turned and said to him in Hebrew, "Rabbouni!" (which means Teacher). [17] Jesus said to her, "Do not hold on to me, because I have not yet ascended to the Father. But go to my brothers and say to them, 'I am ascending to my Father and your Father, to my God and your God.'" [18] Mary Magdalene went and announced to the disciples, "I have seen the Lord"; and she told them that he had said these things to her.

Linked themes
The ascension of Christ is described in Acts 1:9–11.

Related works
Art: Duccio, *Noli me Tangere* (*Touch me not*), 1308 (Duomo, Siena); Fra Angelico, *Noli Me* Tangere, 1438–43 (S. Marco, Florence); Titian, *Noli me Tangere*, c.1515 (National Gallery, London); Rembrandt, *The Risen Christ Appearing to Mary Magdalen*, 1638 (H.M. the Queen); William Blake, *The Angels Remove the Stone from the Sepulchre*, c.1800.

Literature: *Resurrection* (York Mystery Cycle); Thomas Wyatt (1503–42), *Who So List to Hunt*; John Donne (1572–1631), 'Death Be Not Proud';

George Herbert, *Easter Wings*, published 1633; Samuel Taylor Coleridge (1772–1834), *Rime of the Ancient Mariner*; Charles Dickens, *The Tale of Two Cities*, 1859; Dostoevsky, 'The Grand Inquisitor' in *The Brothers Karamasov*, 1886; D.H. Lawrence, 'The Man Who Died' (*The Escaped Cock*), 1929; J.R.R. Tolkien, *The Lord of the Rings*, 1954–5; Ezra Pound (1885–1972), *The Ballad of the Goodly Fere*; Michèle Roberts, *The Wild Girl (1984)*, 1991.

Doubting Thomas

This dramatic account paints a stark contrast between the fear of the **Disciples**, hidden away behind locked doors, and the joy and amazement which the appearance of **Jesus** provokes. Here the Disciples are not only reassured but recommissioned – sent out as Jesus' representatives to continue his work. The doubts expressed by **Thomas** are resolved by a further appearance of Jesus in answer to his challenge.

Key concepts

The Disciples' fear of the authorities; joy at the coming of Jesus; Jesus sends them into the world; Jesus promises the **Holy Spirit**; Jesus gives authority to forgive **sins**; Thomas doubts but comes to believe in the **Resurrection** of Jesus.

John 20:19–29

[19] When it was evening on that day, the first day of the week, and the doors of the house where the disciples had met were locked for fear of the Jews, Jesus came and stood among them and said, "Peace be with you." [20] After he said this, he showed them his hands and his side. Then the disciples rejoiced when they saw the Lord. [21] Jesus said to them again, "Peace be with you. As the Father has sent me, so I send you." [22] When he had said this, he breathed on them and said to them, "Receive the Holy Spirit. [23] If you forgive the sins of any, they are forgiven them; if you retain the sins of any, they are retained."

[24] But Thomas (who was called the Twin), one of the twelve, was not with them when Jesus came. [25] So the other disciples

told him, "We have seen the Lord." But he said to them, "Unless I see the mark of the nails in his hands, and put my finger in the mark of the nails and my hand in his side, I will not believe."

²⁶ A week later his disciples were again in the house, and Thomas was with them. Although the doors were shut, Jesus came and stood among them and said, "Peace be with you." ²⁷ Then he said to Thomas, "Put your finger here and see my hands. Reach out your hand and put it in my side. Do not doubt but believe." ²⁸ Thomas answered him, "My Lord and my God!" ²⁹ Jesus said to him, "Have you believed because you have seen me? Blessed are those who have not seen and yet have come to believe."

Linked themes
In John 14:16–17 Jesus promises that he will send the Holy Spirit; in Acts 1:4–5 he tells the Disciples to wait in **Jerusalem** until the Spirit comes. Acts 2:1–4 describes the gift of the Spirit on the Day of **Pentecost**.

Related works
Art: Caravaggio, *Incredulity of St Thomas*, *c.*1600–1; Rembrandt, *Incredulity of St Thomas*, 1634 (Pushkin Museum, Moscow); Guercino, *Doubting Thomas* (Residenzgalerie, Salzburg); Honthorst, *Incredulity of St Thomas*, *c.*1620 (Prado, Madrid).

Jesus on the Emmaus road
Two **Disciples**, one named Cleopas, encounter a stranger as they walk from **Jerusalem** to a nearby town, discussing the death of **Jesus** and the stories of his **Resurrection**. Approached by a stranger who asks about their conversation, they speak of their disappointment and bewilderment. Rebuking them for their lack of understanding, the stranger explains to them, using passages from the **Old Testament**, why it was necessary for the **Messiah** to suffer. Arriving at Emmaus, the Disciples persuade the stranger to eat with them. It is only when he takes bread, blesses and breaks it and gives it to them (actions which Jesus performed at the **Last Supper** and probably on other occasions) that they recognise him as Jesus.

Key concepts
The bewilderment of the Disciples; the need for the Messiah to suffer;
Jesus recognised as he breaks the bread.

Luke 24:13–31
[13] Now on that same day two of them were going to a village
called Emmaus, about seven miles from Jerusalem, [14] and talking
with each other about all these things that had happened. [15] While
they were talking and discussing, Jesus himself came near and
went with them, [16] but their eyes were kept from recognizing him.
[17] And he said to them, "What are you discussing with each other
while you walk along?" They stood still, looking sad. [18] Then one
of them, whose name was Cleopas, answered him, "Are you the
only stranger in Jerusalem who does not know the things that
have taken place there in these days?" [19] He asked them, "What
things?" They replied, "The things about Jesus of Nazareth, who
was a prophet mighty in deed and word before God and all the
people, [20] and how our chief priests and leaders handed him over
to be condemned to death and crucified him. [21] But we had hoped
that he was the one to redeem Israel. Yes, and besides all this, it
is now the third day since these things took place. [22] Moreover,
some women of our group astounded us. They were at the tomb
early this morning, [23] and when they did not find his body there,
they came back and told us that they had indeed seen a vision of
angels who said that he was alive. [24] Some of those who were
with us went to the tomb and found it just as the women had
said; but they did not see him." [25] Then he said to them, "Oh,
how foolish you are, and how slow of heart to believe all that the
prophets have declared! [26] Was it not necessary that the Messiah
should suffer these things and then enter into his glory?" [27] Then
beginning with Moses and all the prophets, he interpreted to
them the things about himself in all the scriptures.

[28] As they came near the village to which they were going, he
walked ahead as if he were going on. [29] But they urged him
strongly, saying, "Stay with us, because it is almost evening and

the day is now nearly over." So he went in to stay with them.
[30] When he was at the table with them, he took bread, blessed and broke it, and gave it to them. [31] Then their eyes were opened, and they recognised him; and he vanished from their sight.

Linked themes
A key **Old Testament** passage which was seen by the **Church** as foretelling the suffering of Jesus was Isaiah 53 (see Chapter 4).

Related works
Art: Caravaggio, *The Supper at Emmaus*, 1601–2 (National Gallery, London); Velázquez, *The Supper at Emmaus*, c.1620 (Metropolitan Museum of Art, New York); Rembrandt, *The Supper at Emmaus*, 1648 (Louvre, Paris).

Literature: Medieval *peregrinus* (pilgrim) plays; George Eliot, *Adam Bede*, 1859; T.S. Eliot, *The Waste Land*, V, 1922.

Jesus appears to the Disciples beside the Lake of Galilee
The **Disciples** have returned to **Galilee**, and, as when **Peter**, James and **John** were first called to follow **Jesus**, they are fishing. Once again, the resurrected Jesus is recognised only after some time, as the Disciples experience a repetition of the miraculous catch of fish (told in Luke 5:1–11) and Jesus once again shares a meal with them. Peter, who had three times denied Jesus after his arrest, is repeatedly questioned about his love for Jesus and instructed to demonstrate it by caring for Jesus' followers.

Key concepts
Jesus meets the Disciples by Galilee; miraculous catch of fish; Jesus is recognised; Jesus questions and recommissions Peter.

John 21:4–8, 12–17
[4] Just after daybreak, Jesus stood on the beach; but the disciples did not know that it was Jesus. [5] Jesus said to them, "Children,

you have no fish, have you?" They answered him, "No." [6] He said to them, "Cast the net to the right side of the boat, and you will find some." So they cast it, and now they were not able to haul it in because there were so many fish. [7] That disciple whom Jesus loved said to Peter, "It is the Lord!" When Simon Peter heard that it was the Lord, he put on some clothes, for he was naked, and jumped into the sea. [8] But the other disciples came in the boat, dragging the net full of fish, for they were not far from the land, only about a hundred yards off. [...]

[12] Jesus said to them, "Come and have breakfast." Now none of the disciples dared to ask him, "Who are you?" because they knew it was the Lord. [13] Jesus came and took the bread and gave it to them, and did the same with the fish. [14] This was now the third time that Jesus appeared to the disciples after he was raised from the dead.

[15] When they had finished breakfast, Jesus said to Simon Peter, "Simon son of John, do you love me more than these?" He said to him, "Yes, Lord; you know that I love you." Jesus said to him, "Feed my lambs." [16] A second time he said to him, "Simon son of John, do you love me?" He said to him, "Yes, Lord; you know that I love you." Jesus said to him, "Tend my sheep." [17] He said to him the third time, "Simon son of John, do you love me?" Peter felt hurt because he said to him the third time, "Do you love me?" And he said to him, "Lord, you know everything; you know that I love you." Jesus said to him, "Feed my sheep."

Linked themes

This story contains a number of echoes of incidents earlier in the ministry of Jesus such as his initial calling of the Disciples, the miraculous catch of fish, the miracle of the loaves and fishes, Peter's denial and the imagery of Jesus as the **Good Shepherd**.

Related works

Art: Konrad Witz, *The Miraculous Draught of Fishes*, 1443–4 (Musée d'Art et d'Histoire, Geneva); Raphael, *The Miraculous Draught of Fishes*, c. 1519 (The Vatican Museum, Rome).

Jesus commissions his Disciples

Each of the **Gospels** ends with an account of **Jesus** instructing his **Disciples** to go out to all nations, not just to the Jews, to tell others about him and continue his work. Here there are only eleven of Jesus' closest Disciples present because **Judas**, the twelfth, betrayed Jesus and then killed himself. The uncertainty of some is answered by Jesus' claim of authority given by God. Jesus promises to be with his followers to the end of time.

Matthew 28:16–20

[16] Now the eleven disciples went to Galilee, to the mountain to which Jesus had directed them. [17] When they saw him, they worshipped him; but some doubted. [18] And Jesus came and said to them, "All authority in heaven and on earth has been given to me. [19] Go therefore and make disciples of all nations, baptizing them in the name of the Father and of the Son and of the Holy Spirit, [20] and teaching them to obey everything that I have commanded you. And remember, I am with you always, to the end of the age."

Linked themes

The promise that Jesus would be with his Disciples has been seen by Christians as fulfilled in the gift of the **Holy Spirit** on the day of **Pentecost**. The end of the age refers to the concept of the **Second Coming** of **Christ**.

8 THE EARLY CHURCH

THE ASCENSION

THE BIRTH OF THE CHURCH (PENTECOST)

SAUL (ST PAUL) ON THE ROAD TO DAMASCUS

LETTERS TO THE CHURCHES

After the **Crucifixion** of Jesus, his followers went into hiding but the group was subsequently revitalised by the conviction that Jesus had risen from death. The Book of **Acts** shows the disciples receiving the **Holy Spirit** at **Pentecost** and declaring a message of forgiveness of sins for all who would repent, believe in Jesus and be **baptised**. Their numbers grew, despite opposition from the Jewish authorities. Those forced to leave **Jerusalem** by persecution travelled through Palestine and beyond, preaching as they went.

The conversion of **St Paul** was followed by the radical decision by **St Peter** to offer the message of **salvation** to non-Jews, and **Churches** containing both Jews and Gentiles sprang up in Asia Minor, Greece and Rome. Letters were written to these Churches to instruct members about belief and behaviour.

THE ASCENSION

In his final appearance to his **Disciples** before returning to **heaven**, **Jesus** repeats his promise that he will send his **Holy Spirit** to them and states that they will spread out from **Jerusalem** 'to the ends of the earth' to tell others about him.

Key concepts

Forty days after the **Resurrection**; the promise of the gift of the Holy Spirit; the command to bear witness throughout the world; Jesus returns to heaven; Jesus will come back 'in the same way'.

Acts 1:3–5, 8–11

[3] After his suffering he presented himself alive to them by many convincing proofs, appearing to them during forty days and speaking about the kingdom of God. [4] While staying with them, he ordered them not to leave Jerusalem, but to wait there for the promise of the Father. "This,' he said, "is what you have heard from me; [5] for John baptised with water, but you will be baptized with the Holy Spirit not many days from now." [...] [8]... you will receive power when the Holy Spirit has come upon you; and you will be my witnesses in Jerusalem, in all Judea and Samaria, and to the ends of the earth." [9] When he had said this, as they were watching, he was lifted up, and a cloud took him out of their sight. [10] While he was going and they were gazing up toward heaven, suddenly two men in white robes stood by them. [11] They said, "Men of Galilee, why do you stand looking up toward heaven? This Jesus, who has been taken up from you into heaven, will come in the same way as you saw him go into heaven."

Linked themes

The cloud (a common biblical symbol of God's presence) also occurs in the accounts of **Moses** receiving the **Ten Commandments** on Mount Sinai and the **Transfiguration** (see Chapter 6). The promise of the gift of the Spirit is fulfilled at **Pentecost**.

Related works

Art: Giotto, *The Ascension*, 1304–6 (Scrovegni Chapel, Padua); Rembrandt, *The Ascension*, 1636; Perugino, *The Ascension of Christ*, 1496 (Museum of Fine Arts, Lyons).

Literature: The Old English poem *Christ II*; Henry Vaughan (1622–95), 'Ascension'; William Blake, *Jerusalem*, 1804–18; Dylan Thomas, 'And Death Shall Have No Dominion', 1933.

Music: Edward Elgar, *The Apostles*, 1903.

THE BIRTH OF THE CHURCH (PENTECOST)

The coming of the **Holy Spirit** on the day of **Pentecost** is presented as a defining moment in the history of Christianity. The **Disciples** receive understanding of what **Jesus** has done through his death and **Resurrection**, together with the power to communicate this message to others, and become the nucleus of a new and rapidly growing community.

Key concepts

Fulfilment of promises of Jesus; wind and fire as symbols of the Holy Spirit; praising God in many languages; **Peter**'s sermon; fulfilment of **Old Testament prophecy**; the need for **repentance** and **baptism**; the community of the **Church** takes shape.

Acts 2:1–6, 12–17, 22–4, 37–47

When the day of Pentecost had come, they were all together in one place. [2] And suddenly from heaven there came a sound like the rush of a violent wind, and it filled the entire house where they were sitting. [3] Divided tongues, as of fire, appeared among them, and a tongue rested on each of them. [4] All of them were filled with the Holy Spirit and began to speak in other languages, as the Spirit gave them ability.

[5] Now there were devout Jews from every nation under heaven living in Jerusalem. [6] And at this sound the crowd gathered and was bewildered, because each one heard them speaking in the native language of each. [...]

[12] All were amazed and perplexed, saying to one another, "What does this mean?" [13] But others sneered and said, "They are filled with new wine."

¹⁴ But Peter, standing with the eleven, raised his voice and addressed them, "Men of Judea and all who live in Jerusalem, let this be known to you, and listen to what I say. ¹⁵ Indeed, these are not drunk, as you suppose, for it is only nine o'clock in the morning. ¹⁶ No, this is what was spoken through the prophet Joel:
¹⁷ 'In the last days it will be, God declares,
that I will pour out my Spirit upon all flesh,
and your sons and your daughters shall prophesy,
and your young men shall see visions,
and your old men shall dream dreams [...]
²² "You that are Israelites, listen to what I have to say: Jesus of Nazareth, a man attested to you by God with deeds of power, wonders, and signs that God did through him among you, as you yourselves know – ²³ this man, handed over to you according to the definite plan and foreknowledge of God, you crucified and killed by the hands of those outside the law. ²⁴ But God raised him up, having freed him from death, because it was impossible for him to be held in its power. [...]

³⁷ Now when they heard this, they were cut to the heart and said to Peter and to the other apostles, "Brothers, what should we do?" ³⁸ Peter said to them, "Repent, and be baptized every one of you in the name of Jesus Christ so that your sins may be forgiven; and you will receive the gift of the Holy Spirit. ³⁹ For the promise is for you, for your children, and for all who are far away, everyone whom the Lord our God calls to him." ⁴⁰ And he testified with many other arguments and exhorted them, saying, "Save yourselves from this corrupt generation." ⁴¹ So those who welcomed his message were baptized, and that day about three thousand persons were added. ⁴² They devoted themselves to the apostles' teaching and fellowship, to the breaking of bread and the prayers.

⁴³ Awe came upon everyone, because many wonders and signs were being done by the apostles. ⁴⁴ All who believed were together and had all things in common; ⁴⁵ they would sell their possessions and goods and distribute the proceeds to all, as any had need.

⁴⁶ Day by day, as they spent much time together in the temple, they broke bread at home and ate their food with glad and generous hearts, ⁴⁷ praising God and having the goodwill of all the people. And day by day the Lord added to their number those who were being saved.

Linked themes
In the Old Testament the Spirit of God appears in a number of contexts, guiding and empowering individuals to speak or act in particular circumstances. The Holy Spirit is promised to the Disciples by Jesus in John 14:16–17; John 20:22; Luke 24:49 and Acts 1:4–5. The prophecy referred to in verse 17 comes from Joel 2:28–32.

Related works
Art: Giotto, *Pentecost*, 1304–6 (Scrovegni Chapel, Padua); El Greco, *Pentecost*, 1596–1600 (Prado, Madrid); Restout, *Pentecost*, 1732 (Louvre, Paris).

Literature: The late fourteenth-century poem *Piers Plowman* (B-text, Bk 19) includes a Pentecost scene; *Pentecost* (Chester Mystery Cycle); William Shakespeare, *Winter's Tale*, IV, 4, 1610; Francis Bacon, *New Atlantis*, 1626; George Herbert, 'Whitsunday', 1633; Robert Herrick (1591–1674), 'The Country Life'; Nathaniel Hawthorne, *The Scarlet Letter*, 1850; T.S. Eliot, 'Little Gidding', 1944.

SAUL (ST PAUL) ON THE ROAD TO DAMASCUS

The conversion of Saul of Tarsus, a Jewish **Pharisee** and Roman citizen, from persecutor of Christians to outstanding leader within the **Church**, is one of the most significant incidents in the Book of **Acts**. Subsequently known as **Paul** (his Roman name), he went on to found Churches in Asia Minor and Greece and a number of the letters included in the **New Testament** bear his name.

Key concepts

Saul's antagonism; his encounter with **Jesus**; Saul blinded by light; Saul healed and baptised; he begins to preach.

Acts 9:1–6, 11–15, 17–18, 20

… Saul, still breathing threats and murder against the disciples of the Lord, went to the high priest [2] and asked him for letters to the synagogues at Damascus, so that if he found any who belonged to the Way, men or women, he might bring them bound to Jerusalem. [3] Now as he was going along and approaching Damascus, suddenly a light from heaven flashed around him. [4] He fell to the ground and heard a voice saying to him, "Saul, Saul, why do you persecute me?" [5] He asked, "Who are you, Lord?" The reply came, "I am Jesus, whom you are persecuting. [6] But get up and enter the city, and you will be told what you are to do." […]

[11] The Lord said to [Ananias], "Get up and go to the street called Straight, and at the house of Judas look for a man of Tarsus named Saul … [13] But Ananias answered, "Lord, I have heard from many about this man, how much evil he has done to your saints in Jerusalem; [14] and here he has authority from the chief priests to bind all who invoke your name." [15] But the Lord said to him, "Go, for he is an instrument whom I have chosen to bring my name before Gentiles and kings and before the people of Israel" […] [17] So Ananias went and entered the house. He laid his hands on Saul and said, "Brother Saul, the Lord Jesus, who appeared to you on your way here, has sent me so that you may regain your sight and be filled with the Holy Spirit." [18] And immediately something like scales fell from his eyes, and his sight was restored. Then he got up and was baptized […] [20] and immediately he began to proclaim Jesus in the synagogues, saying, "He is the Son of God."

Linked themes

Paul describes his conversion in Acts 22 and 26, Galatians 1:12–24 and Philippians 3:4–11. Paul's work in taking the message about **Jesus** to the **Gentiles** is referred to in Romans 1:1–16 and 15:14–21.

Related works

Art: Michelangelo, *The Conversion of St Paul*, 1542–5; Caravaggio, *The Conversion on the Way to Damascus*, 1600 (S. Luigi dei Francesi, Rome); Parmigianino, *The Conversion of St Paul* (Kunsthistorisches Museum, Vienna).

Literature: The Digby *Conversion of St Paul*, play; Isaak Walton, *Life of Dr John Donne*, 1640; John Bunyan, *Grace Abounding*, 1666; Daniel Defoe, *Robinson Crusoe*, 1719; Charles Dickens, *A Christmas Carol*, 1843–4; Flannery O'Connor, *Wise Blood*, 1949.

LETTERS TO THE CHURCHES

The Christian communities which sprang up across Asia Minor and Greece needed instruction and guidance in matters of belief, relationships within the Church and with the various cultural and social contexts in which they lived. Letters dealing with these topics, some of which bear the names of leaders such as **Paul** and **Peter**, make up a considerable part of the **New Testament**.

From death to life

In this passage, experiencing God's love and forgiveness is described in the starkest possible terms as making the difference between spiritual life and death. Entering into a relationship with God cannot be earned by good deeds; it can only come through faith (trusting God's offer of rescue from the consequences of living in disobedience) and is a gift, freely offered by God and therefore available to all.

Key concepts

Spiritual 'death' resulting from living in disobedience; God's loving initiative towards humankind; forgiveness and a new relationship with God are a gift and cannot be earned by human deeds.

Ephesians 2:1–10

You were dead through the trespasses and sins ² in which you once lived, following the course of this world, following the ruler of the power of the air, the spirit that is now at work among those who are disobedient. ³ All of us once lived among them in the passions of our flesh, following the desires of flesh and senses, and we were by nature children of wrath, like everyone else. ⁴ But God, who is rich in mercy, out of the great love with which he loved us ⁵ even when we were dead through our trespasses, made us alive together with Christ – by grace you have been saved – ⁶ and raised us up with him and seated us with him in the heavenly places in Christ Jesus, ⁷ so that in the ages to come he might show the immeasurable riches of his grace in kindness toward us in Christ Jesus. ⁸ For by grace you have been saved through faith, and this is not your own doing; it is the gift of God – ⁹ not the result of works, so that no one may boast. ¹⁰ For we are what he has made us, created in Christ Jesus for good works, which God prepared beforehand to be our way of life.

Linked themes

In the **Garden of Eden**, **Adam** and **Eve** are warned that to disobey God by eating the fruit of the **Tree of the Knowledge of Good and Evil** will bring death. God's initiative towards humankind and the **grace** which he offers to human beings is a theme found in other letters which bear Paul's name, such as Romans and Galatians.

Related works

Literature: John Donne (1572–1631), 'Elegy upon the Death of Mrs Boulstred', Holy Sonnets; George Herbert, 'Grace'; John Bunyan, *Pilgrim's Progress*, 1678; Christopher Smart (1722–71), *Jubilate Agno*; John Newton, 'Amazing Grace', 1773.

Christ's death for humankind

Here a link is made between the suffering which members of the **Early Church** are experiencing for their faith (possibly due to persecution by the Roman authorities) and the willing sacrifice which **Jesus Christ** made for the sake of others. By dying on the **Cross** to take the consequences of human **sin**, he has made it possible for human beings to be **forgiven** and return to a close relationship with God, like sheep which once wandered away but have returned to the shepherd.

Key concepts

Jesus Christ suffered willingly for the sake of others without retaliation; Jesus took the consequences of human sin; those who had been alienated from God are now reconciled to him.

1 Peter 2:21–5

[21] ... Christ also suffered for you, leaving you an example, so that you should follow in his steps.
[22] He committed no sin,
   and no deceit was found in his mouth.
[23] When he was abused, he did not return abuse; when he suffered, he did not threaten; but he entrusted himself to the one who judges justly. [24] He himself bore our sins in his body on the cross, so that, free from sins, we might live for righteousness; by his wounds you have been healed. [25] For you were going astray like sheep, but now you have returned to the shepherd and guardian of your souls.

Linked themes

This passage echoes the description of the 'Suffering Servant' in Isaiah 53 (see Chapter 4). The Crucifixion is described in the Gospels (see Chapter 7). The **Parable** of the Lost Sheep is told in Luke 15:1–7 (see Chapter 6).

Related works
Art: Bartolomé Esteban Murillo, *The Good Shepherd*, *c.*1660 (Getty Museum).

Music: Handel, *The Messiah* ('He was despised').

Love
This passage, though frequently used nowadays in the context of weddings, is in fact directed at the relationships within the whole Christian community at Corinth and designed to overcome competitiveness and conflict.'Love'(**AV** 'charity') here is an attitude, rather than an emotion, which is to motivate and direct all actions and words. This love, demonstrated in the life and death of **Jesus**, is of eternal value, outlasting all human gifts and achievements.

Key concepts
Gifts, understanding and actions are worthless unless motivated by love; the characteristics of true love; love lasts forever.

1 Corinthians 13
If I speak in the tongues of mortals and of angels, but do not have love, I am a noisy gong or a clanging cymbal. [2] And if I have prophetic powers, and understand all mysteries and all knowledge, and if I have all faith, so as to remove mountains, but do not have love, I am nothing. [3] If I give away all my possessions, and if I hand over my body so that I may boast, but do not have love, I gain nothing.

[4] Love is patient; love is kind; love is not envious or boastful or arrogant [5] or rude. It does not insist on its own way; it is not irritable or resentful; [6] it does not rejoice in wrongdoing, but rejoices in the truth. [7] It bears all things, believes all things, hopes all things, endures all things.

[8] Love never ends. But as for prophecies, they will come to an end; as for tongues, they will cease; as for knowledge, it will come to an end. [9] For we know only in part, and we prophesy only in

part; [10] but when the complete comes, the partial will come to an end. [11] When I was a child, I spoke like a child, I thought like a child, I reasoned like a child; when I became an adult, I put an end to childish ways. [12] For now we see in a mirror, dimly, but then we will see face to face. Now I know only in part; then I will know fully, even as I have been fully known. [13] And now faith, hope, and love abide, these three; and the greatest of these is love.

Linked themes

In John 13:34 Jesus tells his **Disciples**, 'I give you a new commandment, that you love one another. Just as I have loved you, you also should love one another.'

Related works

Literature: Edmund Spenser, Charissa in *The Faerie Queene*, 1590; Thomas Traherne (*c.* 1636–74), *Centuries of Meditation*; William Cowper, *Charity*, 1782; Geoffrey Hill, *The Mystery of the Charity of Charles Peguy*, 1983.

9 THE BOOK OF REVELATION (THE APOCALYPSE)

ST JOHN'S VISION OF CHRIST

THE LAMB OF GOD AND THE OPENING OF THE SCROLL

COSMIC CONFLICT BETWEEN GOOD AND EVIL

THE LAST JUDGEMENT

THE NEW HEAVEN AND THE NEW EARTH

The Book of **Revelation**, also known as the **Apocalypse**, has undergone many different interpretations over the centuries. Apocalyptic writings claimed to provide insights into a hidden spiritual world and Revelation uses dramatic language, vivid imagery and numerology to convey its message. The text is traditionally ascribed to **John the Evangelist**, writing from exile on the island of Patmos. It may date from the reign of the Roman emperor Nero (c.CE65) or that of Domitian (c.CE95).

The text offers a sequence of visions which interweave glimpses of God's power with dramatic scenes of conflict and horror on earth. The opening vision of **Jesus** speaking to the **Churches** of Asia Minor is followed by a glimpse of worship in **heaven**. Here Jesus is shown as the **Lamb** who has been slain (a reference to the **Crucifixion**). He alone is able to open a scroll with seven seals which will reveal the future.

A dramatic sequence of events follows, illustrating the cosmic battle between good and evil. A woman 'clothed with the sun' gives birth to a boy, the archangel **Michael** casts down the great dragon (**Satan**) and two fearsome beasts come forth to lead the world astray. In heaven, one hundred and forty-four thousand followers of the **Lamb** are shown in worship and the 'Son of Man' appears in the clouds to harvest the earth. Seven golden bowls empty plagues upon the earth and judgement is pronounced on Babylon, a symbol of corruption, and upon the Scarlet Woman or 'Whore of Babylon'. The wedding feast of the Lamb, symbolic of Christ's union with his 'bride' the Church, is proclaimed in heaven.

The book concludes with visions of the end of history and the beginning of a new era. At the Last Judgement the living and the dead stand before the throne of God as books revealing their lives are opened and their deeds disclosed. Those whose names are not written in the 'book of life' are condemned. A new heaven and a new earth appear, together with the New Jerusalem, a city free from pain and death, lit by the glory of God and the presence of the Lamb. An epilogue emphasises that Jesus Christ, the Alpha and Omega, 'the beginning and end', will return to earth and the need for all to be prepared for his coming.

ST JOHN'S VISION OF CHRIST

The opening vision of Jesus Christ portrays a figure 'like the Son of Man', using imagery drawn from the Old Testament. He stands amidst seven golden lampstands and dictates messages of warning and encouragement to the seven Churches in Asia Minor which the lampstands represent: Ephesus, Smyrna, Pergamum, Thyatira, Sardis, Philadelphia and Laodicea.

Key concepts
Vision of Jesus Christ as Son of Man; messages of warning and encouragement for the seven Churches.

Revelation 1:10–19
[10] I was in the spirit on the Lord's day, and I heard behind me a loud voice like a trumpet [11] saying, "Write in a book what you see and send it to the seven churches, to Ephesus, to Smyrna, to Pergamum, to Thyatira, to Sardis, to Philadelphia, and to Laodicea."

[12] Then I turned to see whose voice it was that spoke to me, and on turning I saw seven golden lampstands, [13] and in the midst of the lampstands I saw one like the Son of Man, clothed with a long robe and with a golden sash across his chest. [14] His head and his hair were white as white wool, white as snow; his eyes were like a flame of fire, [15] his feet were like burnished bronze, refined as in a furnace, and his voice was like the sound of many waters. [16] In his right hand he held seven stars, and from his mouth came a sharp, two-edged sword, and his face was like the sun shining with full force.

[17] When I saw him, I fell at his feet as though dead. But he placed his right hand on me, saying, "Do not be afraid; I am the first and the last, [18] and the living one. I was dead, and see, I am alive for ever and ever; and I have the keys of Death and of Hades. [19] Now write what you have seen, what is, and what is to take place after this.

Linked themes
The Son of Man is described in Daniel 7:9, 13–14 and Ezekiel 1.

Related works
Art: Albrecht Dürer, *St John's Vision of Christ and the Seven Candlesticks*, 1497–8 (Staatliche Kunsthalle, Karlsruhe).

Literature: William Blake, *Milton: Marriage of Heaven and Hell*, c.1793; D.H. Lawrence, *Apocalypse*, 1929.

THE LAMB OF GOD AND THE OPENING OF THE SCROLL

The narrator sees the throne of God surrounded by twenty-four **elders**, **four living creatures** (resembling a lion, an ox, a human being and an eagle) and Jesus, portrayed as the **Lamb** who has been sacrificed (a reference to his death on the **Cross**). He alone can open the **Scroll of the Seven Seals** which will reveal the future. The first four seals opened loose the **four horsemen of the apocalypse**: the white horse representing conquest; the red horse, war; the black horse, famine; and the pale horse signifying death. The fifth seal reveals the **martyrs**, the sixth a series of natural disasters. At the opening of the seventh seal there is silence in **heaven** before further horrors and plagues are unleashed.

Revelation 5:6–7, 11–12

[6] Then I saw between the throne and the four living creatures and among the elders a Lamb standing as if it had been slaughtered ... [7] He went and took the scroll from the right hand of the one who was seated on the throne [...]

[11] Then I looked, and I heard the voice of many angels surrounding the throne and the living creatures and the elders; they numbered myriads of myriads and thousands of thousands, [12] singing with full voice,

"Worthy is the Lamb that was slaughtered

to receive power and wealth and wisdom and might

and honour and glory and blessing!"

Linked themes

Jesus is described as 'the Lamb of God who takes away the sins of the world' by John the Baptist (see Chapter 5). The Lamb is a reference to the death of Jesus on the Cross.

Related works

Art: Jan van Eyck, *The Adoration of the Mystic Lamb*, 1432 (Cathedral of St Bavo, Ghent); Albrecht Dürer, *The Adoration of the Lamb and the Hymn of the Chosen*, 1497–8 (Staatliche Kunsthalle, Karlsruhe).

Literature: The fourteenth-century poem *Pearl*; Camus, *The Fall*, 1956.

Music: Handel, *The Messiah* ('Worthy is the Lamb'), 1741.

COSMIC CONFLICT BETWEEN GOOD AND EVIL

The woman clothed with the sun and war in heaven
The woman 'clothed with the sun' and menaced by the dragon has been interpreted as symbolising the **Church** threatened by **Satan**. The dragon is then cast down from heaven by the archangel **Michael**.

Revelation 12:1–9
A great portent appeared in heaven: a woman clothed with the sun, with the moon under her feet, and on her head a crown of twelve stars. [2] She was pregnant and was crying out in birth pangs, in the agony of giving birth. [3] Then another portent appeared in heaven: a great red dragon, with seven heads and ten horns, and seven diadems on his heads. [4] His tail swept down a third of the stars of heaven and threw them to the earth. Then the dragon stood before the woman who was about to bear a child, so that he might devour her child as soon as it was born. [5] And she gave birth to a son, a male child, who is to rule all the nations with a rod of iron. But her child was snatched away and taken to God and to his throne; [6] and the woman fled into the wilderness …

[7] And war broke out in heaven; Michael and his angels fought against the dragon. The dragon and his angels fought back, [8] but they were defeated, and there was no longer any place for them in heaven. [9] The great dragon was thrown down, that ancient serpent, who is called the Devil and Satan, the deceiver of the whole world – he was thrown down to the earth, and his angels were thrown down with him.

Linked themes
Isaiah 14:12–15 refers to the 'Day Star' (or **Lucifer**) falling from heaven. These references were influential in creating the concept of the **Fall of the Angels**.

Related works
Art: Albrecht Dürer, *The Woman Clothed with the Sun and the Seven-headed Dragon*, 1497–8 (Staatliche Kunsthalle, Karlsruhe); Albrecht Dürer, *St Michael Fighting the Dragon*, 1498 (Staatliche Kunsthalle, Karlsruhe); Luca Giordano, *The Fall of the Rebel Angels*, 1666 (Kunsthistorisches Museum, Vienna).

Literature: Edmund Spenser, *The Faerie Queene*, Bk 1, 1589.

The scarlet woman (the whore of Babylon)
The woman clothed in purple and scarlet bears the name of **Babylon**, a city which often represents corruption in the **Old Testament**. Here the reference to the martyrdom of Christians in verse 6 and the later identification of the woman in verse 18 as 'the city that rules over the kings of the earth' seem to indicate that she in fact represents Rome, then ruling much of the known world.

Key concepts
Enmity to God characterised by blasphemy, immorality and persecution of Christians.

Revelation 17:3–6
[3] ... I saw a woman sitting on a scarlet beast that was full of blasphemous names, and it had seven heads and ten horns. [4] The woman was clothed in purple and scarlet, and adorned with gold and jewels and pearls, holding in her hand a golden cup full of abominations and the impurities of her fornication; [5] and on her forehead was written a name, a mystery: "Babylon the great, mother of whores and of earth's abominations." [6] And I saw that the woman was drunk with the blood of the saints and the blood of the witnesses to Jesus.

Linked themes
In Chapter 18 the destruction of Babylon is announced.

Related works

Art: Albrecht Dürer, *The Whore of Babylon*, 1497–8 (Staatliche Kunsthalle, Karlsruhe); William Blake, *The Whore of Babylon*, 1809.

Literature: Lady Mede in *Piers Plowman* (Passus II); Duessa in Edmund Spenser, *The Faerie Queene*, Bk I, 1590; Thomas Dekker, *The Whore of Babylon*, 1605; Nathaniel Hawthorne, *The Scarlet Letter*, 1850; William Blake, *Four Zoas*, published 1893.

THE LAST JUDGEMENT

At the end of time all humankind are summoned to stand before the throne of God. Books detailing their lives are opened and all their deeds disclosed. Those whose names are not written in the '**Book of Life**' are condemned.

Key concepts
All called to account for their deeds; the **Book of Life**.

Revelation 20:11–15

[11] Then I saw a great white throne and the one who sat on it; the earth and the heaven fled from his presence, and no place was found for them. [12] And I saw the dead, great and small, standing before the throne, and books were opened. Also another book was opened, the book of life. And the dead were judged according to their works, as recorded in the books. [13] And the sea gave up the dead that were in it, Death and Hades gave up the dead that were in them, and all were judged according to what they had done. [14] Then Death and Hades were thrown into the lake of fire. This is the second death, the lake of fire; [15] and anyone whose name was not found written in the book of life was thrown into the lake of fire.

Linked themes
Jesus speaks of the **Last Judgement** in Mt 25:31–46.

Related works

Art: Giotto, *Last Judgement*, 1306 (Scrovegni Chapel, Padua); Jan/Hubert van Eyck, *The Last Judgement*, c.1420–5; Fra Angelico, *Last Judgement*, 1432–5 (Convent of St Mark, Florence); Petrus Christus, *Last Judgement*, 1452 (Staatliches Museum, Berlin); Rogier van der Weyden, *The Last Judgment*, 1446–52; Michelangelo, *The Last Judgement*, 1536–41; John Martin, *Last Judgement* (Tate Gallery, London).

Literature: The Old English poems *Judgement Day II, the Dream of the Rood, Christ III*; *Last Judgement* (York Mystery Cycle); Christopher Marlowe (1564–93), *Dr Faustus*; John Donne, 'A Hymn to God the Father'; George Herbert, 'Judgement'; Henry Vaughan, 'The Dawning'. The theme of judgement is parodied in Pope, *The Dunciad*, 1728; Byron, *Vision of Judgement*, 1821.

THE NEW HEAVEN AND THE NEW EARTH

A **new heaven and a new earth** are revealed, together with the **New Jerusalem**, a city free from pain and death, lit by the glory of God and the presence of the **Lamb**. An epilogue emphasises that **Jesus Christ**, the **Alpha and Omega**, 'the beginning and end', will return soon and the need to be prepared for his coming.

Key concepts

A new heaven and earth; God dwelling with his people; the beauty of the New Jerusalem; Jesus will return.

Revelation 21:1–4, 19–23

Then I saw a new heaven and a new earth; for the first heaven and the first earth had passed away, and the sea was no more. [2] And I saw the holy city, the new Jerusalem, coming down out of heaven from God, prepared as a bride adorned for her husband. [3] And I heard a loud voice from the throne saying,

"See, the home of God is among mortals.

He will dwell with them;

they will be his peoples,
and God himself will be with them;
[4] he will wipe every tear from their eyes.
Death will be no more;
mourning and crying and pain will be no more,
for the first things have passed away." [...]
[19] The foundations of the wall of the city are adorned with
every jewel; the first was jasper, the second sapphire, the third
agate, the fourth emerald, [20] the fifth onyx, the sixth carnelian,
the seventh chrysolite, the eighth beryl, the ninth topaz, the tenth
chrysoprase, the eleventh jacinth, the twelfth amethyst. [21] And
the twelve gates are twelve pearls, each of the gates is a single
pearl, and the street of the city is pure gold, transparent as glass.

[22] I saw no temple in the city, for its temple is the Lord God
the Almighty and the Lamb. [23] And the city has no need of sun
or moon to shine on it, for the glory of God is its light, and its
lamp is the Lamb.

Revelation 22:12–13

[12] "See, I am coming soon; my reward is with me, to repay
according to everyone's work. [13] I am the Alpha and Omega, the
first and the last, the beginning and the end."

Linked themes
The Letter to the Hebrews speaks of the city prepared by God for his
people (11:16) and the 'heavenly Jerusalem' (12:22).

Related works
Art: Norman Adams, *A New Heaven and Earth*, 1991.

Literature: Images of the Lamb and of the heavenly city are central to
the late fourteenth-century poem *Pearl*, and apocalyptic themes and
imagery strongly influence *Piers Plowman*. See also Francis Bacon, *New
Atlantis*, 1626; John Bunyan, *Pilgrim's Progress*, 1678; William Blake,
Jerusalem, 1804; Charlotte Brontë, *Jane Eyre*, Ch 38, 1847; Thomas Hardy,
Jude the Obscure, 1895.

THE BOOKS OF THE BIBLE

THE OLD TESTAMENT

Books of the Law (the Pentateuch or Books of Moses)
Genesis: **Creation. Adam** and **Eve.** The **Fall of Humankind. Cain** and **Abel. Tower of Babel. Noah** and the **Flood. The Patriarchs:** Abraham, Isaac, Jacob, Joseph.
Exodus: **Israel's** deliverance from Egypt and journey through the desert to the **Promised Land. Moses** and **Aaron.**
Leviticus: Religious laws.
Numbers: Life in the wilderness, the Twelve Spies, **Balaam** and his ass.
Deuteronomy: The **Ten Commandments.**

Historical Books
Joshua: Entry into the **Promised Land,** Rahab, Fall of Jericho.
Judges: **Samson** and **Delilah, Gideon.**
Ruth: Story of **Ruth,** Naomi and Boaz.
1 & 2 Samuel: **Hannah** and **Samuel, Saul, David.**
1 & 2 Kings: **Solomon, Elijah, Jezebel, Elisha.**
1 & 2 Chronicles: **David, Solomon.**
Ezra
Nehemiah
Esther

Poetry and wisdom
Psalms (Psalter).
Wisdom literature: **Job, Proverbs**, *Ecclesiastes*, **Song of Solomon** (Song of Songs, Canticles).

The Prophets
Isaiah, Jeremiah (with *Lamentations*) *Ezekiel*, **Daniel**, *Hosea, Joel, Amos, Obadiah,* **Jonah**, *Micah, Nahum, Habakkuk, Zephaniah, Haggai, Zechariah, Malachi.*

Old Testament Apocrypha
Books found in the **Septuagint** text, but not in the Hebrew: *1 & 2 Esdras, Tobit, Judith*, the rest of *Esther*, the *Wisdom of Solomon, Ecclesiasticus, Baruch*, the *Letter of Jeremiah*, the *Prayer of Azariah*, and the *Song of the Three Young Men, Susanna, Bel and the Dragon*, the *Prayer of Manesseh* and *1 & 2 Maccabees.*

THE NEW TESTAMENT

The Four Gospels
Matthew, Mark, Luke and *John* describe the life and ministry of **Jesus**.

The Acts of the Apostles
Acts: The birth and expansion of the **early church**.

Epistles
Letters to Christian communities and individuals which outline Christian belief and provide practical teaching. Romans, 1 & 2 Corinthians, Galatians, Ephesians, Philippians, Colossians, 1 & 2 Thessalonians, 1 & 2 Timothy, Titus, Philemon, Hebrews, James, 1 & 2 Peter, 1, 2 & 3 John, Jude.

Revelation (Apocalypse)

Vision of the **Son of Man**; Letters to the Seven Churches; Vision of **heaven** and the **Lamb**; Vision of the unfolding of history; the **Last Judgement**; A **new heaven and a new earth**; The **New Jerusalem**.

New Testament Apocrypha

There are various 'Gospels', 'Acts' and 'Epistles', falsely attributed to **New Testament** authors, which are not included in the New Testament **Canon**. The most influential include the *Gospel of Pseudo-Matthew*, the *Gospel of Thomas*, the *Book of James* (the *Protevangelion*) which purport to provide additional information about **Christ's** birth, infancy and teaching, and the *Gospel of Nicodemus* which describes the **Harrowing of Hell**.

TIMELINE

OLD TESTAMENT

Estimated date	Significant events	Characters	Old Testament books recording these events
Prehistory	**Creation**, the **Garden of Eden**, the **Fall**	**Adam, Eve, Cain, Abel,**	**Genesis**
1900BCE	The Call of **Abraham**	**Abraham, Sarah**	Genesis
1800BCE	The **Sacrifice of Isaac**	**Isaac**	Genesis
1750BCE		**Jacob, Esau**	Genesis
1700BCE		**Joseph**	Genesis
1700–1300BCE	**Israel** in Egypt		Genesis
1300BCE	Birth of **Moses**, the **Burning Bush**	Moses	**Exodus**
1270BCE	The **Exodus**	Moses	Exodus
1230BCE	Entering the **Promised Land**	Joshua	**Leviticus, Numbers, Deuteronomy, Joshua**
1200–1100BCE		**Gideon, Samson, Ruth**	Judges, **Ruth**

continued…

OLD TESTAMENT, continued

Estimated date	Significant events	Characters	Old Testament books recording these events
1050–1000BCE		**Samuel, Saul, David**	1 & 2 Samuel
1000–800BCE		**David, Solomon, Elijah, Elisha**	1 Kings, 1 Chronicles, **Psalms, Proverbs**
740–700BCE		**Isaiah**	2 Kings, 2 Chronicles, Isaiah
620–580BCE		**Jeremiah**	2 Kings, 2 Chronicles, Jeremiah
597–539BCE	**Exile** in **Babylon**	**Daniel** Ezekiel	2 Kings, 2 Chronicles, Daniel, Ezekiel
539–331BCE	Palestine under Persian rule, **Temple** and walls of **Jerusalem** rebuilt	Ezra, Nehemiah	Ezra, Nehemiah, **Esther**

NEW TESTAMENT

Estimated date	Significant events	Characters	New Testament books recording these events
4BCE	Birth of **Jesus**	**Mary, Joseph,** Jesus	**Matthew, Luke**
2BCE	Visit of the **Magi**	Jesus, Magi, **Herod**	Matthew
CE27	**Baptism** of Jesus	Jesus, **John the Baptist**	Matthew, **Mark,** Luke, **John**
CE27–30	Ministry of Jesus	Jesus, his **Disciples**	Matthew, Mark, Luke, John
CE30	Death and **Resurrection** of Jesus, **Ascension, Pentecost,** growth of **Early Church**	Jesus, **Judas, Pontius Pilate, Peter, Paul**	Matthew, Mark, Luke, John, **Acts**
CE33	Conversion of **Paul**	Paul	Acts
CE46–65	Paul's missionary journeys, growth of **Early Church**	Paul	Acts, Romans, 1 & 2 Corinthians, Galatians, Ephesians, Philippians, Colossians, 1 & 2 Thessalonians, 1 & 2 Timothy, Titus, Philemon
CE66–70	Jewish revolt against Rome, **Jerusalem** destroyed		
CE70–100	Growth of Early Church	John	Hebrews, James, 1 & 2 Peter, 1, 2 & 3 John, Jude, **Revelation**

A–Z OF PEOPLE, PLACES AND TERMS

Aaron. High priest. Brother of **Moses**, who accompanied him during the **Exodus**. Allowed the **Israelites** to commit idolatry by worshipping a golden calf.

Abel. Second son of **Adam** and **Eve**, murdered by his brother **Cain**.

Abraham. See **Abram**.

Abram, later called **Abraham**. First of the **patriarchs** of **Israel** and father of **Ishmael** and **Isaac**. Called by God to leave his home and go in search of a land which God would show him.

Absalom. Handsome third son of King **David** who rebelled against his father. Was murdered by one of David's followers after his long hair became entangled in the branches of a tree.

Active life. A way of life which manifests holiness through involvement in the everyday world. Leah (**OT**) and **Martha** (**NT**) are seen as representing the active life. See **Contemplative life**.

Adam. According to the Book of **Genesis**, Adam was the first human being. Chose to eat the forbidden fruit and was, as a result, banished with **Eve** from the **Garden of Eden**. See **Fall of Humankind**.

Advent. The liturgical season from the fourth Sunday before **Christmas** Day until Christmas Eve. Preparation for the coming of **Jesus Christ** as a baby at Christmas and for his **Second Coming** as Judge at the end of the world. Marks the beginning of the **Church** year.

Agnus Dei. (Latin, **Lamb of God**.)

Allegory. A story offering, or susceptible to, multiple levels of inter-pretation.

Alpha **and** *Omega*. First and last letters of the Greek alphabet. Used in the Book of **Revelation** for God the Father and **Christ**. Signifies God's presence at **Creation** and at the end of time.

Ambrose, St (*c*.339–97), **Bishop** of Milan. Famous for sermons. Other writings include commentaries, hymns and letters.

Ancient of Days. Term used to describe God as Judge (reflecting the association of wisdom with age in Jewish thought) in the Book of **Daniel** (7:9, 13, 22). God's clothing is described as being 'white as snow' and his hair as being 'like pure wool'. It is from this description that Christian art has taken its general approach to depicting the first person of the **Trinity**.

Andrew, St, Apostle. Brother of **St Peter** and one of the **twelve Apostles**. Later traditions held that he visited Scythia and was **martyred** in Achaia.

Angel. Greek *angelos*, 'messenger'. Heavenly messenger traditionally portrayed as having a winged human form. See **Gabriel, Michael**.

Anglo-Saxon. Term used to describe the Germanic tribes who settled in England from the mid fifth century onwards; also used of their history, culture and language until the Norman Conquest in 1066.

Anna. Prophetess who rejoiced to see **Jesus** at the **Presentation in the Temple**.

Anne, St. The parents of the **Virgin Mary** are not mentioned in the **canonical gospels** but the **apocryphal** *Protevangelium* of James states that they were called Joachim and Anne and offers a detailed account of the Virgin's birth and early life.

Annunciation. The **Angel Gabriel's** announcement to the **Virgin Mary** that she is to be the mother of **Jesus** (Lk 1:26–38).

Antetype. Earlier form or symbol. See **Type**.

Anti-Christ. Chief enemy of **Christ** (See 1 and 2 Jn). Figure expected to emerge before the end of the world (2 Thess 2:3–10 and Rev 13).

Antitype. That which a **type** represents or **prefigures**.

Apocalypse. A **revelation** or unveiling of future events or the **heavenly** world, e.g. **Daniel (Old Testament)** and **Revelation (New Testament)**.

Apocrypha (Greek 'the hidden' [things]). **Old Testament Apocrypha**: books found in the **Septuagint** text but not in the Hebrew: 1 & 2 Esdras, Tobit, Judith, the Rest of **Esther**, the Wisdom of Solomon, Ecclesiasticus, Baruch, the Letter of Jeremiah, the Prayer of Azariah, the Song of the Three Young Men, Susanna, Bel and the Dragon, the Prayer of Manasseh and I & 2 Maccabees. Included in the **Vulgate** but not in all subsequent **Bibles**. See **Canon of Scripture. New Testament Apocrypha**: various '**Gospels**', 'Acts' and 'Epistles', incorrectly attributed to New Testament authors, which have been excluded from the New Testament **Canon**. The most influential include the *Gospel of Pseudo-Matthew*, the *Gospel of Thomas*, the *Book of James* (*Protevangelium*) which claim to provide additional information about **Christ**'s birth and infancy and the *Gospel of Nicodemus* which describes the **Harrowing of Hell**.

Apostle. One of the group of **twelve** originally chosen by **Christ** and commissioned to preach the **Gospel** to the nations. In Acts 1, Matthias was chosen to replace **Judas Iscariot. St Paul** also claimed the status of an Apostle.

Ark. The ship built by **Noah** at God's instruction in which he and his family are saved from the **Flood**.

Ark of the Covenant. Portable shrine containing the **Tablets of the Law** and symbolising the presence of God with the people of **Israel**. Kept first in the Tabernacle (tent) which the **Israelites** carried with them on their journey through the wilderness, and later in the **Temple**.

*Arma Christi***.** See **Instruments of the Passion**.

Ascension. The withdrawal of **Christ** into **heaven** after the **Resurrection** (Acts 1:6–11) celebrated on the fortieth day after **Easter**.

Athanasius, St, Father of the Church. Drew up the final list of books which form the **New Testament Canon**.

Atonement. The reconciliation of humankind to God through the death of **Christ**.

Augustine, St, of Hippo (CE354–430). **Bishop** in North Africa. Author of many influential theological works including *On Christian Doctrine*, *Confessions* and *City of God*.

Authorised Version (**AV**). See *King James Version* (**KJV**).

Ave Maria (**Hail Mary**). 'Hail (Mary) full of **grace**, the Lord is with thee, blessed art thou amongst women and blessed is the fruit of thy womb **Jesus**'. A prayer based on Lk 1:28, 42.

Baal. Term used in the **OT** for a local or pagan deity other than the God of **Israel**. (See Chapter 4.)

Babel. Hebrew name for **Babylon**.

Babylon. City on the river Euphrates, capital of Babylonia and traditional enemy of the Israelites, to which they were eventually exiled. Often carries connotations of pride, sinfulness and oppression.

Balaam. **Old Testament** character known because his donkey was able to see an angel sent from God to block his path whereas Balaam was not (Num 22:1–35).

Baptism. The **Sacrament** of admission into the Christian **Church**. The candidate is immersed in or sprinkled with water in the name of the **Trinity**.

Bathsheba. Wife of Uriah the Hittite with whom King **David** commits adultery before murdering her husband and taking her as his own wife. Mother of **Solomon**.

Beatitudes (Latin *Beatus*, 'blessed'). Blessings promised by **Christ** in Mt 5:3–11.

Benedictus (Latin 'Blessed'). Song of thanksgiving and **prophecy** uttered by **Zechariah** after the birth of his son **John the Baptist** (Lk 1:68–79).

Bernard, St, of Clairvaux (1090–1153). **Abbot** of Clairvaux. Writings show a strong mystical character and emphasis on God's love and **grace**.

Bethlehem. A town south of **Jerusalem**. Birthplace of **David** and **Jesus**.

Bible (Greek *Biblia*, books). The **Christian** Bible comprises the **Old Testament scriptures** inherited from Judaism, together with the **New Testament**, drawn from writings produced from *c.*CE40–125.

Biblia Pauperum (Latin 'Bible of the poor'). A series of captioned miniatures illustrating the parallels between the **Old Testament** and **New Testament**.

Bishop (Greek *episkopos,* 'overseer'). Leader of the Christian community within a limited geographical area.

Bishop's Bible. English language version of the **Bible** authorised by the **Bishops** of the Church of England and published in 1568.

Book of Acts. Also known as the Acts of the Apostles. Recounts the growth of the **Early Church in Jerusalem.**

Book of Enoch. An **apocryphal** collection of **revelations** on topics such as the origin of evil, the **Fall of the Angels, Heaven** and **Hell.** Originally written in Hebrew during the two centuries before the birth of **Jesus Christ.**

Book of James. See *Protevangelium.*

Book of Life. The book, referred to in the Book of **Revelation,** as containing the details of each person's earthly life which, at the **Last Judgement,** will be referred to in the final judgement of each individual.

Book of Revelation. See **Revelation.**

Bride. See **Bride of Christ.**

Bride of Christ. Image used of the **Church** in the Book of **Revelation.**

Burning bush. Scene in which **Moses** encounters God speaking from a bush which burns but is not consumed by the flames (Ex 3:2).

Cain. Son of **Adam** and **Eve** who failed to win God's approval and became the first murderer when he killed his brother **Abel** in a jealous rage and was condemned to exile (Gen 4).

Calvary (Latin *Calvaria,* Hebrew *Golgotha,* both meaning skull). Place of **Christ's** execution just outside **Jerusalem.**

Canaan. Country described to **Moses** as a land 'flowing with milk and honey' (Ex 3:7–8) and settled by the **Israelites** after the **Exodus.**

Candlemas. Festival to mark the **purification of the Virgin Mary** and **Christ's presentation in the Temple** (Lk 2:22–38) celebrated on

2 February. Candles carried in procession to symbolise Christ, 'a light for **revelation** to the **Gentiles**' (Lk 2:32).

Canon of scripture (Greek *kanon*, measuring rod, rule). The list of books which were accepted as authoritative by the **Christian Church**. See *Apocrypha*.

Canonical. Included in **canon of scripture**, authoritative.

Canticles. Biblical texts sung in worship. See *Magnificat, Nunc Dimittis, Benedictus, Venite*.

Christ (Greek *Christos*, translation of the Hebrew '**Messiah**', the anointed one of Jewish **prophecy**). Title (eventually used as name) given to **Jesus**, as fulfilling this **prophecy**.

Christmas. Celebration of the birth of **Christ** on 25 December. Festivities last for 12 days.

Church. Term for a worshipping community of Christians.

Circumcision. Removal of the foreskin of a male infant at eight days old, practised by Jews as a sign of the **covenant** established by God with **Abraham** (Gen 17:9–12).

Consecrate. To make holy by a decision or act of dedication to God.

Contemplative life. A way of life which achieves or demonstrates holiness through prayer, meditation and withdrawal from the world. Rachel (OT) and **Mary of Bethany** are seen as **types** of the contemplative life. See **Active life**.

Contrition. Form of inner **repentance**, genuine sorrow for **sin**.

Corpus Christi (Latin, the 'body of Christ'). Feast celebrated sixty days after **Easter** to mark the institution of the **Eucharist**.

Covenant. A binding agreement or treaty. Used in the **Bible** of God's relationship with his people. Important covenants in the **Old Testament** include those made with **Noah** and **Abraham**. At the **Last Supper**, **Jesus** speaks of a 'new covenant' which will come into effect through his death.

Coverdale Bible. First complete Bible printed in English, produced by Miles Coverdale, assistant to **Tyndale**, in 1535.

Creation. Creation can refer both to the process by which the universe was made and to the created order which emerged. Christian **doctrine**, based on the first two chapters of the Book of **Genesis** and amplified by the theologians, stated that God created 'heaven and earth' *ex nihilo*, out of nothing.

Creed (Latin *credo*, 'I believe'). A brief summary of **Christian** belief. Three creeds are used in Western **liturgy**: the short Apostles' Creed; the Nicene Creed, which originated at the Council of Constantinople in 381; and the longer Athanasian Creed, which probably dates from *c*.500.

Cross. Instrument of torture and execution used in the Roman Empire. The means by which **Christ** was put to death and therefore the primary symbol of the **Christian faith**, representing the means by which he is believed to have won **forgiveness** for humankind. The Cross may be represented as Tau-shaped (like a capital T), with a shorter cross-bar or with a circle enclosing the upper intersection (Celtic). In medieval art a cross made of living branches signifies the Tree of Life.

Crossing of the Red Sea. The waters of the Red Sea parted miraculously during the Exodus to let the **Israelites** cross, while the pursuing Egyptian army were later drowned (Ex 14:1–30).

Crucifixion. Execution by nailing or binding to a cross. Used frequently in Roman Empire. The crucifixion of **Jesus**, recorded in all four **Gospels**, is believed by Christians to have made **salvation** available to humankind.

Daniel. **Apocalyptic** prophet and hero of **Israel** who interpreted dreams. Daniel survived imprisonment in a den of lions for refusing to give up praying to God. Also the hero of the **Apocryphal** books *Susanna and the Elders* and *Bel and the Dragon*.

David. The second king of **Israel**, successor to **Saul**. Slayer of **Goliath**; penitent following adultery with **Bathsheba**; writer of **Psalms**.

Day of Judgement. See **Last Judgement**.

Deborah. A judge of Israel at the time of the Judges.

Delilah. Wife of **Samson** who betrayed him to the **Philistines**.

Demon. Evil spiritual force opposing God and seeking to lead human beings away from him.

Deposition. The taking down of **Christ's** dead body from the **cross** by **Joseph of Arimathea** (and, in **John's Gospel**, with **Nicodemus**).

Deuteronomy. Fifth book of the **Old Testament.** Contains the **Ten Commandments.**

Devil (Greek *diabolos*, accuser). Chief of the **fallen angels.**

Disciple. New Testament term meaning learner or follower and used of the **Twelve Apostles** as well as of the followers of **Jesus** in general. See **Apostle.**

Divine inspiration. The idea that the writers of the **Bible** were directly inspired by God.

Doctrine. Teaching about an aspect of Christian belief.

Douay-Rheims Bible. Translation of the **Vulgate Bible.** The **New Testament** was published at Rheims in 1578, the **Old Testament** at Douai in 1582.

Early Church. Term used for the first few centuries of the growth of the Christian **Church,** first in **Jerusalem** and then across the Roman Empire.

Easter Sunday. Day on which the **Resurrection** of **Christ** is celebrated.

Eden. See **Garden of Eden.**

Elder. (1) The heads of families in **Israelite** society. (2) Leaders of congregations in the **Early Church.** (3) The twenty-four crowned figures shown seated on thrones in the Book of **Revelation.** These figures may together symbolise the **Twelve Tribes of Israel** and the **Church.**

Elijah. Important **Old Testament prophet.** Spoke out against the worship of heathen gods in **Israel** and was persecuted by King Ahab and his wife Jezebel. Confronted the priests of the pagan god **Baal** in a contest on Mount Carmel. Said to have been taken up to **heaven** in a chariot of fire (2 Kings 2:11–12).

Elisha. OT Prophet and successor to **Elijah.**

Elizabeth. The mother of **John the Baptist** and cousin of the **Virgin Mary.**

Emmanuel (Hebrew 'God with us'). Title used of **Jesus** in Mt 1:23, referring to a **prophecy** of **Isaiah** (Isa 7:14).

Entry into Jerusalem. Christ is described in the **Gospels** as riding into **Jerusalem** on an ass, greeted by crowds who placed palm branches on the ground in front of him. See also **Palm Sunday**.

Epiphany. 6 January. In the Western Church this festival celebrates the manifestation (Greek *epiphaneia*) of Jesus to the **Magi** and hence to the **Gentiles**.

Epistle (Greek *epistole*). (1) Letter written to a **Church** or individual in the **New Testament**. (2) Passage, usually from the New Testament letters but sometimes from the **Book of Acts** or the **Old Testament**, read as part of **Christian** worship.

Esther. Hebrew queen who saves her people from persecution.

Eternal life. A new quality of life, received by those who accept the forgiveness and relationship offered by Jesus, which begins in this life and is fulfilled after death in the presence of God.

Eucharist (Greek *eukharistia*, thanksgiving). The central act of the **Church's** worship in which bread and wine are **consecrated** and consumed. See Mt 26:26–8, Mk 14:22–4, Lk 22:17–20, 1 Cor 11:23–5. Also known as **Holy Communion**, the Lord's Supper and the **Mass**.

Evangelist. Used of the four **Gospel** writers: **Matthew, Mark, Luke** and **John**.

Eve. The first woman, created by God as **Adam's** companion. Persuaded by the serpent to use her **free will** to choose to eat the forbidden fruit and, as a result, banished with Adam from the **Garden of Eden**.

Exegesis. A critical interpretation of a text, especially biblical.

Exile. Periods when the **Israelites** were compelled to leave their land. (See Chapter 2.)

Exodus. (1) The departure of the **Israelites** from Egypt and their forty-year journey through the wilderness towards Canaan. (2) Second book of the **Old Testament**.

Fall of Humankind. Adam and **Eve's** act of disobedience in the **Garden of Eden** (Gen 2 and 3) which led to estrangement from God for them and their descendants.

Fall of the Angels. According to an account pieced together by some of the **Fathers of the Church** from scattered biblical allusions, a number of **angels** had rebelled against God. Their leader, **Lucifer** ('light bearer'), had sought to claim equality with God (Isa 14:12–15) and together with his followers had been cast out of **heaven** (Rev 12:7–9) to dwell henceforth in **Hell**. Lucifer became **Satan** (Hebrew *satan*, adversary), the **Devil**, and his followers became **demons** seeking constantly to alienate humankind from God, thus turning the world into a spiritual battlefield.

Fast. Period of abstinence from food.

Fathers of the Church. Christian leaders and thinkers, living mostly between the end of the first century and the eighth century, whose writings (including biblical commentaries, sermons, histories, poetry and biography) were considered to carry particular authority. Key figures included **St Ambrose** (b.340), **Bishop** of Milan (374–397), **St Jerome** (330/347–420) and **St Augustine** (b.354), **Bishop** of Hippo in North Africa (396–430). The term can also refer more generally to the many churchmen who were deemed to be authoritative commentators on **doctrinal**, theological, **liturgical** and biblical matters between the first and twelfth centuries.

Flight into Egypt. Journey made by **Joseph**, the **Virgin Mary** and **Jesus**, from **Bethlehem** to Egypt, following a warning in a dream that King **Herod** wished to kill Jesus.

Flood. In **Genesis**, God destroys the world with a flood because of the wickedness of humankind, saving only **Noah** in his **ark** (Gen 6:5–9:29).

Forgiveness. Reconciliation with God made possible by his forgiveness of the **sins** of humankind through his **grace**. See **Cross**.

Four living creatures. Also known as tetramorphs (Greek 'four forms'). The **prophet** Ezekiel describes four living creatures, each with four wings and four faces: man, lion, ox and eagle (Ezek 1:5–10). The Book of **Revelation** depicts four living creatures who surround the throne of God: one like a lion, one like an ox, the third has the face of a man, the fourth is like an eagle. As individual figures these creatures became the symbols for the four **Evangelists: Matthew** (man), **Mark** (lion), **Luke** (ox), **John** (eagle).

Four horsemen of the Apocalypse. Four horses representing conquest, war, famine and death loosed on the world in Rev 6:1–8.

Free will. The idea that God gave to humankind the free will to choose between good and evil, as exercised by Adam and Eve at the **Fall of humankind.**

Gabriel. The archangel who told **Mary** at the **Annunciation** that she would conceive **Jesus.**

Galilee. Lake and area in northern **Israel**, home of **Jesus** and many of his **Disciples**, and scene of much of his **ministry.**

Garden of Eden. Original idyllic home of humankind at the **creation**, thought to be located in Mesopotamia.

Garden of Gethsemane. Garden outside Jerusalem where **Jesus** prayed and was arrested.

Genesis (Book of Genesis). First book of the **Old Testament.**

Geneva Bible. English-language Bible published in Geneva in 1560 by Protestant exiles.

Gentiles. Biblical name given to non-Jews.

Gideon. One of the Judges of **Israel** (Judg 6–9).

Gloria in Excelsis (Latin 'Glory be to God on high'). Opening words of **Christian** hymn used in worship. Modelled on the **Psalms**, it incorporates words from the message of the **angels** at the **Annunciation** to the shepherds in Lk 2:14.

Glossa Ordinaria. The standard medieval commentary on the **Bible**, composed chiefly of extracts from the **Fathers.**

Golgotha. See **Calvary.**

Goliath. A **Philistine** giant who threatened the **Israelite** army but was killed by **David** with a slingshot.

Good Friday. Day commemorating the **Crucifixion** of **Christ.**

Good Samaritan. One of the most famous parables of **Jesus** (Lk 10:25–37). (See Chapter 6.)

Good Shepherd. Title used by Jesus of himself (Jn 10:14). (See Chapter 6.)

Gospel (Greek *evangelion*, Old English *godspel*, good news). (1) The central message of the **Christian faith** concerning **salvation**. (2) Title given to the four **New Testament** books which describe the life of **Christ**, i.e. **Matthew, Mark, Luke** and **John**. (3) A reading taken from one of the four **Gospels** used in the **Eucharist/Holy Communion/Mass**.

Gospel of Bartholomew. An **apocryphal** text whose existence was known to **Jerome** and which may be the same as the manuscript called 'Questions of Bartholomew'. Contains material on the **Fall of the Angels** and the **Harrowing of Hell**.

Gospel of Nicodemus. An **apocryphal** text of the fifth to sixth centuries containing the *Acts of Pilate* and the highly influential *Descent into Hell* which describes the **Harrowing of Hell**.

Gospel of Pseudo-Matthew. **Apocryphal** infancy gospel which draws on the *Protevangelium* of James and *Gospel of Thomas*. Contains material about the birth of **Jesus** including the earliest extant reference to the presence of the ox and ass.

Gospel of Thomas. Second-century **apocryphal** gospel which contains material claiming to describe the childhood of **Jesus**.

Grace. The undeserved favour of God, whereby individuals may receive **salvation** and grow spiritually.

Hades. A Greek word for the world of the dead, where they await final judgement.

Hail Mary. See *Ave Maria*.

Hannah. Mother of **Samuel** in one of the Bible's several miraculous birth stories (1 Sam 1–2).

Harrowing of Hell. The belief, based on an interpretation of 1 Pet 3:18–20, that while **Christ's** body rested in the tomb his spirit descended into **Hell** to free the souls of the **righteous**.

Heaven. The dwelling place of God and the **angels** and eventually all those redeemed by **Christ**.

Hell. The abode of devils and the place to which the unrepentant will pass after the **Last Judgement**.

Heresy. Belief considered contrary to the generally accepted teaching of the **Church.**

Herod Antipas. Son of **Herod the Great** and ruler of **Galilee.** Responsible for the execution of **John the Baptist.** Also questioned **Jesus** after his arrest (Lk 23:6–12).

Herod the Great. King of the Jews 37–34BCE. Ruthless ruler who is described in **Matthew's Gospel** as threatened by news of the birth of **Jesus** and responded by ordering the killing of all male infants under the age of two years.

Hexateuch. The first six books of the **Old Testament: Genesis, Exodus,** Leviticus, Numbers, Deuteronomy and Joshua, which were sometimes contained in a separate volume.

Holy Communion. See **Eucharist.**

Holy Saturday. The day between **Good Friday** and **Easter Sunday.** A vigil was kept in preparation for **Easter** day.

Holy Spirit (Holy Ghost). Third Person of the **Trinity.**

Holy Week. Week before **Easter Sunday.**

Hortus conclusus (Latin, 'enclosed garden'). Taken from Song 4:12: 'My sister, my spouse, is a garden enclosed.' Used by medieval theologians and artists as a symbol of the purity of the **Virgin Mary.**

Incarnation. Belief that, in the person of **Jesus Christ**, God became a human being and willingly offered himself to die on the **Cross** in order to save men and women from their **sins.**

Instruments of the Passion (Latin *Arma Christi*). The objects used in the arrest, trials and **Crucifixion** of **Christ**. They include the cock which crowed when **Peter** denied Christ, the scourge (whip) and pillar or column used during Christ's flogging, the crown of thorns, the rope, nails, hammer, sponge, lance, pincers, dice used by the soldiers to play for Christ's robe and the thirty pieces of silver paid to **Judas Iscariot.**

Isaac. Son of **Abraham** and **Sarah**, husband of Rebekah and father of Esau and **Jacob**.

Isaiah. **Prophet** and author of at least part of the book of **prophecy** that bears his name, which predicts the coming of a servant king in the line of **David** who came to be thought of as **Messiah**. Many Christians believe that these prophecies are fulfilled in **Jesus**.

Ishmael. Son of **Abraham** by Hagar, his wife's Egyptian slave. Traditionally regarded as the father of the Arab peoples.

Israel. (1) The name given by God to **Jacob**, who became the father of the **Twelve Tribes of Israel** and gave his name to (2) the kingdom settled by those tribes. At the division of the **Israelites** in two after the death of **Solomon** in 922BCE, the northern kingdom was called **Israel**.

Israelites. Descendants of **Israel** (**Jacob**) and occupants of **Israel**.

Jacob. Son of **Isaac** and Rebekah and brother of **Esau**, renamed **Israel** or 'one who fights with God' in Gen 32:24–30.

James, St, 'the Great' (*Santiago De Compostela*), **Apostle**. Son of Zebedee, brother of **St John**. Witnessed **Transfiguration of Christ**. First of the **Twelve** to be **martyred** (CE44). Seventh-century tradition claimed he visited Spain.

James, St, 'The Lord's Brother'. See Mk 6:3; Gal 1:19. Shared leadership of the **Early Church** in **Jerusalem** with **St Peter**. The apocryphal infancy **Gospel** the *Book of James* (also known as the *Protevangelium*) was attributed to him.

Jehovah. Archaic anglicised form of the OT abbreviation YHWH which was used to indicate the personal name of God, now usually translated as LORD.

Jerome, St. (CE330/347–420). Biblical scholar. Main translator of the **Vulgate**.

Jerusalem. City captured and made into the capital city of Israel by King David. Site of the Temple built by Solomon, and of the Crucifixion and Resurrection of Jesus, it is a holy city for Jews, Christians and Muslims.

Jesse. Father of King **David**.

Jesse Tree. An allegorical interpretation of the genealogy of **Christ**, very popular in Western medieval art.

Jesus (Greek form of Hebrew 'Joshua' meaning '**Yahweh** [God] is **salvation**'). Also given the title **Christ**, meaning 'anointed one' or **Messiah**. His life is recorded mainly in the four **Gospels** although he is also mentioned by the Jewish historian Josephus (c.CE37–c.100) and the Roman historian Tacitus (c.CE110).

Job. Main character of the Book of Job and an example of patient suffering.

John The Baptist, St, son of **Zechariah** and **Elizabeth** and cousin of the **Virgin Mary**. Appeared c.CE27 by the banks of the Jordan preaching **repentance**. Baptised **Jesus**. Later beheaded by **Herod Antipas** at the instigation of **Salome** (Mt 14:1–12).

John, St, Evangelist, brother of **St James the Great**. One of the three **Apostles** closest to **Christ**. Tradition states that he wrote the Fourth **Gospel**, the three Epistles of John and possibly the Book of **Revelation**. Often portrayed standing with the **Virgin Mary** at the foot of the **Cross**. Symbol an eagle.

Jonah, Old Testament prophet. While trying to escape God's command to preach to the people of Ninevah, Jonah was swallowed by a large fish and remained in its stomach for three days. Jonah's experience was later interpreted as prefiguring the three days which **Jesus** spent in the tomb between the **Crucifixion** and the **Resurrection**.

Joseph of Arimathea. Member of the **Sanhedrin** and a secret follower of **Jesus**. Requested Jesus' body after the **Crucifixion** and had him buried in his own tomb.

Joseph, St, husband of the **Virgin Mary**. According to the **Gospels**, a carpenter and descendant of **David**. The second-century *Book of James* (*Protevangelium*) describes him as very old at the time of his marriage.

Joseph. Son of **Jacob**.

Joshua. Assistant and successor to **Moses**. Led the **Israelites** into the land of **Canaan**.

Judah. (1) One of the twelve sons of **Jacob** and (2) one of the **Twelve Tribes of Israel**. (3) The name taken by the southern kingdom after the division of the **Israelites** into two after the death of **Solomon** in 922BCE.

Judas Iscariot. One of the original **Twelve Disciples** of **Christ**. According to the **Gospels** he betrayed Christ to the Jewish authorities and later hanged himself.

Judge (ruler, governor). Title given to leaders of **Israel** in the period between Joshua and the beginning of the monarchy (*c*.1200–1000BCE). Among the most famous were **Deborah**, **Gideon** and **Samson** whose stories are told in the Book of Judges.

Judgement. See **Last Judgement**.

Kingdom of God, Kingdom of Heaven. The central theme in Jesus' teaching, this refers to God's rule and power at work among people who accept his authority in their lives. Already evident in Jesus' **ministry**, God's rule will be fully revealed at Jesus' **Second Coming**.

King James Version (**KJV**). Also known as the *Authorised Version* (**AV**). Very influential version of the Bible commissioned by James I and first published in 1611, and was used by English-speaking Protestants well into the twentieth century.

Lamb of God (Latin *Agnus Dei*). Symbolic description of **Jesus Christ** based on the words of **John the Baptist**:'Behold the Lamb of God who takes away the sins of the world' (John 1:29), a reference to his death for the **sins** of others. In Rev 5:6 Jesus is represented as a lamb who has been slain. The symbolism of the sacrificial lamb is found in the **Old Testament** stories of **Abel**, **Abraham** and **Isaac**, the **Passover** and the practice of offering **sacrifices** for sin.

Last Judgement. The final judgement on mankind when all will have to give account of their lives to **Christ** as Judge (Mt 25:31–46).

Last Supper. The **Passover** meal **Jesus** eats with his **Disciples** before his betrayal and arrest, at which he institutes the **Eucharist/Holy Communion/Mass**.

Law. (1) The Law given to **Moses** on **Mount Sinai** and recorded in (2) the first five books of the **Old Testament (Pentateuch)**.

Lazarus. Brother of **Mary** and **Martha.** According to Jn 11:1–44, **Christ** raised Lazarus from the dead, an event later held to **prefigure** his own **Resurrection.**

Lectionary. Arrangement of extracts from **scripture** to be read at public worship.

Legend. Traditional story popularly regarded as historical.

Lent. Forty-day period of penitence and **fasting** before **Easter,** lasting from Ash Wednesday to **Holy Saturday,** which recalls **Christ**'s forty days in the wilderness (Lk 4:1, 2).

Levi. (1) One of the twelve sons of **Jacob** and (2) one of the **Twelve Tribes of Israel,** the tribe from which priests came. (3) One of the **Disciples** of **Jesus,** later renamed **Matthew.**

Leviathan. A monstrous sea creature mentioned in a number of **Old Testament** passages, notably Job 41. The gaping jaws of Leviathan were used in medieval imagery to symbolise the mouth of **Hell.**

Levite. Descendant of **Levi;** also a subordinate priest in Judaism.

Leviticus. Third book of the **Old Testament,** part of the **Pentateuch,** records the Laws given by God to Moses.

Liturgy. The written text of the formal services of the **Church.**

Logos. See **Word.**

Longinus. The name given in the apocryphal *Acts of Pilate* (part of the **Gospel** of **Nicodemus**) to the Roman soldier said to have pierced **Christ**'s side with a spear during the **Crucifixion** (Jn 19:34). Later **legends** claimed that he had been cured of blindness when his eyes were touched by the blood which ran down the spear.

Lord's Prayer (Latin *Paternoster*). Taught by **Jesus** to his **Disciples** (Mt 6:9–13).

Lucifer (Latin 'light bearer'). Synonym for the **Devil.**

Luke, St, Evangelist. Author of the Third **Gospel** and the **Book of Acts.** **New Testament** references suggest he was a **Gentile** physician who accompanied **St Paul** for part of his missionary journeys. His symbol is an ox.

Luther, Martin (1483–1546). German Protestant Reformer who believed that the **Bible** should be available in the vernacular and translated it into German.

Magi (Greek *magoi*, 'wise men, sages'). The 'wise men from the East' (Mt 2:1) who brought gifts of gold, frankincense and myrrh to the infant **Jesus**. The **New Testament** account says nothing of their rank, number or names. It was **Tertullian** (*c*.160–*c*.225) who described them as kings, and **Origen** (b.*c*.185) who gave their number as three. A sixth-century work names them as Gaspar, Melchior and Balthasar (see Chapter 5).

Magnificat ('*Magnificat anima mea Dominum*', 'My soul magnifies the Lord'). Song of the **Virgin Mary** taken from Luke 1:46–55 and used as a **canticle** in worship.

Malchus. Name given to the high priest's servant, whose ear was cut off by **Peter** and subsequently restored by **Jesus** during the arrest of Jesus in the **Garden of Gethsemane**.

Manna. The food said to have been miraculously provided for the **Israelites** as they travelled through the wilderness. In Ex 16:4 God promised **Moses** that he would rain down bread from **heaven** which was to be gathered daily, except on the **Sabbath**. According to Ex 16:31, manna was 'like coriander seed' and tasted 'like wafers made with honey'.

Mark, St, Evangelist. Author of the second **Gospel**. His symbol is a lion.

Martha. Sister of **Mary of Bethany** and **Lazarus**, whose home was visited by **Christ**. In Lk 10:38–42 she was described as 'busy with much serving'; as a result she became a symbol of the **active life** (practical service and involvement in the world) whilst Mary symbolised the **contemplative life**.

Martyr (Greek *martus*, 'witness'). One who suffers death for their **faith**.

Mary Magdalene, St. According to the **Gospels,** Mary was delivered by **Christ** from 'seven demons' (Lk 8:2), stood by the **Cross** (Mk 15:40), discovered the empty tomb, and was the first to encounter the Risen Christ (Mk 16, Jn 20:11–18). Tradition also identified her with the 'sinner' who anointed Christ's feet (Lk 7:37–50) and with **Mary of Bethany**, the sister of **Martha**.

Mary of Bethany. Sister of **Martha** and **Lazarus**. Described in Lk 10:38–42 as sitting at **Christ**'s feet, listening to his word; as a result Mary was held to typify the **contemplative life** of prayer and meditation whilst her sister **Martha** represented the **active life**.

Mary Salome. One of the women present at the **Crucifixion** (Mk 15:40) and after the **Resurrection** (Mk 16:1–4).

Mary, the Blessed Virgin, Mother of Jesus. The account of Mary's life in the **New Testament** was amplified by **apocryphal** documents and a number of **doctrines** concerning her person and role developed in succeeding centuries.

Mass (also called the **Eucharist, Holy Communion** or Lord's Supper). The chief **sacramental** service of the **Church**, incorporating praise, intercession and readings from **scripture**. The central action is the consecration of the bread and wine by the priest, recalling the words and actions of **Christ** at the **Last Supper** and commemorating the **sacrifice** which he offered for the **sins** of mankind on the **Cross**.

Massacre of the Innocents. The slaughter by **Herod the Great** of all male infants under two years old in an attempt to kill the newly born **Jesus** (Mt 2:1–18).

Matthew, St (Levi), Apostle and **Evangelist**, author of the first **Gospel**. Also called Levi, son of Alphaeus (Mk 2:14). According to the **Gospels** he was a publican (tax-collector) before he was called by **Christ** to become one of the **Twelve**. His symbol is a man.

Maundy Thursday (Holy Thursday) (Latin *mandatum*, 'commandment'). Thursday before **Easter Sunday**. Commemorates the **Last Supper** (**Christ**'s sharing of the **Passover** meal with his **Disciples**) at which he instituted the **Eucharist**, washed the Disciples' feet and commanded that they should love one another as he loved them.

Messiah (Hebrew 'anointed one'). Equivalent to the Greek *christos*. See **Christ**.

Michael, St, Archangel. In Revelation 12:7–9 he casts down **Satan** from **Heaven**.

Midrash. A rabbinical exegesis of Biblical texts.

Ministry. Period or type of work, including public teaching and preaching, prayer and worship, often accompanied by **miracles**.

Miracle. An event evoking wonder, in which a person is believed to be the agent of God's power. In the Bible, miracles tend to be associated with key people at critical periods of history, such as the **Exodus**, the **ministry** of **Jesus** and the **Apostles**.

Miriam. Sister of **Aaron** and half-sister of **Moses**, she accompanied them during the **Exodus**, leading the **Israelites** in worship after the **Crossing of the Red Sea**.

Moralised Bible (*Bible Moralisée*). A type of illustrated Bible popular in the medieval period which establishes correspondences between events in the **Old** and **New Testaments**.

Moses. Led the people of **Israel** out of slavery in Egypt. Received the **Ten Commandments** on **Mount Sinai**. Following an encounter with God, Moses comes down from the mountain with his face 'shining' (Ex 34:29–30). The mistranslation in the **Vulgate** of the Hebrew word for 'shining' as 'horned' instead of 'giving rays' led to Moses being depicted with horns in many medieval images.

Mount of Olives. Hill outside **Jerusalem**. Scene of **Jesus'** arrest.

Mount Sinai (Mount Horeb). Mountain in the Sinai Desert where **Moses** met God and received the **Tablets of the Law**.

Mystery plays. Medieval play cycles based on Biblical narratives and traditionally performed by trade guilds at the feast of **Corpus Christi**.

Mystic. A person who seeks direct spiritual encounter with God, usually through a life of self-denial and contemplation.

Nativity. Birth of **Christ**.

Nazirite. A person dedicated to the service of God who made vows to abstain from alcohol, not to cut their hair and not to touch a corpse. Included **Samson**, **Samuel** and **John the Baptist**.

New Heaven and New Earth. Renewed creation where God will live with humankind, seen by **John** in a vision recorded in Revelation 21:1–8.

New Jerusalem. Part of the **New Heaven and New Earth**, dwelling place of the **Lamb** (Rev 21:1–8).

New Revised Standard Version (NRSV). Modern translation of the Bible used in this book.

New Testament (NT). Writings produced by the **Christian** community c.CE50–100 and subsequently affirmed as authoritative by the **Church**. See **Canon of scripture**. (1) The Four **Gospels: Matthew, Mark, Luke, John**. (2) Acts (the **Early Church**). (3) Epistles (letters to churches and individuals): Romans, 1 & 2 Corinthians, Galatians, Ephesians, Philippians, Colossians, 1 & 2 Thessalonians, 1 & 2 Timothy, Titus, Philemon, Hebrews, James, 1 & 2 Peter, 1, 2 & 3 John, Jude. (4) **Revelation (Apocalypse)**. Description of the **Heavenly Jerusalem**. See also *Apocrypha*.

Nicodemus. A Jewish religious leader who visited **Jesus** at night and appears to have been a secret **Disciple**. Assisted **Joseph of Arimathea** with the burial of Jesus.

Noah. Righteous man saved from destruction in the **Flood** because, at God's command, he built an **ark** (Gen 6:5–9:29).

NT. Abbreviation for the **New Testament**.

Numbers. Fourth book of the **Old Testament**, part of the **Pentateuch**, records the **Laws** given by **God** to **Moses** as well as some **Israelite** history.

Nunc Dimittis. Also called the Song of **Simeon**. **Canticle** based on Luke 2:29–32 and named from its opening words in Latin.

Old English. The language and vernacular (English) literature of the **Anglo-Saxons** in England between the fifth and eleventh centuries.

Old Latin. The collective term for the many biblical texts that were in circulation before **St Jerome** collated them into the single **Vulgate** text of the **Bible**.

Old Testament (the Hebrew **Bible** or **OT**). The sacred writings of Judaism which also form the first part of the **Christian** Bible. (1) Books of the **Law: Genesis, Exodus, Leviticus, Numbers, Deuteronomy**. (2) Historical books: Joshua, Judges, **Ruth**, 1 & 2 **Samuel**, 1 & 2 Kings, 1 & 2 Chronicles, Ezra, Nehemiah, Esther. (3) Books of teaching: **Psalms**;

Wisdom literature: **Job**, Proverbs, Ecclesiastes, Song of Solomon (Song of Songs, Canticles). (4) The **Prophets: Isaiah**, Jeremiah (with Lamentations) Ezekiel, **Daniel**, Hosea, Joel, Amos, Obadiah, **Jonah**, Micah, Nahum, Habakkuk, Zephaniah, Haggai, Zechariah, Malachi. (See also *Apocrypha*.)

Original Sin. The state of disobedience to and alienation from God which is believed to have characterised mankind since the **Fall**.

OT. Abbreviation for the **Old Testament**.

Palm Sunday. The Sunday before **Easter** marked by the blessing of palms and a procession commemorating **Christ's entry into Jerusalem** (Mt 21:1–11).

Parable. A story form often used by **Jesus** in his teaching (see **Good Samaritan, Prodigal Son**).

Paradise. See **Heaven**.

Passion of Christ (Latin *passio*, 'suffering'). The physical and psychological suffering endured by **Jesus** on behalf of mankind during the vigil in the **Garden of Gethsemane**, arrest, trial, scourging and **Crucifixion** (Mt 26–7, Mk 14–15, Lk 22–3, Jn 18–19).

Passion Sunday. Two weeks before **Easter**.

Passover. Jewish spring festival celebrating the deliverance of the people of **Israel** from slavery in Egypt (see Ex 12, where the **Israelites** were told by God to kill a lamb per household and mark the doorway with its blood, so that their homes would be 'passed over' when God struck down the first-born of the Egyptians). According to the **Gospels**, it was at the Passover meal before his death (the **Last Supper**) that **Christ** instituted the **Eucharist**, comparing himself to a sacrificial lamb whose blood would save sinners (see Mt 26:26–9).

Paternoster (Latin 'Our Father'). The **Lord's Prayer** (Mt 6:9–13, Lk 11:2–4).

Patriarchs. The principal ancestors of the **Israelites: Abraham, Isaac** and **Jacob**.

Patristic (Latin *pater*, 'father'). Relating to the **Fathers of the Church**, particularly to their writings.

Paul, St, 'Apostle to the Gentiles' (d.*c.*CE65). Born Saul of Tarsus, a Jew and Roman citizen. His initial hostility to the **Early Church** was overcome by his conversion on the **road to Damascus** (Acts 9:1–19). Using the Roman version of his name, Paul travelled through Asia Minor and into Europe preaching to both Jews and **Gentiles**. Eventually arrested and taken to Rome for trial. Tradition holds that he was executed during the persecution under Nero. The **New Testament** letters bearing his name stress that **salvation** is offered as a gift (by God's **grace**) through **faith**, as a result of the **forgiveness** won by **Christ**'s death on the **Cross**, and is available to Jews and non-Jews alike (e.g. Eph 2).

Pentateuch. The first five books of the **Old Testament: Genesis, Exodus, Leviticus, Numbers, Deuteronomy.**

Pentecost (Whitsun). Seventh Sunday after **Easter**. The Jewish feast of Weeks (harvest). Day when the **Holy Spirit** descended upon the **Disciples** (Acts 2).

Peter, St, Apostle. Originally called Simon, he was given the name Cephas (Aramaic equivalent of the Greek 'Peter', meaning rock) by **Christ**. His profession of **faith** (Mt 16:13–20) evoked the promise:'Thou art Peter; and upon this rock I will build my church … I will give to thee the keys of the kingdom of **heaven**.' His later denial of Christ (Mt 26:69–75) was followed by **repentance** and a fresh commission to care for Christ's followers (Jn 21:15–19). In Acts he emerges as the leader of the **Early Church**. Early traditions describe him as the first **bishop** of Rome who was **crucified** head downwards during the reign of Nero. Often portrayed as the gate-keeper of **heaven**, holding the keys promised by Christ.

Pharaoh. Title of the King of Egypt.

Pharisee. An elite group of strictly observant Jews active at the time of **Jesus** and often critical of his **ministry**.

Philistines. Traditional enemies of the **Israelites** in the territory of **Israel**.

Pietà. Depiction of the **Virgin Mary** holding the dead **Christ** in her arms following the **Crucifixion**.

Pilate, Pontius. Roman prefect in charge of the province of Judea from CE26 to 36/37.

Prefiguration. A foreshadowing, particularly by the use of **typology**.

Priest. One who is ordained by the **Church** to serve in a particular role.

Prelapsarian ('Before the Fall'). The state of innocence and **grace** in which **Adam** and **Eve** existed before they disobeyed God's commandment not to eat from the **Tree of Knowledge of Good and Evil**.

Presentation in the Temple. The **circumcision** and naming ceremony performed in the **Temple** for every male Jewish infant at eight days old, which was for **Jesus** an occasion for **prophecy** by **Simeon** and **Anna** about his life and death (Lk 2:21–40).

Prodigal Son. One of the most famous **parables** of Jesus (Lk 15:11–32) in which a father, representing God, forgives the sins of one of his sons.

Promised Land. The land promised by God to the people of **Israel**. (See **Canaan**.)

Prophecy. Disclosure of the message or plans of God through a human messenger. (See **Prophet**.)

Prophet. Person who conveys God's message to human beings or speaks about the future.

Prophets. Term used of individuals, male or female, who communicated God's message, sometimes through words alone, sometimes through dramatic actions.

Protevangelium (Book of James). Its name (Latin 'first **Gospel**') comes from its claim to relate events, particularly in the life of the **Virgin Mary**, earlier than those recorded in **Luke**. **Apocryphal** infancy narrative also known as the *Book of James*. Probably dates from the second century. Incorrectly attributed to **James, the Brother of the Lord**.

Psalms, Book of. Contains 150 Hebrew poems or songs, many attributed to King **David**, on a variety of themes including praise, lament, pilgrimage and prayer for God's help and **forgiveness**. Daily repetition of the psalms lay at the heart of medieval worship. (See **Psalter**.)

Psalter. A book used in worship containing the **Psalms** and **Canticles**.

Pseudepigrapha (Greek, 'false writings'). Jewish religious writings not considered **canonical**. Many try to achieve legitimacy by claiming to have been written by well-known authors, but have been proved to be fake.

Purgatory. Upon death, human beings faced a personal **judgement** to determine their immediate destination. It was believed that many would have to endure a period of punishment in Purgatory (a kind of antechamber to **heaven**) before they would be ready to enter the presence of God.

Purification of the Virgin Mary. Jewish **law** required that a mother should undergo ritual cleansing forty days after the birth of her child. It is likely that this event would have taken place at the same time as the **Presentation in the Temple** (Lk 2:22–39) and these two events are often portrayed together.

Queen of Sheba. Queen, from Africa or Arabia, who visited King **Solomon** to test his wisdom.

Rabbi. Jewish teacher.

Remnant. A small group who will return from exile to worship **God** (Isa 10:20–3).

Repentance. Renunciation of **sin** coupled with determination to obey God in the future.

Resurrection. That **Jesus** rose from the dead, thus conquering death, and that everyone will rise from the dead for the **Last Judgement** is a central **Christian** belief.

Revelation. (1) The idea that God reveals himself to humankind in various ways, including through **Jesus**, the **Holy Spirit** and **Creation**. (2) The Book of Revelation, also called **Apocalypse**. The final book of the **Bible** which records the **Apocalyptic** visions of **St John** on the island of Patmos.

Righteous. Holy, or made right with God through the **Cross**.

Road to Damascus. Scene of the dramatic conversion of **St Paul**. (See Chapter 8.)

Ruth. Daughter-in-law of Naomi, wife of Boaz and ancestor of **David**.

Sabbath. (Hebrew, 'rest'). Seventh day of the Jewish week, on which the people were to rest from work.

Sacrament. Rite or ceremony.

Sacrifice. Biblical worship required the offering of gifts to God. These offerings expressed a range of attitudes including praise, thanksgiving, acknowledgement of guilt and submission to God's will

Sacrifice of Isaac. As a test of faith God asks **Abraham** to sacrifice his much-loved son, Isaac, but provides a substitute at the last moment (Gen 22).

Saint. A title conferred by the **Church** recognising a **martyr** or a Christian of particular holiness after their death.

Salome. Stepdaughter of **Herod Antipas** who requested and was given the head of **John the Baptist** as a reward for her dancing at a banquet.

Salvation. The teaching that God became a human being in the person of **Jesus Christ** and willingly offered himself to die on the **Cross** in order to save men and women from their sins. There were a variety of interpretations of the **doctrine** of **Atonement** (i.e. the reconciliation of mankind to God through the death of Christ). **Origen** (c.185–254) viewed **Christ**'s death as a ransom paid to **Satan**, who had acquired rights over man through the **Fall of Humankind**; but this interpretation was later largely superseded by that of **St Anselm** (c.1033–1109), who taught that Christ died to take the punishment due to human sin, thus paying the debt owed to God and appeasing his **righteous** anger.

Samaritan. The Samaritans, whose ancestors had been moved into the land of **Israel** during the Jewish exile in **Babylon** (2 Kings 17:24–41), were regarded with distrust and hostility by Jews. Originally worshippers of many gods, the Samaritans later adopted the worship of the one God but only accepted part of the Jewish scriptures.

Samson. Old Testament figure, possessed of enormous strength, who protected **Israel** against their enemies, the **Philistines**. Eventually betrayed by **Delilah**, he was captured and blinded by the Philistines and pulled down their temple, causing his own death in the process. Events in his life were subsequently interpreted by Christian commentators as prefiguring events in the life of **Jesus**. His story is told in Judges 13–16.

Samuel. Old Testament prophet and the last of the Judges of **Israel**. He anointed **Israel's** first two kings, **Saul** and **David**.

Sanhedrin. The Jewish ruling council.

Sarah. Wife of **Abraham** and mother of **Isaac** in her old age.

Satan (Hebrew *satan*, 'adversary'). See **Devil, Fall of the Angels.**

Saul. First king of **Israel** who was eventually rejected by God because of disobedience and overshadowed by his son-in-law **David** of whom he was intensely jealous. Died in battle against the **Philistines.**

Saviour (Latin *salvator*, 'redeemer', 'deliverer'). Used in the **Old Testament** to refer to God who rescues the **Israelites** from captivity and exile, and in the **New Testament** to refer to **Jesus Christ** as the one who offers deliverance from sin to all human beings.

Scripture. Term used for the holy writings of Judaism, Christianity and Islam.

Scroll of the Seven Seals. Scroll opened in the Book of **Revelation** (**Apocalypse**) after which a number of calamitous events follow, including the appearance of the **Four Horsemen of the Apocalypse.**

Scarlet Woman, The (Whore of Babylon). Woman clothed in purple and scarlet, representing corruption at the **Apocalypse** in Revelation 17–18. (See Chapter 9.)

Second Coming [of Christ]. The expected return of **Christ** in glory to judge the living and the dead and to bring to an end the present world order. (See **Last Judgement.**)

Septuagint (LXX). Greek translation of the Hebrew **Old Testament.** Jewish tradition states that it was made for the Jews of Alexandria in the third century BCE by a group of seventy scholars (hence LXX). Probably completed by 132BCE. It differs from the Hebrew Bible in the order of Biblical books and includes additional books.

Sepulchre/Holy Sepulchre. Tomb; term used to refer to the tomb in which **Christ's** body was laid after the **Crucifixion.**

Sermon on the Mount. Christ's teaching in Mt 5–7.

Seven Last Words from the Cross. The seven utterances of **Jesus** while on the **Cross** recorded in the **Gospels**. See Lk 23:34, Lk 23:43; Jn 19:26–7; Mt 27:46; Mk 15:34; Jn 19:28; Jn 19:30; Lk 23:46.

Seven Penitential Psalms. Psalms 6, 32, 38, 51, 102, 130 and 143.

Simeon. A faithful worshipper of God who had been promised that he would not die before he saw the **Messiah**.

Simon of Cyrene. Man conscripted to carry **Christ's Cross** on the way to **Calvary**.

Sin. Disobedience to the known will of God. According to **Christian** theology, human beings have displayed a pre-disposition to sin since the **Fall of Humankind**.

Sodom and Gomorrah. Two sinful towns destroyed by God with sulphur and fire (Gen 18:16–19:28).

Solomon. Son of **David**; third king of **Israel**; renowned for his wisdom. The **Old Testament** books Proverbs and Song of Songs (Song of Solomon) are traditionally attributed to him.

Son of Man. In the **New Testament** this phrase is often linked to Daniel 7:13 which describes 'one like a son of man' coming on the clouds of **heaven** and being given dominion over all peoples and nations. **Jesus** is shown using this phrase of himself in the **Gospels**.

St. Abbreviation of **Saint**.

Stephaton. Name later given to the man who held up a sponge soaked in vinegar to **Christ** at the **Crucifixion**.

Synoptic. Term used of the **Gospels** of **Matthew**, **Mark** and **Luke** which reflect a similar approach and use much common material in portraying the life of **Christ**.

Tablets of the Law. Two stone tablets inscribed by **God** with the **Ten Commandments** and given to **Moses** on **Mount Sinai**. (See Chapter 2.)

Talmud. The fundamental code of Jewish civil and canon law, composed in the first to fifth centuries CE.

Temple. The centre of Jewish worship in **Jerusalem**.

Ten Commandments. Commandments given by God to **Moses** on Mount Sinai, found in Deut 5:6–21 and Ex 20:1–17. In summary, the Commandments are: (1) I am the LORD your God … Worship no God but me. (2) Do not make for yourselves images of anything … Do not bow down to any idol or worship it. (3) Do not use my name for evil purposes. (4) Observe the **Sabbath**. (5) Respect your father and mother. (6) Do not commit murder. (7) Do not commit adultery. (8) Do not steal. (9) Do not accuse anyone falsely. (10) Do not covet.

Tertullian (*c.*CE160–*c.*CE225). Highly influential **Father of the Church**.

Theophany. A moment when the divine is made visible to humanity.

Thomas. One of the **Twelve Disciples** known for his doubting of **Jesus' Resurrection**. (See Chapter 7.)

Torah (Hebrew 'law' or 'teaching'). The **Law** given to **Moses** and its interpretation.

Tower of Babel. Episode in Genesis 11:1–9 in which God thwarts an attempt to build a tower to reach **Heaven** by causing humankind to speak in different languages.

Transfiguration of Christ. Event described in the **Gospels** of **Matthew**, **Mark** and **Luke** in which **Jesus** is seen by **Peter**, **James** and **John**, revealed in glory and accompanied by **Moses** and **Elijah**.

Tree of Jesse. See **Jesse Tree**.

Tree of Knowledge of Good and Evil. Tree in the **Garden of Eden** whose fruit was forbidden. **Adam** and **Eve** disobey this order, resulting in the **Fall of Humankind**. (See Chapter 1.)

Trinity. The **Church** taught that God was three persons – Father, Son (**Jesus Christ**) and **Holy Spirit** – who shared one divine nature and together brought about the **Creation** and **Salvation** of the world.

Trope. Brief elaboration of passage of **scripture** or **liturgical** text.

Twelve Disciples ('the Twelve'). A group chosen by **Jesus** to accompany, work with and learn from him and in due course take his message to others. They were Simon **Peter, Andrew, James** and **John** (sons of Zebedee), Philip, Bartholomew, **Thomas, Matthew** (**Levi**), James son of Alphaeus, Thaddeus (Jude), Simon the Cananean, and **Judas Iscariot** who betrayed Jesus.

Twelve Tribes of Israel. The twelve tribes were descended from the twelve sons of Jacob (Israel): Reuben, Simeon, **Levi**, Judah, Dan, Napthali, Gad, Asher, Issachar, Zebulun, **Joseph** and Benjamin.

Tyndale, William (1494–1536). Translator of the first printed New Testament in English, which was published in Germany in 1526. His translation of the Old Testament was only partially completed before he was executed for heresy.

Type (Greek *tupos*, 'example', 'figure'). A person or event (usually in the **OT**) which, while accepted as historical, was also held to foreshadow some aspect of **Christ** or the **Church** e.g. **Abraham**'s **sacrifice of Isaac** was seen as a **type** of God's **sacrifice** of his much-loved son.

Typology The interpretation of people and events (particularly in the **OT**) as foreshadowing elements of **Christian revelation**. (See **Type**.)

Venite. **Canticle** beginning 'O come, let us sing unto the Lord', based on Psalm 95.

Virgin Birth. The understanding that **Mary** retained her virgin status during both the conception and birth of **Jesus**. This belief is part of the **doctrine** of the perpetual virginity of **Mary**, recorded first by **St Jerome** in c.CE383, which claims that she also maintained her virgin state throughout the remainder of her life.

Virgin Mary. See **Mary, the Blessed Virgin.**

Visitation. The **Virgin Mary's** visit to her cousin **Elizabeth** (Lk 1:39–56).

Vulgate. Latin version of the **Bible** most widely used in the West. Assembled by **St Jerome** from the various Old Latin versions of the **Bible** and his translations of Greek and Hebrew texts around the end of the fourth century CE.

Washing of the Disciples' feet. Christ washes the feet of the disciples at the **Last Supper** as a symbol of cleansing, humility and service.

Wilderness. Traditional place of trial and temptation.

Whitsun. Name given to the festival of **Pentecost** in England.

Whore of Babylon. (See **Scarlet Woman, The.**)

Word (Greek *logos*). Title used for **Jesus** in the opening passage of **John's Gospel**, suggesting his distinct existence before creation as well as his specific **incarnation** in it.

Writings, The. Final section of the Jewish sacred writings which includes short stories, poetry, wisdom and later Israelite history, including the books of Proverbs and **Psalms**.

Wyclif, Johan (*c.*1330–84). English philosopher, theologian and reformer. A group of his followers translated the **Bible** into English.

Zechariah. Priest, husband to **Elizabeth** and father of **John the Baptist**. Temporarily struck dumb by God when he does not believe that his aged wife will conceive and bear him a son (Lk 1:5–20).

FURTHER READING

ART HISTORY

Drury, John, *Painting the Word: Christian Pictures and their Meanings*, Yale University Press in association with The National Gallery, London, 1999.

McGregor, Neil with Langmuir, Erica, *Seeing Salvation: Images of Christ in Art*, Yale University Press, 2000.

Mühlberger, Richard, *The Bible in Art: The New Testament*, Portland House, 1990.

Mühlberger, Richard, *The Bible in Art: The Old Testament*, Portland House, 1991.

Usherwood, Nicholas, *The Bible in 20th Century Art*, Pagoda, 1987.

Zuffi, Stephano, *Gospel Figures in Art*, The J. Paul Getty Museum, 2003.

Zuffi, Stephano, *Old Testament Figures in Art*, The J. Paul Getty Museum, 2003.

LITERATURE

Alter, Robert and Kermode, Frank (eds), *The Literary Guide to the Bible*, William Collins & Co. Ltd, 1987.

Fisch, Harold, *Biblical Presence in Shakespeare, Milton and Blake*, Oxford, 1999

Jasper, David and Prickett, Stephen (eds), *The Bible and Literature: A Reader*, Blackwell Publishers Ltd, 1999.

Jeffrey, David Lyle (General Editor), *A Dictionary of Biblical Tradition in English Literature*, Eerdmans, 1992.

Marx, Steven, *Shakespeare and the Bible*, Oxford, 2000.

FILM

Cawkwell, Tim, *The Filmgoer's Guide to God*, London, 2004.

THE BIBLE

Alexander, P. (ed), *The New Lion Handbook to the Bible*, Lion, 1999.
Barton, John, *What is the Bible?* SPCK, 1997.
Brownrigg, Ronald, *Who's Who in the New Testament*, Routledge, 2001.
Comay, Joan, *Who's Who in the Old Testament, together with the Apocrypha*, Routledge, 2001.
Gabel, John B., Wheeler, Charles B. and York, Anthony D., *The Bible as Literature: An Introduction*, Oxford University Press, 2000.
Metzger, Bruce M. and Coogan, Michael D. (eds), *The Oxford Companion to the Bible*, Oxford University Press, 1993.
Riches, John, *The Bible: A Very Short Introduction*, Oxford University Press, 2000.
Selman, Martin and Manser, Martin, *The Bible A–Z (Collins Gem Series)*, Harper Collins, 2004.

BIBLE TRANSLATIONS

There are many modern translations and paraphrases of the Bible which include:
The Good News Bible, Collins, 2004.
The *Holy Bible New Revised Standard Version Anglicized Edition*, Oxford University Press, 1998.
The Holy Bible New International Bible, Hodder and Stoughton, 1997.
The New Jerusalem Bible, Oxford University Press, 2000.